D1044720

REPORT ON
HUMAN RIGHTS
IN
EL SALVADOR

353-2
1-

REPORT ON HUMAN RIGHTS IN EL SALVADOR

COMPILED BY
AMERICAS WATCH COMMITTEE
AND
THE AMERICAN CIVIL LIBERTIES UNION

JANUARY 26, 1982

VINTAGE BOOKS
A DIVISION OF RANDOM HOUSE
NEW YORK

First Vintage Books Edition, March 1982
Copyright © 1982 by the Center for National
Security Studies
All rights reserved under International and
Pan-American Copyright Conventions.
Published in the United States by Random House, Inc.,
New York, and simultaneously in Canada by Random
House of Canada Limited, Toronto.
Originally published by the Center for National
Security Studies in January, 1982.
Manufactured in the United States of America
ISBN: 394–71141–6

ACKNOWLEDGMENTS

This report was prepared by a team of authors organized and directed by Roberto Alvarez. The other authors were Cynthia Arnson, Robert Goldman, Francesca Jessup, Juan Mendez, Michael Posner and Nina Shea. Heather Foote drafted the initial version of Chapter 7, and Michelle Meier drafted the initial version of Chapter 13. Pat Breslin prepared a draft of the summary and did editing. Consultants to the authors included Leyda Barbieri, Piero Gleijeses, Hurst Hannum, Ann Nelson and Roger Plant. Research assistance was provided by Patricia Krackov, Anne Laurent and Lisette Nunez. Morton Halperin edited the report.

A number of institutions provided assistance of various kinds including Americas Watch Committee, Amnesty International, Center for National Security Studies, Comision de Derechos Humanos de El Salvador, International Committee of the Red Cross (ICRC), International Commission of Jurists, International Human Rights Law Group, International League for Human Rights, Lawyers Committee for International Human Rights, the National

Council of the Churches of Christ, U.S.A., Socorro Juridico del Arzobispado de San Salvador, the Unitarian Universalist Service Committee and the Washington Office on Latin America.

The assistance of Philippe Villers is gratefully acknowledged.

INTRODUCTION

We delivered this report to President Reagan on January 25, 1982, with a call to the President not to certify to Congress that El Salvador is complying with the human rights conditions of the foreign assistance act. Copies were also delivered to Congressional leaders. The following day, we released this report publicly.

Despite the evidence compiled in this report, on January 28, the President certified "that the Government of El Salvador is making a concerted and significant effort to comply with internationally recognized human rights" and "that the Government of El Salvador is achieving substantial control over all elements of its armed forces, so as to bring to an end the indiscriminate torture and murder of Salvadoran citizens." Without certification, all military aid and arms sales to El Salvador would have had to stop and U. S. troops would have had to be withdrawn. A further certification must be made on July 27, 1982, for military aid to continue beyond that point.

This report demonstrates, we believe, that the President's January 28 certification is a fraud. Regrettably, there is no mechanism in the foreign assistance act for Congress to reject a certification. It is possible, however, for Congress to demonstrate that it meant what it said in the foreign assistance act by adopting legislation suspending military aid to El Salvador so long as the gross human rights abuses documented in this report persist. That will happen only if Congress is prompted to act by public outrage. In publishing this report, we hope to provoke that outrage.

Aryeh Neier
Americas Watch Committee

Morton Halperin
American Civil Liberties Union

PREFACE

Since mid-1980, the small Central American nation of El Salvador has been wracked by a generalized armed conflict. The toll in lost lives is high and continuing to mount. Suffering is widespread among the people; hundreds of thousands of poor peasants have been forced to abandon their homes to escape the conflict.

A great deal of international attention has focused on El Salvador over the past year because some see the struggle there as part of East-West confrontation and because of the disturbing and persistent reports of massive human rights violations.

This is a report about the violations of human rights in El Salvador as that term is generally understood in international law: that is, deprivations of life and liberty by a government without due process of law and not in the course of armed combat. We limit ourselves to human rights matters because those are the exclusive concerns of the sponsors of this report. We do not take sides in the armed conflict now under way in El Salvador nor do we attempt to deal comprehensively with various aspects of

that conflict. We do not discuss the geopolitical significance of the conflict. This report refers to the armed conflict under way in El Salvador only to the extent necessary
to help readers understand the violations of human rights
that are taking place. The various individual rights generally covered by the term "human rights" are examined
against the backdrop of domestic and international laws
which are part of El Salvador's legal system, and which
are designed to protect their exercise.

Obviously, in any generalized conflict, violence stems
from many sources. In the case of El Salvador, there have
been many violations of Salvadoran law by armed revolutionaries. These have included summary executions, kidnappings and the destruction of public and private
property. This report does not question the use of military
force to resist such acts nor the use of legal process, in
accordance with internationally recognized legal norms,
to punish violations of domestic law. It is, obviously, the
right of any government to defend itself against violent
efforts to overthrow it. Nor does this report take a position
on whether conditions in El Salvador are such as to justify
rebellion against the government—a right recognized
under appropriate circumstances in the constitution of El
Salvador as well as in the Universal Declaration of Human
Rights. This issue aside, even in circumstances as difficult
as those in which the government of El Salvador finds
itself, however, a government must be required to adhere
to certain fundamental standards of human rights. International law requires that such norms be observed and the
government of El Salvador is committed to observing this
basic rule.

The idea that the way a sovereign government treats its
citizens within its borders is of legitimate concern to the
international community is relatively new in the history of
relations among nations. Its origins lie in international
condemnation of the massive human rights violations of

World War II and the formation of the United Nations in the aftermath of the War and its dedication to human rights. Since then, a series of international and regional instruments have been promulgated, many of them legally binding for the states that ratify them, which specify fundamental rights that states agree to respect and protect.

The system of international human rights that has developed since World War II is premised on the assumption that international concern with and attempts to redress human rights abuses in any country are appropriate whenever: a) the rights in question are specified in an international instrument of general application; b) violations of rights are attributable to a government or an agent of the government as it is involvement of a government that makes domestic redress difficult or impossible; and c) that remedies for abuses under domestic law have been exhausted or that it is plain that it would be fruitless to seek remedies under domestic law.

International concern with human rights abuses in any country is most pressing when it is demonstrated that a government is engaging in a systematic pattern of gross violations of internationally recognized human rights. This report attempts to present a comprehensive review of human rights violations by the current government of El Salvador. After presenting a brief overview of the history of El Salvador and of the much-discussed land-reform program, a series of chapters deal with major human rights and describe the evidence of violations by the government. The U.S. role in El Salvador is then discussed. An Appendix describes the domestic and international laws which are part of El Salvador's legal system, and which commit the government to protect these human rights.

Extensive documentation from numerous and varied sources has been obtained for this report. The data have included information, as well as testimony and documentation expressly furnished for this study. As part of the research, co-authors of this report visited El Salvador, Mexico, Nicaragua, and New York City to interview witnesses and representatives of inter-governmental and non-governmental international organizations, such as the Inter-American Commission on Human Rights, the Office of the U.N. High Commissioner for Refugees, Amnesty International, the International League for Human Rights, *Socorro Juridico* (the legal aid office of the Archdiocese of San Salvador), the Commission on Human Rights of El Salvador, members of the Salvadoran, U.S. and international press, and many victims and relatives of victims of violations attributed to the Salvadoran authorities. The Report describes events in El Salvador through September 12, 1981.

CONTENTS

APPENDICES

SUMMARY

This report contains much detailed information including testimonials from individuals whose rights were violated. Here the information can be presented only in a generalized form.

A. *Background to tragedy*

The underlying causes of the present crisis in El Salvador are the highly concentrated system of land tenure, the denial of basic rights to a peasant majority still prevented by law and practice from forming independent organizations, and a half century of hardline military rule by an army that has traditionally represented the interests of the landed oligarchy.

El Salvador is a small country, about the size of Massachusetts, with approximately 4.8 million people. Excepting Haiti, its population density is the highest in the Western Hemisphere. Clearly, the pattern of land distribution in such a country affects all else. (See Chapter 2 for data on economic and social conditions.)

In the last century, land ownership has become increasingly concentrated. The coffee boom of the late nineteenth century led to the abolition of communal lands farmed by indigenous peasants in favor of private property. In this century, the cotton and sugar booms of the past three decades accelerated concentration.

Commercial agriculture required large landholdings demarcated by legal titles and a pool of readily-available and preferably cheap labor. Massive evictions of peasants facilitated both. The only missing factor was coercion to keep the newly landless laborers in line. Around the turn of the century, a rural mounted police force was created, first in the coffee departments of Ahuachapan, Sonsonate, and Santa Ana, and then throughout the country. It was the precursor of the National Guard, which was formally created in 1912.

An agrarian law of 1907 confirmed the virtual serfdom of rural workers. Landless workers could be arrested for vagrancy. They had to carry workbooks showing to whom they owed their labor. Agrarian judges, assisted by the army, pursued anyone who tried to escape the estate on which he was to work.

Popular unrest in the countryside finally spilled over in 1932 under the pressure of the collapsing coffee market during the world-wide depression. General Maximiliano Hernandez Martinez, who had recently taken power, responded to a small peasant uprising with fire and blood. (See Chapter 3.) As many as 30,000 peasants were slaughtered in a campaign starkly known in Salvadoran history as "La Matanza," the massacre.

El Salvador's small Communist Party was blamed for the uprising. Its leader, Agustin Farabundo Marti, was arrested and executed. Today's guerrillas fight under the banner of the Farabundo Marti Front for National Liberation (FMLN).

General Martinez's twelve-year rule set the pattern for military-oligarchical control of the country for the next fifty years. Presidents came from military ranks; cabinet members were generally civilians representing the coffee oligarchy.

Economic transformation after World War II introduced significant changes into El Salvador. There was a measure of industrialization, and an urban-based working class took shape. The 1960s, the era of the Alliance for Progress, saw substantial light industry develop. However, the border war with Honduras in 1969 cut off a major market and exacerbated domestic problems as thousands of Salvadorans who had settled in Honduras returned home.

Labor leaders shared briefly in power during a short-lived provisional government in 1960–1961, and during the following decade new civilian political parties—principally the Christian Democrats (PDC) and also the social democratic MNR—appeared and grew.

Despite political and economic changes in the cities, rural El Salvador remained almost feudal. Attempts to organize rural workers were ruthlessly suppressed. In 1950, an amended agrarian law reaffirmed vagrancy as a punishable offense. The National Guard was detailed to maintain order on private estates. Landowners themselves appointed law enforcement officials. Eviction of superfluous tenant farmers was streamlined. With rapid expansion of sugar and cotton plantations in the Pacific lowlands, the percentage of landless laborers soared, to 40 percent by 1975, according to one estimate.

During the 1960s, a new instrument to insure control of rural areas appeared: ORDEN (Spanish for "order"). This intelligence and paramilitary apparatus grew to an estimated 80,000 members and penetrated every hamlet in the country.

By the early 1970s, tension in El Salvador was increasing. In 1972, voters expressed their repudiation of the five-decades-old system of military rule by casting their ballots for presidential and vice-presidential candidates of a civilian coalition, Jose Napoleon Duarte of the PDC and Guillermo Manuel Ungo of the MNR. As their lead piled up in unofficial returns, the army suspended radio broadcasts, and later simply announced that its candidate, Colonel Arturo Armando Molina, had won.

With electoral paths to change and reform blocked, new forms of opposition took shape. In the cities, mass popular organizations appeared outside the traditional political party structures. Migrants forced from the rural areas had swelled the city slums. They combined in the new organizations with urban workers disillusioned with official unionism, university students, and low-paid teachers. Between 1974 and 1978, three such organizations appeared: the Front for Unified Popular Action (FAPU), based on urban workers, in 1974; the Popular Revolutionary Block (BPR), based mainly on the peasantry, in 1975; and the February 28 Popular Leagues (LP-28), based in San Salvador's slums, in 1977.

Meanwhile, three guerrilla groups had begun to operate in El Salvador: the Popular Forces of Liberation (FPL), formed in 1970 from the radical faction of the Salvadoran Communist Party and left-wing university students; the Revolutionary People's Army (ERP), which appeared in 1971 and emphasized sabotage and individual acts of terrorism; and the Armed Forces of National Resistance (FARN), formed from an ERP splinter group in 1975.

Soon, the guerrilla bands and the mass organizations linked up—FAPU with the FARN, the BPR with the FPL, and the LP-28 with the ERP.

In 1977, the electoral farce was played out again. General Carlos Humberto Romero won presidential elections which were stage-managed by the military. On recorded tapes played for a subcommittee hearing in the U.S. House of Representatives, military officers were heard using a crude code to communicate the number of votes they wanted registered in various sections of the country (see Chapter 10).

After 1977, the opposition abandoned reliance on elections and the government turned to increasingly savage repression in an attempt to stem the rising tide of demonstrations, strikes, and protests. But it was an event in neighboring Nicaragua that doomed the Romero government. The victory of the Sandinistas over the Somoza dictatorship in July 1979 seemed to signal the twilight of the military tyrants in Central America. The conviction grew, in San Salvador and in Washington, that reforms were urgently needed if El Salvador was not to follow the path of Nicaragua.

On October 15, 1979, a group of younger military officers removed Romero and promised far-reaching changes in Salvadoran society. But the officers were fatally divided among themselves. At one end of the spectrum were the younger and more progressive officers grouped around Colonel Adolfo Arnoldo Majano; at the other, conservatives who recognized the need for a new public image led by Colonels Jose Guillermo Garcia and Jaime Abdul Gutierrez.

The officers invited prominent civilian politicians to join the Revolutionary Governing Junta, among them Guillermo Ungo. Popular pressure for reform, including an end to repression, intensified, but the level of repression actually increased. The Majano-led wing soon found that its influence over the army was limited or, in the case of the National Guard and the Treasury Police, virtually non-existent. Members of the latter two branches of the security forces also belonged to various paramilitary groups that played an ever-more-violent role in the last months of 1979. By year-end, the civilian members of the government made executive control over the armed forces the central condition for their continued participation and when the military rejected their demands, most resigned.

With the fall of this "First Junta," the centrist alternative was effectively closed, and the conservatives in the military were back in unquestioned control.

The opposition popular organizations had meanwhile come together in the *Coordinadora Revolucionaria de Masas* (CRM) which called a mass demonstration in San Salvador on January 22, 1980 to mark the anniversary of the uprising of 1932. This demonstration, the largest ever in the country, was attacked by units of the armed forces, marking the end of peaceful protest in El Salvador. By April further development of the opposition culminated in the establishment of the Democratic Revolutionary Front (FDR). It included civilian political leaders and organizations, former government officials, trade unions, professional organizations, and the popular mass organizations. The FDR is the political arm of a now revolutionary opposition. The guerrilla organizations also began to coalesce, and in October 1980, formed the Farabundo Marti National Liberation Front (FMLN). By mid-1981, the FMLN's regular forces numbered some 5,000 combatants, compared with some 15,000 in the combined Salvadoran armed forces.

Events in March 1980 hastened the onset of open warfare in El Salvador. On March 24, the popular Archbishop of San Salvador, Oscar Romero (no relation to the former President), was assassinated at his altar while saying mass. Archbishop Romero, who had championed the cause of the poor using his influence to promote a political solution, in his last homily, had called on the Junta's troops to disobey orders to fire on their own people. With his death, El Salvador lost its most important symbol of resistance to political violence.

In the same month, the government announced a sweeping agrarian reform program—if carried out—by Latin American standards. All estates over 500 hectares (1,235 acres) were expropriated with compensation. A second stage, aimed at estates between 100 and 500 hectares, has now been indefinitely postponed. The third stage, known as Land to the Tiller, was intended to give all small renters and share-croppers outright ownership of the land they had previously rented.

The program has been troubled from the start, and has apparently failed in its attempt to undermine peasant support for the guerrillas. Large landowners bitterly opposed the first stage; suspension of the second stage leaves the coffee oligarchy untouched; and the third stage does not deal with the thousands of laborers left landless by the spread of commercial agriculture in recent decades. In addition, the widespread violence in the countryside, particularly when military sweeps take place, forced hundreds of thousands of peasants onto the roads as refugees. (See Chapter 2 for an analysis of the agrarian reform program.)

Perhaps most destructive to the program was the fact that its implementation was accompanied by a wave of repression by military and security forces operating without restraint under a state of siege.

Violence and repression mounted throughout 1980. Colonel Majano, considered the principal progressive leader within the military, was forced out of the Junta and into exile. In November, six of the top leaders of the FDR were kidnapped in broad daylight in San Salvador by civilians operating inside a military cordon. Their mutilated bodies were found scattered around the city a few hours later. In December, four U.S. women, religious workers, were killed on a road outside San Salvador in circumstances which convinced then U.S. Ambassador Robert White that the security forces were responsible.

At present, the military situation seems to be at a stalemate. A "general offensive" by the guerrillas in January 1981 was beaten back by government forces, but the guerrillas still seem able to move about at will in the countryside. The Junta, now nominally headed by Jose Napoleon Duarte, with backing from the Reagan administration, proposes elections in 1982 and 1983 to resolve the conflict. The opposition says that widespread repression and violence makes free elections impossible and asserts its willingness to negotiate a political solution. The FDR-FMLN recently scored a diplomatic victory in August 1981 when France and Mexico recognized it as a "representative political force."

There are no signs of a quick solution to the crisis and neither the government nor FMLN forces appears capable of a decisive military victory.

B. *The human rights situation in El Salvador*

There are two salient facts about the violation of human rights in El Salvador today: first, the violations are directly related to the structure of Salvadoran society described in the preceding pages; second, the intensity and frequency of violations have increased since the "reform" government took power in a coup on October 15, 1979, and particularly since it was reshuffled on January 9, 1980.

As throughout contemporary Salvadoran history, the violence and repression is most severe in the rural areas. It has fallen most heavily on peasants, particularly those who have emerged as leaders of peasant organizations. And, in a steadily widening circle, the violence has touched those individuals and institutions who have espoused the cause of the peasants and protested their fate: priests and nuns, civilian political leaders, labor leaders, journalists, teachers, students, refugee workers. By now, it has engulfed the whole society.

• In 1980 alone, the conservative estimate of the U.S. State Department is that 9,000 died in political violence in El Salvador. *Socorro Juridico,* the legal aid office of the Archdiocese of San Salvador, placed the figure at 10,000. Of them, it said over 8,000 were killed by government forces, and of them over 3,700 were peasants, 400 industrial workers, 100 teachers, and 10 were priests.

• Since the October 15, 1979 coup, 602 cases of prisoners disappearing after detention have been documented by *Socorro Juridico.*

• Torture of the most brutal kind is common in El Salvador. Statistics are difficult to compile partly because relatively few victims survive to give testimony, but a high proportion of the corpses of individuals arrested by security forces or abducted by paramilitary groups show signs of barbaric torture. As a commission investigating attacks on health workers noted in 1980:

The brutality involved in the killings of health workers and patients and the accompanying torture suggest that this is a deliberate tactic aimed at striking terror into the hearts of others. Victims have been decapitated, emasculated or found with the initials "EM" which stands for Esquadron de la Muerte [Death Squad], in their flesh. [See Chapter 4.]

• Arbitrary arrests by Salvadoran authorities are widespread, and are clearly used against the political opposition.

• Rights to due process of law and a fair trial have been abrogated and the independence of the judiciary eliminated.

• Priests and nuns have been marked as targets of repression. The best-known cases involved the assassination of Archbishop Oscar Arnulfo Romero on March 24, 1980, and of three American nuns and a lay worker on December 2, 1980.

• Constitutional guarantees of freedom of expression have been suspended, and opposition newspapers no longer publish. Since January 1980, seventeen news offices and radio stations have been bombed or machine-gunned, twelve journalists have been killed by the security forces, and three have disappeared.

• Union leaders and organizers have been special targets for the government's security forces. Unions have been dissolved and guarantees of workers' rights abolished.

• Elections are planned for March 1982 but guarantees of safety and freedom for opposition leaders do not exist. The armed forces in mid-1981 published a list of 128 people it accuses of being terrorists, among them the top leaders of the opposition.

• At least 350,000 refugees, mainly peasant families, have abandoned their homes and fled to other areas of El Salvador, or to neighboring countries.

1. *Legal guarantees of rights*

Salvadoran law contains many guarantees of the rights which are today violated with impunity by the security forces. In addition, El Salvador is a party to several international conventions that mandate protection of human rights. (See Appendix I.)

Although many of the provisions of the 1962 Constitution have been suspended by the Junta, ostensibly it is still partially in force. It provides for executive, legislative, and judicial branches. It guarantees various rights, including equality before the law; the right of asylum; freedom of movement and residence; freedom from extradition or expatriation; freedom of conscience, religion, thought, and expression; protection and defense of life, honor, liberty, labor, property, and possessions; and the right to justice, due process of law, and of *habeas corpus.* The home is recognized as inviolable and arbitrary detention is forbidden, as is the retroactive application of laws.

During emergencies such as war, rebellion, and general disasters, the rights of freedom of movement and residence, of thought and expression, of assembly and of the inviolability of correspondence, may be suspended for 30 days. A new decree is necessary to prolong the suspension.

Under the "organic law of the judicial branch," the Supreme Court has final jurisdiction on the constitutionality of laws, decrees, and regulations, and writs of *habeas corpus* and of *amparo* (a remedy to stop or redress acts or omissions of any official which violate constitutional rights).

In addition to its domestic laws, El Salvador has signed several international conventions that are legally binding domestically. It is a founding member of both the United Nations and the Organization of American States and voted for both the UN Declaration on Human Rights and the OAS Declaration of the Rights and Duties of Man. It has ratified the four Geneva Conventions of 1949 on the laws of war as well as its 1977 Protocols. It has also ratified the American Convention on Human Rights and the UN Covenants on Civil and Political Rights and on Economic, Social and Cultural Rights. It has signed treaties guaranteeing asylum and political and civil rights for women, and condemning genocide, forced labor, racial discrimination, and apartheid.

2. *Recent legislation affecting human rights*

In spite of these guarantees and promises El Salvador has recently enacted a series of laws and decrees which negate or threaten the exercise of human rights.

On November 25, 1977, the Romero government enacted a Law of Defense and Guarantee of Public Order. It defined 18 categories of activity as crimes against public order in such broad and vague terms that they could be used to harass and repress anyone who opposed the Romero government. The U.S. State Department, the Inter-American Commission on Human Rights (IACHR) of the OAS, and the International Commission of Jurists all criticized the law as a severe threat to civil liberties. It was repealed on February 27, 1979 but most of its provisions and procedures, often in even harsher form, have been reinstated under the Revolutionary Governing Junta, in power since October 15, 1979.

The first decree of the new government, issued the day of Romero's overthrow, was the Proclamation of the Armed Forces. It set forth the reasons for the coup and the objectives of the new government. It accused the Romero government of violating human rights, fostering corruption, causing economic and social disaster, and disgracing the country and the armed forces. It criticized what it called El Salvador's "antiquated economic, social and political structures." It acknowledged past electoral frauds, and blamed previous governments for failing to push through necessary structural changes. Claiming that the armed forces had always been identified with the people, the Proclamation promised to end violence and corruption, guarantee human rights observance, equitably distribute the national wealth while increasing it, and improve the country's foreign relations, mainly with its Central American neighbors.

Specifically, the armed forces promised to dissolve ORDEN to assure freedom for political parties of all ideologies, to grant amnesty to all political exiles and prisoners, to permit labor unions to organize. In addition, the armed forces committed themselves to agrarian reform, and housing, food, education, and health care for all.

Decree No. 114 of February 8, 1980, introduced a major legal change. It accepted the Constitution of 1962 only "insofar as it is compatible with the nature of the present Regime and does not contravene the postulates and objectives of the Proclamation of the Armed Forces of October 15, 1979, and its line of government." Many of the decree's measures concerned economic changes the Junta wished to institute, but its most important result was to make the Constitution subordinate to proclamations of the Armed Forces, and to the armed forces themselves.

Constitutional guarantees were no longer the supreme law of the land and enforcement of them could no longer be sought as a matter of right.

Decree No. 155 of March 6, 1980, imposed a state of siege on the country. Its ostensible purpose was to allow smooth implementation of the agrarian reform which was announced at the same time. Under the Constitution, as mentioned above, state of siege provisions suspend the freedoms of movement and residence and of thought and expression, the inviolability of correspondence, and the right of assembly for 30 days. They also give the military courts jurisdiction over civilians accused of certain crimes including treason, espionage, rebellion, sedition, other offenses against the peace or independence of the state, and offenses against the law of nations. Despite the constitutional restrictions on extending the state of siege, it has been renewed each month and is by now permanent in El Salvador.

Decree No. 43 of August 21, 1980, placed certain autonomous government agencies under military control, including the National Administration for Aqueducts and Sewerage (ANDA), the National Telecommunications Administration (ANTEL), the Hydroelectric Executive Commission for the Lempa River (CEL), and the Autonomous Executive Commission of the Port Authority (CEPA). All workers and employees became members of the armed forces and are subject to any military order. The measure was aimed at preventing strikes.

Decree No. 507 of December 3, 1980, drastically changed the administration of justice, effectively ending judicial independence. It permits the military to hold a person for 180 days of preventive detention or 120 days of corrective detention on suspicion or whim. Even children, no matter how young, are subject to military justice. The investigation phase of proceedings can be carried out in secrecy. Security forces need not bring a prisoner before a judge until 15 days after the arrest. Standards of evidence are practically eliminated. (See Chapter 6 for an analysis of Decree No. 507.)

On January 10, 1981, the Junta imposed a 7 P.M. to 5 A.M. curfew on the country and declaration of martial law. Subsequent events indicate that troops carried orders to shoot to kill curfew violators. From January 12 to February 19, 1981, alone, *Socorro Juridico* compiled a list of 168 persons killed. Many were on their way home and were killed a few minutes after 7 P.M. Others were simply standing outside their houses. (See Chapter 3.)

3. *The right to life*

The various international agreements on human rights which El Salvador has ratified guarantee the right to life as the most basic and precious of rights. The Constitution of El Salvador says: "No person may be deprived of his life . . . except after being tried and sentenced in accordance with provisions of law . . ." (Article 164).

Massacres carried out by military and security forces stain the pages of recent Salvadoran history. In 1972 and 1977 protests of fraudulent elections were crushed by troops firing on crowds. A 1975 student demonstration against government expenditures on the "Miss Universe" pageant was fired upon by National Guardsmen; at least 16 students died. In May 1979, 23 demonstrators were killed by police outside the Cathedral in San Salvador. There were many similar incidents.

The killing continued after the October 1979 coup. The International Commission of Jurists reported: "Violence has not abated following the overthrow of General Romero. Many people have died in almost daily clashes of demonstrators and police." On January 22, 1980, the largest demonstration in the country's history came under fire from sharpshooters on the roof of the National Palace. Between 20 and 52 persons died. During the funeral ceremony for Archbishop Romero, 22 church leaders from several countries saw shots fired from the Presidential Palace at the crowd. During 1980, the killings escalated to a level of approximately 200 a week and continued close to that level in 1981.

4. *The right to humane treatment*

Prohibitions against torture in international agreements ratified by the government of El Salvador and in the Constitution of El Salvador are absolute. As the 1978 OAS General Assembly reaffirmed in Resolution 371: ". . . there are no circumstances that justify torture, summary execution, or prolonged detention without due process of law. . . ." (See Chapter 4.)

Investigations by the OAS Inter-American Commission on Human Rights and by a British Parliamentary delegation found "unequivocal proof" of torture during visits to El Salvador in late 1979 and early 1980. The U.S. State Department report on human rights for 1978 said:

There have been numerous detailed allegations of torture of prisoners by security guards, many of which are credible. Accusations against the National Guard and other security forces include denial of food and water, electric shock and sexual violations.

The State Department's findings the following year were in the same vein.

Despite promises of improvement in human rights conditions after the October 15, 1979, coup, torture continued to be employed by the security forces. Decree No. 507, discussed above, contains clauses which are practically invitations to the use of torture. They permit convictions based on uncorroborated confessions made in the presence of only police, army, or other security personnel. They also permit security forces to hold prisoners for 15 days after arrest before bringing them before a judge.

Torture has been widely used prior to killings. By mid-January 1980, tortured and mutilated corpses were appearing every day throughout El Salvador. In the following months, reports of killings, abductions and torture in the countryside mounted sharply.

Documented cases of torture during interrogation by security forces are numerous. Torture has been reported to occur in the central headquarters of the National Guard, the Treasury Police, and the National Police in El Salvador, and in police and National Guard headquarters in other towns. The most frequent types of tortures reported are severe blows to all parts of the body, death threats, choking, electric shock to lips, mouth, and genitals, hooding, drugging, submersion in water, cigarette burns, and simulated execution.

Information regarding the use of torture points unequivocally to the involvement of all branches of the security forces, as well as of paramilitary groups acting with impunity. The systematic, massive character of the practice leads to the inescapable conclusion that the authorities approve of it.

5. *The right to personal liberty*

The right to freedom from arbitrary arrest is guaranteed in the Constitution of El Salvador and in various international agreements to which it is a party. In spite of these protections, that right is seriously undermined by recent decrees of the Junta, and by the actions of its security forces.

The Law for the Defense and Guarantee of Public Order, passed under the Romero government in 1977, permitted the security forces to conduct arbitrary and unacknowledged arrests. The Inter-American Commission on Human Rights, after its January 1978 visit to the country, reported:

The security bodies have committed serious violations of the right to liberty, in making arbitrary arrests. They have maintained secret places of detention, where some persons, whose capture and imprisonment have been denied by the government, were deprived of liberty under extremely cruel and inhuman conditions. [See Chapter 5.]

The government that took power with the October 1979 coup promised to end arbitrary arrests. But in less than five months, it reimposed a state of siege and other measures which permitted arbitrary arrests, even though the Constitutional right to personal liberty is not subject to suspension under Salvadoran law.

On December 3, 1980, the Junta issued Decree No. 507 (discussed above) which permits prolonged, even indefinite, detention of prisoners at a military judge's whim. The decree has been applied selectively against political opponents of the regime, although not against well-known, right-wing figures with ties to the armed forces, such as former Major Roberto D'Aubuisson nor Ricardo Sol Meza (accused of killing two American labor advisors). The cases of both men were handled in the ordinary courts.

The main protection against arbitrary arrest, the right of *habeas corpus,* is no longer effective in El Salvador. Lawyers seeking writs have been mistreated and sometimes arrested by the security forces. Many have been threatened, some killed. And the Supreme Court, empowered by the Constitution to enforce the writs, declines to involve itself.

6. *The right to due process and to a fair trial*

Guarantees of due process and fair trial are found in El Salvador's Constitution:

No person may be deprived of his life, liberty, property, or possessions except after being tried and sentenced in accordance with provisions of law; nor shall anyone be tried twice for the same offense . . . every person has the right of *habeas corpus* . . . [Article 164, Title X]

No person shall be tried except under laws that were promulgated prior to the commission of the offense in question, and by a court that was previously established by law. . . . [Article 169, Title X]

Various other provisions of the Constitution and of the Code of Criminal Procedure contain guarantees of the rights of prisoners.

However, these legal standards have not ensured consistent, non-discriminatory justice in El Salvador's modern history. As the Inter-American Commission on Human Rights concluded in its 1978 report on El Salvador: ". . . in practice the legal remedies are not effective for protecting the persons arbitrarily deprived of their basic human rights." (See Chapter 6.)

Despite its promises of an end to human rights abuses, the government that took power in October 1979 has virtually eliminated guarantees of due process and fair trial in security cases. Decree No. 155 of March 6, 1980, placed civilians accused of security offenses under military courts whose procedures differ significantly from those in ordinary criminal proceedings. For example, the constitutional right against self-incrimination by refusing to answer a judge's questions during the investigation phase does not exist in military court proceedings. Also, military judges can order arrests on the basis of a "simple presumption" of a crime rather than the "sufficient elements of proof that the person participated in the offense," the standard required in the ordinary courts. And, unlike the regular criminal investigation, the military investigation phase is secret.

The independence of the civilian judiciary was eliminated after October 15, 1979. The Junta replaced all the magistrates on the Supreme Court with its own appointees. Under the state of siege law, civilian judges may not review in any meaningful way the procedings of the military courts. Decree No. 507 finally ended judicial independence by militarizing the administration of justice. "The judiciary," a former civilian judge has charged, "is an appendage of the military high command."

Fear has been as effective in undermining judicial independence and authority as the Junta's decrees. The International Commission of Jurists concluded that:

The judiciary has been made impotent by fear, while magistrates who have attempted to investigate crimes attributed to the security forces or right-wing groups have been immediately attacked, and several of them have been murdered.

7. *The right to freedom of conscience and religion*

El Salvador is a predominantly Catholic country, and the Catholic Church has played a pivotal role in the events of recent years. It has been in the forefront in implementing the changing role sketched for the Latin American church at bishops' conferences in Medellin, Colombia, in 1968 and in Puebla, Mexico, in 1979. Over the last two decades, the church in much of Latin America has shucked off the social conservatism which characterized it for centuries, and has become a leading voice for reform and social change.

This change has caused much controversy within the Latin American church, and in Latin American society in general. In El Salvador, as elsewhere, there have been divisions and disagreements, but the direction has been clear. It has supported the struggle of poor people for justice.

Violence against the church for its identification with the poor began several years ago. In June 1977, the Salvadoran church's Inter-Diocesan Social Secretariat published a report on attacks on the church in the preceding 18 months. It listed

. . . ten bomb explosions, two searches; one ransacking and desecration of the Blessed Sacrament; one threat to close the church radio; seven prohibitions for priests wishing to enter El Salvador; three priests tortured and two mistreated; three priests arrested; two priests and four laypersons assassinated; three priests forced to leave the country due to death threats. A defamation campaign. Threats to expel an order of religious women. Fifteen parishes without priests.

The incidence of attacks declined in the first few weeks after the October 1979 coup, but resumed with ferocity in 1980. The assassination of Archbishop Romero took place on March 24, and the four American churchwomen were killed on December 2. In addition, dozens of attacks by government forces on church members were documented during that year and continue up to the present. Priests, catechists, seminarians, Catholic relief workers, and nuns have been killed, or arrested and tortured. Churches have been raided and shot up with machine guns.

8. *The right to freedom of thought and expression*

El Salvador's constitution and the international conventions it has ratified guarantee freedom of expression, but limitations on that freedom, by law, military intervention, or threat, have been a constant feature of Salvadoran reality. The Law for the Defense and Guarantee of Public Order, enacted in 1977, formalized those limitations. The International Commission of Jurists described that law in 1978 as "a serious attack on freedom of expression particularly that of the press . . ." (See Chapter 8). Bombs, machine gun attacks, and death threats against independent newspapers and editors complemented statutory limitations on the press during the Molina and Romero governments.

The October 15, 1979, Proclamation of the Armed Forces promised to guarantee human rights observance in part "by stimulating free expression of thought, in accordance with ethical standards." Five months later, the Junta declared a state of siege which suspended constitutional guarantees of freedom of expression. Again, bombs and machine guns have complemented the restrictions. From January 1980 to June 1981, according to *Socorro Juridico,* 17 news offices and radio stations were bombed or machine-gunned, twelve journalists killed, eleven by official security forces, and three disappeared.

No independent newspapers currently publish. The last two, *El Independiente* and *La Cronica del Pueblo,* had closed by January 1981 after numerous bombings, threats, military interventions, and assaults on employees. The government has failed to investigate any of those incidents thoroughly.

9. *The rights of assembly and association*

According to the Constitution (Title X, Article 160), "the inhabitants of El Salvador have the right to assemble and to meet peacefully without arms, for any lawful purpose." In practice, those perceived to be opponents of the government have not enjoyed that right in recent decades. Restrictions on the rights to assembly and association have been particularly severe in the countryside. After the peasant uprising of 1932, all organizations of agricultural workers were banned. When peasant unions began to organize in the late 1960s and 1970s, the government responded with repression. The International Commission of Jurists observed: "It is from late 1976 that the detention, torture, disappearance and murder of peasant leaders began to be reported with alarming frequency." (See Chapter 9.)

In 1977, the Law for the Defense and Guarantee of Public Order, aimed at peasant organizations as well as urban-based unions, made public meetings and all strikes illegal.

The October 15, 1979, coup brought to power a government promising, among other things, to recognize and respect "the right to unionize, in all labor sectors." The next day, it ousted striking workers from several factories in San Salvador, killing 18, arresting 78, and torturing many. "Within a week," Amnesty International reported, "the new government was responsible for more than 100 killings of demonstrators and striking workers who had been occupying farms and factories."

In the following weeks, political demonstrations in the streets of San Salvador regularly came under fire from security forces. In March 1980, after its agrarian reform program was announced, government troops swept rural areas where labor groups were strong. "There appears to be no doubt whatsoever," Amnesty International concluded, "that members of the major *campesino* groupings, all of them affiliates of oppositionist political coalitions, are being systematically persecuted in areas to be affected by the agrarian reform."

Groups which have sought to monitor human rights conditions, particularly the Archdiocese's *Socorro Juridico* and the Salvadoran Commission on Human Rights, have had their offices raided repeatedly and bombed, their files ransacked, and their employees threatened and, in some cases, killed.

Academic freedom of association has also been denied. Teachers and students have been killed, schools and the university closed down.

Since mid-1980, several unions have been dissolved and their leaders imprisoned. A strike at the Rio Lempa hydroelectric plant in August 1980 ended when authorities arrested the entire leadership of the Sindicato de Trabajadores de la Electricidad de la Central Electrica del Rio Lempa (STECEL).

10. *Political rights*

The 1962 Constitution established a "republican, democratic, and representative" form of government with power emanating from the people who enjoy universal suffrage as well as the rights to form and join political parties and to be candidates for public office. Nevertheless there has not been a fair election in El Salvador for the last 50 years. The U.S. State Department summarized Salvadoran political history this way in 1980:

Authoritarian military governments allied with a wealthy elite have been the trademarks of Salvadoran politics. A democratic facade has been maintained over the years through regularly scheduled elections resulting in the periodic changing of Presidents, Legislative Assembly members, and municipal administrations. Since the early 1970s, the results of the elections inevitably have been challenged as fraudulent, and although personnel have changed, the character of the governing coalition and its *modus operandi* have not. As a result, the Government party controlled all but four of the fifty-four Legislative Assembly seats and all two hundred sixty-one mayoralties at the time of the October 15 coup. . . .

Legally, participation in the political system is open to all citizens. However, the functioning of the opposition political parties allegedly had been inhibited through repression, harassment, and collusion that have prevented effective recruitment, organization, and campaigning, including denial of access to the media. The new government has pledged to open the political process.

—Country reports on human
rights practices for 1979

The long history of manipulated elections, and particularly the blatant frauds of 1972 and 1977, undermined faith in elections. The OAS Inter-American Commission on Human Rights concluded after a 1978 visit that:

There is widespread skepticism among the citizenry regarding the right to vote and to participate in government. In particular, the political parties of the opposition, in this connection, came to have no confidence in the possibility of having full and honest elections, not only in the light of their experiences during the course of recent elections, but also because of the structure of the electoral system and of the obstacles the parties encounter in trying to organize in the interior of the country. . . .

The Proclamation of the October 1979 coup acknowledged "scandalous election frauds" in the past and promised "a truly democratic system," with free elections open to parties of all ideologies. But the Junta later suspended several rights basic to political participation and its denial of those rights has been selectively directed against the political opposition.

The Junta has announced elections in March 1982 for delegates to a constituent assembly, to be followed by presidential and legislative elections in 1983. One of the features of its provisional law for registering parties is that in the present climate of unrestricted political violence against the opposition, it requires the names *and addresses* of at least 3,000 members to register a new party.

Government officials have made contradictory statements in recent months as to whether the opposition coalition, the Democratic Revolutionary Front (FDR) and its head, Guillermo Ungo, would be allowed to participate in elections. For its part, the opposition favors political negotiations with international mediation to end the conflict. It has said it would consider elections as part of the comprehensive process of political negotiations.

11. *The rights of refugees and displaced persons*

The conflict in the rural areas forced at least 350,000 Salvadorans to become refugees, mainly peasant families who abandoned their homes for safety in less dangerous areas or in neighboring countries. (See Chapter 11.) Government attitudes toward peasant organization, and the counter-insurgency campaign against the guerrillas have been the major factors spurring their flight.

Even after the October 1979 coup and the promises of reform by the new government, according to Amnesty International, military authorities continued to regard *campesino* organizations as suspect and "subject to the same degree of repression dealt out to members of avowedly violent guerrilla groups . . ." *Socorro Juridico* noted sharp increases in reports of killings, arrests, torture, and forced displacement of rural inhabitants coinciding with 171 military operations carried out in different farming areas between January and March 13, 1980. The implementation of the Junta's agrarian reform program in March 1980 produced a new surge of refugees. National Guard and Army units ostensibly deployed to implement the program were allegedly involved in the disappearance, torture, and execution of hundreds of rural inhabitants of villages where the population included members of opposition labor organizations.

The military strategy is to eliminate bases for guerrilla organizations by depopulating villages, and to isolate the guerrillas and create food supply and other logistical problems. This has led to the slaughter of livestock, the theft of food, the razing of villages, cropburning, and direct assaults upon the civilian population.

Of those refugees who have stayed within the country, estimated to number over 150,000, some 80 percent have gone to other rural areas where they may receive some relief assistance from the government or domestic and international humanitarian agencies. Some 5,000 have gone to camps run by the Archdiocese of San Salvador where food and medicine are reported in critically short supply. Health workers aiding refugees have been harassed and some of them killed. Fear is an additional problem. Refugees dare not leave the sites provided by the Church for fear of further persecution by the military. Nor are they safe inside the camps. Between August 20, 1980 and March 17, 1981, *Socorro Juridico* documented 67 separate instances of killings, detentions, robberies, encirclements, threats, searches, and military occupations of refugee centers by the security forces.

At least 200,000 other Salvadoran refugees have fled to neighboring countries, principally Mexico, Guatemala, Honduras, Nicaragua, and Costa Rica. The refugees in Honduras, estimated to number anywhere from 33,000 to 70,000, generally live near the border with El Salvador. After surviving the traumatic events that drove them from their homes, many were further victimized as they attempted to cross the border. In two widely reported cases, at the Sumpul and Lempa rivers, thousands of Salvadoran peasants allegedly were attacked by Salvadoran troops while Honduran troops blocked the border. In the second of these incidents, March 17, 1981, at the Lempa River, doctors, priests, and relief workers present witnessed the Salvadoran air force dropping bombs and strafing the fleeing refugees while the army fired on them with mortars and machine guns.

Nor are the refugees safe within Honduras. Substantial testimony indicates a pattern of murder, harassment, assault, abduction and forcible return to El Salvador by Salvadoran security forces and members of ORDEN operating in Honduras, as well as crimes by Honduran army personnel against the refugees, including rape and murder.

C. *U.S. involvement*

Since the October 15, 1979, coup, the United States has become deeply involved diplomatically, economically, and militarily in the affairs of El Salvador. Since the coup, U.S. economic aid, including proposals for FY1982, has climbed over $300 million, much higher than for any other Latin American nation. Security assistance to the Junta through FY1982 will total $62 million, four times what it was in all the years from 1950 to 1979. Despite deep concern both in Congress and among the public about parallels to the early days of U.S. involvement in Vietnam, U.S. military personnel have been sent to El Salvador to help that country's armed forces. U.S. military aid and training are going to units repeatedly accused of massive violations of the human rights of El Salvador's people.

U.S. military involvement in El Salvador began modestly enough with a military mission in the mid-1940s, and with training and assistance programs in pursuit of hemispheric security. After the Cuban Revolution in 1959, U.S. hemispheric strategy shifted to defense against internal subversion rather than external attack. Under the Public Safety Program, the U.S. helped train and equip the Salvadoran police and National Guard. An evaluation of this program in 1967 was satisfied that it had "efficiently trained the National Guard and National Police in basic tactics so that authorities have been successful in handling any politically-motivated demonstrations in recent years." (See Chapter 13.)

The first interruption in U.S. military aid to El Salvador came, not because of the Carter administration's human rights policies, but because in 1976 Salvadoran army chief of staff Gen. Manuel Alfonso Rodriguez was convicted in New York of trying to sell 10,000 machine guns to people he thought belonged to the Mafia. The next year, El Salvador announced it was rejecting military aid to protest U.S. criticism of the Romero government's human rights record.

Less than three weeks after the 1979 coup, the U.S. shipped $205,000 worth of riot control equipment to El Salvador, along with four Army advisers. Training in non-lethal forms of crowd control, it was argued, was essential to reduce human rights violations. Archbishop Romero spoke out against the sale and, in a letter to President Carter shortly before his death, charged that "the security forces, with better personal protection and effectiveness, have repressed the people even more violently using deadly weapons."

Despite Romero's protests, U.S. military aid to the Junta increased steadily. Most of it was for training and "non-lethal" equipment (vehicles, communications gear, night vision devices). Some aid was held up for approximately five weeks after the December 2, 1980, murder of the four American churchwomen and reports implicating Salvadoran security forces. When it resumed, in the context of a major offensive by guerrilla forces, two leased helicopters were included. On January 17, 1981, during the Carter administration's last week in office, overtly lethal weapons—grenade launchers, rifles, ammunition, etc.—were sent for the first time.

On February 23, 1981, the new Reagan administration issued a "White Paper" alleging clandestine military support given by the Soviet Union, Cuba and their Communist allies to Marxist-Leninist guerrillas now fighting to overthrow the established government of El Salvador. U.S. military aid to the government increased dramatically. By spring, the Administration had sent $20 million in emergency funds and asked Congress to reprogram or appropriate $31 million more. Additional U.S. military personnel were sent as well. By mid-March, 56 were in El Salvador. Their missions included training in use and maintenance of helicopters; training the Salvadoran navy to interdict seaborne infiltration of arms; liaison with the Salvadoran army; intelligence; assisting Salvadoran commanders at the national and regional levels with planning, communications, and coordination; and the training of a new quick-reaction force, the 2,000 man Atlacatl Battalion, by counterinsurgency specialists (Green Berets).

The U.S. commitment to the Junta in El Salvador has increased dramatically in spite of congressional attempts to apply legislative brakes to the process. The U.S. experience in Vietnam produced a body of legislation aimed at limiting the discretionary authority of the President in similar situations. (See Chapter 13 for an analysis of the War Powers Resolution and of legislation linking security assistance and human rights.) But it is becoming increasingly evident that the law is still vague, that the executive branch has a great deal of room to maneuver and that congressional brakes are difficult to apply.

D. *Conclusions*

The analysis of the information developed for this report led the authors to the following major conclusions:

1. The Revolutionary Governing Junta of El Salvador, both by commission and omission, is responsible for a widespread and systematic pattern of gross violations of human rights.

2. Despite its avowedly reformist character, the human rights situation in El Salvador has steadily worsened since the Revolutionary Governing Junta came to power on October 15, 1979. In fact, not since *la Matanza,* the 1932 massacre of as many as 30,000 peasants, has the human rights situation in El Salvador been as bad as it is now.

3. The violations of human rights taking place in El Salvador are not aberrations. Rather, they are selectively directed against those perceived as opposing the country's economic and political system.

4. The U.S. government has increased its diplomatic, economic, and military support for El Salvador precisely during the period when human rights violations there have accelerated. Both the Carter and Reagan administrations have followed this policy, but the levels of support,

and therefore the U.S. stake in El Salvador, have increased dramatically under President Reagan.

5. Under present conditions, the solution to the crisis favored by the Revolutionary Governing Junta and the Reagan administration—elections in 1982 and 1983—offers little hope for an end to the tragedy of El Salvador.

PART I

BACKGROUND TO TRAGEDY

CHAPTER 1
A BRIEF HISTORY OF EL SALVADOR

Just a few years ago, the tiny Central American republic of El Salvador was a forgotten country; today it is on the world stage as a bitter internal conflict claims scores of lives every day.

Why has El Salvadoran society become so polarized? Why, despite pressure from abroad, has it proved impossible to enact reform within a peaceful climate? Why is it that social tensions which erupted in the past—as long ago as 1931—have exploded again into all-out civil conflict?

El Salvador's social indicators tell part of the tale. It is a very poor country, lacking strategic or mineral resources, and attracting relatively little foreign investment. It is an overwhelmingly agricultural economy, with up to 70 percent of the people living on land much of which is rugged terrain unsuitable even for subsistence agriculture. It has by far the highest population density in Central America, with some 500 people per square mile against an average of 94 per square mile in the rest of the isthmus. An average per capita GNP is estimated at 650 US dollars, while 5 percent of the people accounted for 38 percent of national income. The level of social amenities remains extraordinarily low, particularly in the countryside where an average of four people share a room and 85 percent of all houses lack electricity, running water and proper sanitary facilities. In some regions, there is only one doctor for every 25,000 people; life expectancy is 62 years at birth. Sixty-six percent of the children between the ages of 6 months and 5 years in intensive farming regions and 77 percent of the children in the same age group in coffee-growing regions suffer from malnutrition.[1]

Like its Central American neighbors, El Salvador has experienced a *dynamic* process of land concentration and land eviction in the last century. It began during the coffee boom of the late nineteenth century, when communal lands farmed by indigenous peasants were abolished in favor of private property. It reached a second acute phase during the cotton and sugar booms of the last three decades, when the number of landless peasants increased by alarming proportions. In the meantime the military and paramilitary law enforcement agencies have exercised a progressively tighter rein in rural areas, in an attempt to stifle social protest at its inception.

One needs to understand this process, in order to see why an apparently radical agrarian reform after March 1980 bypassed so many of the country's impoverished rural workers; to see why this class had been excluded from the benefits of the few social reforms of the 1960's and has taken an increasingly militant stance as its economic plight has worsened; and, finally, to see why the replacement of a few individuals in the higher echelons of the military had so little effect on the long-standing brutal and repressive practices of the National Guard and local law enforcement agencies.

It was almost exactly one hundred years ago, in February 1881, that a liberal government enacted the legislation abolishing communal patterns of land tenure. The coffee boom was already under way and previous legislation had specified that at least half of communal landholdings had to be dedicated to commercial crops (a demand that few indigenous peasants could afford to fulfill, given the five years it takes a coffee plant to bear fruit). During this period, the heyday of laissez-faire liberalism, similar legislation was enacted all over Latin America. The difference in El Salvador was that the laws were actually enforced. Given the intensive labor requirements of coffee cultivation the new coffee magnates had as much need for a regular supply of manpower as for legal title to the land itself. New rural police forces were established to help rural officials evict and control the rural population. When widespread unrest broke out in the major coffee regions towards the turn of the century, a new mounted police force, the precursor of the National Guard, was created, first in the coffee departments of Ahuachapan, Sonsonate and Santa Ana, and then throughout the country.

The system was refined further over the next fifty years. An Agrarian Law passed in 1907 gives some indication of the virtual slavery to which rural workers had been reduced. Landless laborers could be arrested for vagrancy, and had to carry work books registering their work obligations. Agrarian judges, assisted by the army, were appointed in each village to keep lists of all day-laborers, and arrange for the capture of all those who ran away from the estates. In 1912 the rural National Guard and the *patrullas cantonales* consisting of army reserve units carrying out regular police patrols were created.

Popular pressure built up through the 1920's and when the bottom fell out of the coffee market during the depression, it finally erupted in the uprising of 1932 popularly known by the word "Matanza" (the massacre). In the previous year the oligarchy had been sufficiently disturbed by popular unrest to acquiesce in the election of a reformist liberal named Arturo Araujo, El Salvador's last elected civilian president. Within months, as demonstrations and strikes escalated markedly, Araujo was obliged to surrender power to a military officer, General Maximiliano Hernandez Martinez. General Martinez swiftly knit together the repressive apparatus, bringing the National Guard, the National Police and the *patrullas cantonales* (village patrols) under the direct jurisdiction of the Defense Ministry. After a peasant uprising in the west of the country had been suppressed, General Martinez retaliated with a "scorched earth" policy that cost up to 30,000 lives. This massacre is one of the most important political events in the history of El Salvador. The blame for the uprising was laid at the door of El Salvador's small Communist Party. Its leader, Augustin Farabundo Marti, was arrested and executed. It is a name now internationally known, since its adoption by the insurrectionary movement which is fighting in El Salvador today.

General Martinez, who ruled for 12 years, paved the way for the system of government which (with one brief interlude in 1960–61) was to survive intact until 1979, ensuring that the military would retain political power. The president chosen from military ranks would, in turn, appoint civilian cabinet members who, with few exceptions, would represent the interests of the now entrenched coffee oligarchy.

After the Second World War the Salvadoran economy underwent significant transformations, which in turn had their effect on both political party structures and the attitudes of part of the military toward popular pressure groups. A measure of industrialization took place, in the capital city of San Salvador and such regional towns as Santa Ana. The industrial working class for the first time was permitted relative freedom of trade-union organization, social welfare benefits, and a minimum wage structure. In particular during the Alliance for Progress era of the 1960's, substantial United States aid poured into urban industry. Within the framework of the Central American Common Market, El Salvador developed a substantial light industry in processed foods, paint and paper products, and the assembly of prefabricated items. Many of its exports went to the neighboring country of Honduras, until this market was cut off by the so-called "football war" of 1969.

By 1960, organized labor had gained such influence in urban areas that the military overthrew its own incumbent president, and installed a provisional government including labor representatives. The experiment was short-lived, and another military coup brought Colonel Julio Rivera to power in 1961. However, for the urban sector at least, the nature of government had undoubtedly changed. The early 1960's saw the establishment and rapid rise of the Christian Democratic Party, of which Jose Napoleon Duarte was a founding member. In 1965, Guillermo Ungo's social democratic National Revolutionary Movement (MNR) was founded. In the March 1964 municipal elections the Christian Democrats emerged as the dominant opposition party, and they rapidly increased their share of the vote through the remainder of the decade.

But rural El Salvador was a very different society. The formation of trade-unions remained illegal for agricultural workers in the countryside, and any attempt at organization was ruthlessly suppressed. Under the Agrarian Law, as amended in 1950, the punishable offense of vagrancy was reaffirmed. It was stipulated that National Guard members keep order on private estates, and that law enforcement officials be appointed by the landowners themselves. There were provisions for the summary eviction of unwanted tenant farmers, for the local Mayor and police to destroy the homes of "malefactors," for people out at night to be detained indefinitely by the police on suspicion and for the National Guard to arrest anywhere, at any time, laborers who failed in their obligations to landowners. It was still a society of virtual serfdom.

The dramatic expansion of commercial agriculture put increased pressure on land. Until about 1950, commercial farming was restricted to large-scale coffee cultivation in the highland piedmont. But new crops, primarily cotton and sugar, gradually took over the entire Pacific lowlands, forcing squatters and former subsistence farmers into the position of landless laborers. The most significant expansion occurred during the 1960's, when, during the Alliance for Progress, cotton acreage alone went up from 106,000 acres in 1960 to 302,000 acres in 1965. One researcher estimates that landless rural workers rose from 11 percent of the labor force in 1961 to 29 percent in 1971, and 40 percent in 1975.[2]

In other parts of Latin America the twin poles of the Alliance for Progress were reform (primarily land reform) and counter-insurgency. In El Salvador, the very term "land reform" was equated with communism by the privileged classes, and brought back memories of 1932. The United States government did not press for it, at least until the next decade, but it laid a strong emphasis on counter-insurgency and upgrading the police forces. There was—perhaps surprisingly—no violent opposition in El Salvador throughout this decade. But the United States feared that acute social tensions could lead to violence. As an internal evaluation of the U.S. Public Safety Program commented in 1967:

The Public Safety Program in El Salvador is 10 years old and the advisors have efficiently trained the National Guard and National Police in basic tactics so that authorities have been successful in handling any politically motivated demonstrations in recent years. . . . With the potential danger that exists in a densely populated country where the rich are very rich and poor extremely poor El Salvador is fortunate that the Guard and Police are well trained and disciplined. . . .[3]

During the late 1960's an additional element appeared in the Salvadoran security apparatus, in the form of an 80,-000 strong paramilitary network known as ORDEN, which penetrated every hamlet in the country and established an elaborate system of internal espionage.

As a result of the fraudulent 1967 elections and the labor unrest that occurred in the next two years, by the early 1970's tension was at a high level. In 1972 Jose Napoleon Duarte, a Christian Democrat, who is now president of the military-dominated Revolutionary Governing Junta, and Guillermo Manuel Ungo, leader of the social democratic MNR (National Revolutionary Movement) who now heads the opposition Democratic Revolutionary Front (allied with the guerrillas fighting to overthrow the Junta), ran together as, respectively, the presidential and vice-presidential candidates of an electoral coalition which fought on a platform of human rights and social justice and sought to end forty years of military dictatorship through the ballot box: Fraud by the military deprived them of victory.

On March 25 an unsuccessful military uprising protesting the fraudulent elections left some 100 killed and another 200 wounded.[4] As a wave of reprisals was unleashed, Duarte and numerous political and military leaders were detained and tortured.

A new factor had now appeared in the form of El Salvador's first guerrilla group, the Popular Forces of Liberation (FPL) formed in 1970 from the radical faction of the Salvadoran Communist Party (PCS) and left-wing university students. In the next few years further violent opposition groups were to emerge, first the Revolutionary People's Army (ERP) in 1971 and then the Armed Forces of National Resistance (FARN), formed from an ERP splinter group in 1975. The groups differed in military and political strategy, as the ERP, for example, turned to sabotage and individual acts of terrorism while the others emphasized building popular support. One effect of the renewed land concentration was peasant flight to the cities, and a new class of marginal slum dwellers in urban shanty towns. They—together with landless laborers, urban workers disillusioned with official unionism, university students and low-paid teachers—were to form the basis of a political phenomenon of the 1970's, the emergence of mass popular organizations outside the traditional party structure.

First to be formed, in 1974, was the Front for Unified Popular Action (FAPU) comprised primarily of urban workers. The following year saw the emergence of the Popular Revolutionary Block (BPR), the largest and most radical group, deriving the bulk of its support from the peasantry. Finally the February 28 Popular Leagues (LP-28) was set up in 1978 within the slum population of San Salvador. Each of these organizations soon formed links with the guerrillas, FAPU with the FARN, the BPR with the FPL, and the LP-28 with the ERP. They manifested distinct political and social characteristics, and there was often rivalry, particularly with FAPU, which was accused by the others of "reformist tendencies." However, all concurred on the necessity of implementing a wide-ranging program of reforms and bringing down the military regime through mass action.

The government of Colonel Arturo Armando Molina (1972–77), under pressure from the United States embassy, attempted to counter the growing tensions by enacting a limited agrarian reform, supported by a government-favored peasant organization, *Union Comunal Salvadorena* (UCS), which claimed 100,000 members and received extensive support from US funding sources. An agrarian transformation act was enacted in 1975, but the reform program never got under way. The first stage was to have been extremely limited, distributing only 50,000 acres of land to 12,000 peasant families. Generous compensation was provided, but for the rural oligarchy it was an attack on the concept of private property. Powerful landowner associations such as the Eastern Region Farmer's Front (FARO) and the influential National Association of Private Enterprise (ANEP) launched a publicity campaign against the project. The military itself divided and the conservatives prevailed.

According to a 1978 Report on Human Rights in El Salvador by the Inter-American Commission on Human Rights (IACHR) as well as the Hearings before the Sub-Committees on International Organizations and on Inter-American Affairs of the Committee on International Relations, March 9 and 17, 1977, the presidential elections held February 20, 1977, were marked by intimidation, violence and fraud carried out on a massive scale by the government. Despite the claims of irregularities and fraud, General Carlos Humberto Romero, the official candidate, was declared the winner on February 25, 1978.[5]

There was no more talk of reform but rather an escalating campaign of repression and political killing which has been amply documented by such organizations as the Inter-American Commission on Human Rights. While the victims included politicians, priests and persons from almost every sector of society, poor peasants and rural workers again bore the brunt of the repression. The victory of the Nicaraguan revolutionaries in July 1979 turned the scales against Romero. Perceiving him as lacking the political skill to extract the reforms from the armed forces and oligarchy needed to avoid a repetition of the Nicaraguan experience, military officers, who were by no means united among themselves, staged a military coup against General Romero in October 1979. At one end of the spectrum were the younger and more progressive officers grouped around Colonel Adolfo Arnoldo Majano; at the other end were conservatives who nevertheless saw the need for a new public image. This group was led by Colonels Jose Guillermo Garcia and Jaime Abdul Gutierrez, who today are believed to be the most powerful men in the country. Initially committed to reforms, the first Junta of the new government included civilian representatives of parties such as the National Revolutionary Movement (MNR), the National Democratic Union (UDN), the more radical wing of the Christian Democrats, and individuals drawn from a coalition of trade-unions and professional organizations known as the *Foro Popular* in which the parties also participated.

On the military side, younger officers were promoted who represented reform-oriented sectors within the Armed Forces. Yet there was a distinct effort to preserve the structure of the security forces and to avoid factionalism. As a result, except for the displacement of General Romero himself, and a few other military figures identified with the extreme right wing, such as Major Roberto D'Aubuisson, the lines of command remained unaltered, and security operations remained substantially in the same hands as during the Molina and Romero regimes. Apart from one of the armed groups which at first tried to instigate an insurrection, the attitude of the guerrillas and mass organizations was one of an armed truce, continuous pressure for speedy reforms, and skepticism that the experiment would last.

The Junta stated its intention to restore the rule of law, to create a climate of peace, and recognize "the validity of the current (1962) Constitution . . . and all laws . . . that govern the institutional life of the Republic . . ." (Article IV, Decree No. 1), and on October 16, 1979, it decreed a general amnesty for all political prisoners and Salvadorans in exile. In November, it dissolved ORDEN and created a Special Committee to Investigate Missing Political Prisoners which was granted autonomy and full powers to carry out its task. Composed of the Attorney General, a member appointed by the Supreme Court of Justice and "an honorable citizen" appointed by the Junta, it was given sixty days to carry out the investigation and submit "a detailed report" to the Junta. On November 23, 1979, presenting its first report, the Special Investigative Commission advised the Junta that it had "concrete data" that some officials of previous regimes were responsible for violations of basic human rights and recommended that the following steps be taken to redress past abuses and to prevent their recurrence:

1. the prosecution of former Presidents Molina and Romero for their responsibility as Commanders-in-chief of the Armed Forces.

2. the prosecution of the former Directors General of the National Guard, Treasury Police and National Police under the Molina and Romero regimes.

3. prohibiting the existence of jails or even simple, provisional detention facilities in the headquarters of the Public Security Forces or in any other troop headquarters (since this facilitates illegal detention and the use of torture), and requiring that arrested persons be brought to public jails under the control of the Justice Ministry.

4. action to compensate the families of missing political prisoners whose deaths are confirmed or presumed.

On December 3, 1979, the Ministry of the Presidency announced that the Attorney General's Office had been instructed to investigate and obtain sufficient evidence to begin proceedings against these former officials and stated that compensation would be paid to families of missing persons and police killed in confrontation with the guerrillas. However, the Junta had taken no steps to begin this promised investigation by the time the Special Committee submitted its final report to it on January 3, 1980 (the day most civilian members of the Junta resigned).

The Junta's failure to act apparently convinced the Special Committee that its work was futile. Accordingly, in its final report, the Committee advised the Junta that it was "concluding its mission and declaring itself to be disbanded" and pointedly reiterated its earlier recommendations. The IACHR has confirmed that the Junta "never set in motion" the promised investigations of former Presidents Molina and Romero and the former heads of the security forces.[6] Moreover, the Junta has never taken action to implement the Special Committee's other remedial recommendations: Political detainees remained imprisoned, and ORDEN, though officially proscribed, continued to operate with utter impunity and with the government's complicity.

Although during this period the Junta did not modify any existing laws guaranteeing the rights to a fair trial and due process of law, it regularly denied to its perceived opponents the exercise of these basic rights and took no steps to sanction past or curb ongoing abuses of authority by government officials and agents.

The months following the coup were marked by a series of demonstrations and strikes, occupations of ministries and embassies, led by the popular organizations and demands for a halt in repression. These protests were met with a repression arguably greater than that under Romero. Officers led by Majano attempted to halt the rising violence but found they had only limited authority within the regular army and virtually none over the National Guard and the Treasury Police. It was these forces which were identified as the principal instigators of right-wing terrorism, many of their personnel belonging to the various paramiliary groups. By the end of the year the activities of these groups had reached such a pitch and had become so clearly identified with the regular forces that the civilian members of the Junta made executive control over the armed forces the central issue of their continued participation in government.

Early in January 1980 the military rejected civilian attempts to exercise control over the armed forces, thus precipitating the resignation of two of the three civilian Junta members—Guillermo Ungo and Roman Mayorga —as well as all civilian cabinet members. Many of those who replaced them stayed on only until the spring, by which time they too resigned and left the country, charging that they had no effective voice in decisions with a government that had increasing concentrated control in the hands of the military. With the fall of this "First Junta" the centrist alternative was effectively closed, and the military were back in control.

On January 22, 1980, to commemorate the 48th anniversary of the rebellion of 1932, the *Coordinadora Revolucionaria de Masas* (CRM), into which the mass organizations had united, organized a massive demonstration in San Salvador. This demonstration, the largest ever in the country, was attacked by guards and sharpshooters on the rooftops of the National Palace. As in the case of past massacres, there is disagreement about the exact number of demonstrators killed (one source says "more than twenty," another "at least 52"), but only the Government disputes that those doing the killing were under the control of the ruling Junta.[7]

The U.S. State Department recognized that civilian members of the Junta did not have control over the security forces when it asserted that "despite efforts to make a clean break with the pattern of human rights abuses of previous governments, there were some incidents of excessive violence by the security forces."[8]

The International Commission of Jurists observed that:

Violence has not abated following the overthrow of General Romero. Many people have died in almost daily clashes of demonstrators and police. Some militant left-wing groups have announced that they will suspend their activities to see if the government will put its pledges into action. The Archbishop of

El Salvador, a leading defender of human rights, has also indicated that he favors a dialogue with the Junta. It is to be hoped that the present government will indeed set the country on the course to democracy. If not, violence will probably continue and the likelihood of generalized popular insurrection, a right guaranteed by the Salvadoran Constitution, will increase.[9]

Shortly afterwards, many civilian political groups and former government officials who had left the Junta, Guillermo Ungo among them, combined with various nonaligned trade-unions and professional organizations to form the Democratic Front (FD). In April this group reached agreement with the CRM on a common program of reforms and action which led to the establishment of the Democratic Revolutionary Front (FDR). Since April 1980 the FDR has been the political arm of the revolutionary opposition, incorporating liberal and social-democratic elements as well as those of the Marxist left.

At the same time the various guerrilla groups had been moving towards greater unity, setting up a united command structure, known as the United Revolutionary Directorate (DRU). In October 1980 they incorporated the small military forces of the Communist Party, establishing a combined front called the Farabundo Marti National Liberation Front (FMLN). By mid-1981 the regular forces of the FMLN amounted to some 5,000 combatants, compared with some 15,000 in the combined Salvadoran Armed Forces. Armed confrontations between the military and the guerrillas intensified.

On February 8, 1980, the Junta placed itself beyond *all* legal restraints with the announcement that it would recognize the validity of the 1962 Constitution only insofar as it was "compatible" with the regime's objectives and "line of government" (Decree No. 114, Article 1). On March 6, 1980, the Junta declared a nationwide state of siege that was renewed every 30 days and which significantly changed the nature and administration of the country's legal system.

The preambulatory paragraphs of the State of Siege Decree (No. 155) attempt to justify this action on the grounds that despite the Junta's efforts "to put into practice the basic principles of democracy and . . . to create a climate of peace and tranquility" (Par. I), certain persons

in obstructing this effort, have committed acts designed to create a state of disruption and social disturbance within the country, thereby affecting the economy of the Nation and the public peace so necessary at this time; [Par. II]

These same persons, whose purpose it is to thwart the process of structural change that the current Government is carrying out, have seriously disturbed the public order. . . . [Par. III]

The process of structural change alluded to in Paragraph III apparently refers to the Junta's agrarian reform measures specified in other decrees.

Article I of Decree No. 155 suspended, in accordance with the specific terms of Article 175 of the Constitution, the following four constitutional guarantees: freedom of movement and residence (Article 154); freedom of thought and expression (Article 158, par. 1); inviolability of correspondence (Article 159); and the right of assembly, except for meetings or assemblies for cultural or industrial purposes (Article 160).

Article II of this Decree, pursuant to Article 177 of the Constitution, vested military tribunals with jurisdiction over civilians charged with the commission of the following crimes: treason, espionage, rebellion, sedition, other offenses against the peace or independence of the state, and offenses against the law of nations. For all other crimes, civilians, in theory, continued to be subject to ordinary court proceedings.

The move towards open warfare was precipitated by the

tragic assassination of San Salvador's Archbishop Oscar Arnulfo Romero, who had championed the cause of the poor and used his influence to promote a political solution to the conflict. In his last homily, Romero openly called on the Junta's troops to disobey orders to fire on their own people. With his death, El Salvador lost a symbol of popular resistance to political violence. Throughout the rest of 1980, the reformist image the Salvadoran government sought through the agrarian reform program was undermined by a series of events. Colonel Majano, considered the principal progressive force within the military, was forced out of the Junta by Colonels Garcia and Gutierrez, and sent into exile. In November, six leading members of the FDR (including its then President, former agriculture minister Enrique Alvarez Cordoba) were kidnapped from a meeting in San Salvador by a large group of heavily armed civilians acting with apparent military support. The bodies of the six were discovered a few hours later. In early December, four U.S. religious workers were killed on an isolated road outside San Salvador in circumstances which convinced the U.S. ambassador himself that guilt lay unequivocally with the security forces.

To bolster the Junta's waning image, Jose Napoleon Duarte was elevated to the presidency of what is the fourth transitional government since October 1979.

The FDR-FMLN, which had declared a "general offensive" in January 1981, in what is said was an attempt to present the incoming Reagan administration with a *fait accompli,* in recent months has stated its willingness to negotiate a political solution to the conflict.

CHAPTER 2

THE AGRARIAN
REFORM PROGRAM:
A BRIEF APPRAISAL

The agrarian reform in El Salvador has been a source of substantial controversy. Supporters of the Junta point to it as a sign that the government deserves support. Critics argue that little has actually been accomplished. This chapter assesses the program after providing some background on economic conditions in El Salvador.

A. *Socio-economic background*[1]

El Salvador is the smallest country on the mainland of the Americas with an area of approximately 8,200 square miles, the size of Massachusetts. Its population, now 4.8 million, has quadrupled in the past 60 years and is projected to continue to increase at the high rate of 3.5 percent a year. Even now, El Salvador, with over 500 inhabitants per square mile, is the second most densely populated country in the Americas and one of the highest in the Third World.

The estimated average per capita income is US $650. Median income is much lower, however, since the distribution of income and wealth is extremely skewed. The wealthiest 5 percent of families receive 38 percent of the income, and the wealthiest 20 percent receive 67 percent, while the bottom 40 percent of families receive only 7.5 percent.

In early 1980, the top 10 percent of landowners in El Salvador held 78 percent of the arable land, and the lowest 10 percent, barely 0.4 percent. Other reports indicate that 40 percent of the farmland was owned by fewer than 2,000 families, representing .002 percent of the population. Moreover, the number of landless families in rural areas has been increasing from 30,450 in 1961 to 112,100 in 1971, and to 300,000 in 1980. This situation, exacerbated by the rapid population growth, means that the basic social needs of the vast majority of the population are not being met.

The agricultural sector is the mainstay of the economy. In recent years it has generated nearly 30 percent of the country's Gross Domestic Product (GDP), employed nearly 50 percent of the labor force, and earned more than 60 percent of the foreign exchange. Coffee, the main cash crop, accounts for 15 percent of the GDP. Cotton, sugar cane, and sorghum are next in importance.

The industrial sector generated about 15 percent of GDP, but employs only about 12 percent of the labor force.

1. *Unemployment*

Employment needs in both urban and rural areas are unmet. In 1978, 34 percent of the total rural labor force was unemployed. Lack of training and the low percentage of skilled laborers aggravate the problem.

2. *Health*

Infant mortality rates (50.5 per 1000 live births in 1978) and life expectancy at birth (62.2 years in 1975–80), although improved over past years, are still relatively poor. Intestinal and respiratory disease account for almost 40 percent of all deaths. The frequency of water-borne diseases, due to the lack of proper solid waste facilities, is particularly high. Despite some improvements, in 1978, there were serious shortages in health services—3.4 physicians per 100,000 people; 1.3 hospital beds per 1,000 people. In addition, there are disparities between health services in the capital and in the rest of the country. In 1978 San Salvador, with a sixth of the national population, had 42 percent of the physicians, 30 percent of the nurses and 47 percent of the hospital beds. In 1979 barely 13 percent of the labor force was covered by health care and pension benefits of the social security system.

3. *Nutrition*

Despite improvements since 1970, in the mid-1970's the average calorie consumption of the population was equivalent to only 77 percent of the recommended level. For the poorer half of the population, calorie consumption was also below internationally established requirements. Malnutrition thus afflicts an estimated 66 percent of children between the ages of 6 months and 5 years in intensive farming regions and 77 percent of those in coffee growing regions.

4. *Housing*

There are severe housing shortages, particularly in the rural area. The 1971 census found that more than half of all housing, rural and urban, had only a single room. Electricity, sewage and water services for housing is limited, particularly in rural areas. The inadequate drinking water and sewage service is reflected in the high rates of infections and parasitic diseases.

5. *Education*

The literacy rate and school enrollments have improved in the last decade; however, the situation generally remains deficient. The literacy rate in 1978 was 62 percent, but it is significantly lower in rural areas, reflecting the serious shortage of teachers there. In both urban and rural areas, female enrollment in schools is proportionately lower than that of males.

B. *The agrarian reform*

On March 5, 1980, the government of El Salvador initiated an agrarian reform program of unprecedented scope. It promised to redistribute the major portion of the nation's arable land, including its richest farmland, from the relatively few landowners to the hundreds of thousands of *campesinos* who have traditionally worked the land. The plan was presented as an attempt to address the structural problems which have fostered the growing violence. In part due to the reform program, the US government pictures the ruling Junta as a moderate, centrist body committed to progressive change, and justifies on humanitarian grounds the continuation of economic and military support to it.

Socio-economic conditions in El Salvador demonstrate the need for agrarian reform. The convergence of two factors—a rapidly expanding population in a relatively small territory and an extremely skewed pattern of resource distribution—have pushed the country's economic structures to the breaking point. Widespread poverty reaching levels beyond human tolerance has resulted in extreme levels of social and political conflict. The two major violent confrontations in the country's history, the 1932 peasant massacre and the 1969 "Football War,"[2] both had their roots in the fact that access to land for most of the population is grossly inadequate or altogether lacking.

As a result of government acquiesence to the landed oligarchy's opposition, little was done over the years to effect reform. The most significant previous attempt occurred in 1976 when the government of Colonel Molina, with U.S. support, planned to expropriate some 56,000 hectares of land in the country's cotton-growing region. That plan was shelved because of opposition from cotton growers.

The 1980 plan, the most radical land redistribution plan ever adopted by a Salvadoran government, is the centerpiece of the reforms promised by the Junta which took power on October 15, 1979. The reforms themselves were not implemented until five months later under strong pressure from the U.S. government.

This section will examine the process of implementing the reform, its current status, and the prospects for its completion. An evaluation of the reform process, as compared to alternative plans, is beyond the scope of this study.[3]

1. *The agrarian reform law*

The Basic Agrarian Reform Law, Decree 153, announced on March 6, 1980, and the Land-to-the-Tiller Plan, Decree 207, April 28, 1980, authorize the expropriation of landed estates and establish compensation for former proprietors. Decree 153 lays the groundwork for the formation of peasant-run cooperatives, and Decree 207 converts renters into owners of their parcels. The reform, which has three phases, is applicable throughout the country, regardless of "crop, location, productivity, land tenure system, or quality of soil or any other variable" (Decree 153). Three other May 1980 decrees, Nos. 220, 221 and 222, deal, respectively, with bonds for compensation, the forming of *campesino* groups, and technical modifications to the basic law.

a. *Phase I*

Decree 153 (Phase I) provides for the transfer, through expropriation or purchase, of estates over 500 hectares to *campesino* families who will operate them as private cooperatives. The Junta announced that 376 properties would be affected, covering 225,000 hectares owned by 242 families. This area, some 15 percent of El Salvador's farm land, produces export crops but grows only a small percentage of the basic grains (approximately 14 percent of the country's coffee, 31 percent of cotton, 24 percent of sugar cane, 38 percent of rice, 13 percent of corn, 5.2 percent of sorghum and 7 percent of beans). Between 60,000–70,000 families were to benefit from this phase of the reform.

Decree 256 (June 3, 1980) provides for the sale of these properties to a government agency, the Salvadoran Institute for Agrarian Reform (ISTA), on the terms specified in Decree 153—25 percent cash and 75 percent bonds.

The land so acquired is to be administered as a "joint venture" of ISTA and the *campesino* groups until the latter have acquired "the necessary skills." The law is silent regarding ownership by the *campesino* enterprises.

Decree 153, Article 4, establishes reserve rights for prior owners of affected lands. The right is limited to a legal maximum amount of between 100 and 150 hectares depending on the quality of the land. The ceiling may be increased by 20 percent (Decree 153, Art. 7) if the owner maintained or increased productivity or otherwise improved his land and also complied with labor and social security laws. Under Decree 222, affected landowners were given one year from the expropriation date to claim reserve rights.

The *campesino* organizations receiving land must be comprised exclusively of peasants who do not own any land, whether they are paid workers, lease-holders, secondary lease holders, or tenant farmers *("colonos")*, as well as peasants who own land that is insufficient to meet their basic needs.

Income generated by the properties is to be distributed in the following order of priority:

1. Payment of production costs.
2. Satisfaction of basic needs of beneficiary family groups.
3. Payment of the ISTA's "agrarian debt."

Any surpluses may be distributed within the affected zone with attention to the interests of the national economy and in order to

1. Create a reasonable margin of savings for all the beneficiaries in the affected zone.
2. Develop social programs for the community.
3. Develop other types of productive projects.

The law does not state who determines how the distribution is to be made.

b. *Phase II*

Phase II of Decree 153 provides for the transfer of farms ranging from 100 to 500 hectares. These farms comprise approximately 340,000 hectares, or about 23 percent of Salvador's farm land with an estimated 30 percent of the coffee crop, the backbone of the country's export economy.

There has been no attempt to implement this phase of the reform and there are no foreseeable prospects for its implementation. Many familiar with the reform, including U.S. Ambassador to El Salvador Deane Hinton, doubt that it will ever be put into effect.

c. *Phase III*

Decree Law 207 contains the "Land-to-the-Tiller" program. This third phase of the reform is designed to give renters and sharecroppers ownership of the lands they have been working. The decree expropriates lands not directly exploited by their owners and gives immediate recognition to the ownership rights of former renters. An estimated 125,000 tenant families are to receive 180,000 hectares comprising 12 percent of all farmland under this program. Beneficiaries are limited to plots of under seven hectares.

Former owners of lands under 100 hectares receive 50 percent in cash and 50 percent in bonds, those of properties over 100 hectares, 25 percent in cash and 75 percent in bonds. Beneficiaries have thirty years to pay for their plots. During this period, the plots may not be sold, rented or mortgaged.

Although renters were automatically converted into owners by the decree, no means to prove ownership were provided. On December 22, 1980, the Junta finally issued rules for the titling process: upon application, a beneficiary receives a receipt that confirms use rights and access to production credit; upon verification of the application a provisional title is issued; a definitive title is issued when compensation is determined, payments by beneficiaries scheduled and the documentation meets land registry requirements.

2. *Implementation of the reform law*
a. *Phase I*

Of the three phases, implementation of Phase I has gone the farthest. ISTA technicians backed by the military began taking over properties over 500 hectares the same day Decree 153 was announced and largely completed the process within two months. In all there are about 300[4] farms with approximately 216,000 hectares farmed by 32,-116[5] cooperative members and their families. But, a number of factors reduced the potential scope of this phase. Only a limited number of *campesinos* have been permitted to join the cooperatives and their participation in administration and decision-making is extremely restricted. To date, only one title has been issued in the name of the cooperative; all other titles are still held by ISTA.[6]

Cooperatives were established on approximately 200

estates, nearly 100 fewer than promised. Since each farm is over 500 hectares, that represents a considerable loss of valuable farmland to the reform. ISTA officials say some farms were erroneously included in Phase I due to zoning miscalculations and outdated records. Critics say some farms were returned as a result of pressure by landowners through their military connections.

Several of these [returned] properties had valuable coffee processing plants which with the collusion of government officials were reclassified as urban properties, thus becoming exempt from the agrarian reform process.[7]

Evidence for either claim is difficult to get. However, it is commonly accepted that 12 haciendas expropriated under Phase I have been returned to their original owners. In at least one instance, military corruption is blamed for the return of a large estate (named "Venecia y Prusia," in the province of San Salvador), in spite of protests by ISTA officials.[8]

The owner's right of reserve is another limitation on the program, through which a former owner can claim between 100–150 hectares as his reserve right. According to a recent AID report, between 14,000–21,000 hectares may be returned to former owners.[9]

Nevertheless Phase I encompassed a vast area of farmland and dispossessed a significant portion of the landed elite. Limited *campesino* participation and control has been more significant in undermining the impact of the reform.

Only 32,116 *campesinos* have become cooperative members. According to the AID El Salvador Office Director, Peter Askin, the figure should be twice that.[10] Membership in the cooperatives was severely reduced because most of the expropriations took place during El Salvador's rainy season, when the labor population on the farms is at its lowest. As a result, only the core permanent workers, *colonos,* and administrators were present when the cooperatives were formed. Seasonal workers, the great majority on the large estates, were excluded from cooperatives. They have no share in cooperative decision-making nor potential profits and no job security.

The legal rights and participation of *campesinos* who are cooperative members are also limited. Despite assurances from the government that it does not intend to turn Phase I land into "State-run farms," 18 months after the interventions began, titles of all but one Phase I estates are still held by ISTA. The process of turning over formal titles and control is lagging far behind schedule; all titles were to be distributed by the end of 1981.[11]

Until titles are distributed, ISTA decides how each cooperative's income will be allocated—whether, as profits, for capital improvements, or transferred to other, financially ailing cooperatives. Meanwhile, cooperative members have no security. Given the armed conflict and the volatile position of the Junta, possible claims to the farms by former owners or the military pose serious threats. As a U.S. AID official, who visited El Salvador in May 1980, said, "(t)here is an oppressive atmosphere of uncertainty, insecurity and fear among the people on intervened farms throughout the country."[12] Whether titles will ever be issued to all the cooperatives remains to be seen. At present there seems no movement in this direction.

Another criticism of the reform is that on many of the farms members are excluded from the administration of the cooperatives and little, if anything, is being done to foster their active participation in the future. A U.S. AID report says:

> [The *colonos*] also still conceive of their ties to the hacienda as those which have traditionally defined *colonaje:* they are salaried workers, they must respect the hacienda hierarchy, they have to abide by the same restrictions. They find it difficult to

voice their opinions, and the idea of taking an active role in cooperative management and decision making is simply not part of their conceptual world. In other words, the *colonos* have changed little—if at all—either behaviorally or psychologically.

This is at least in part due to the fact that in many cases the haciendas themselves have changed very little. To keep production from faltering, the ISTA technicians have attempted to make as few modifications as possible in the administrative and labor structure of the hacienda enterprise. They have tried to retain as many of the former management and service employees as possible. The *colonos* are being dispatched on labor assignments around the farms more or less as had been done in the past. The same hacienda hierarchy, the same rules and restrictions, and the same system of salaries (for employees) and daily wages (for *colonos*) have been kept in place with few modifications. All of this was wise, and even necessary, to preserve continuity in the farm operation and to avoid disastrous disruptions of the productivity cycle. At the same time, however, maintenance of the traditional structure—especially on the larger farms—has left most of the agricultural laborers with the feeling that aside from a change in *patrones,* their position within the structure of the hacienda has in reality remained substantially the same.[13]

The procedure following the expropriation by ISTA teams, was to first gather together people living on the Phase I farms and explain the basic design of the reform. Officers forming an administrative council for each farm were elected on the spot and cooperatives were formed. As stated above, ISTA representatives, anxious to maintain as much continuity as possible, urged the retention of managerial staff, which typically served to exclude *campesinos* from the administrative councils. As a result, the *campesinos* have no more control over the farms under the cooperative system than they had in the past. Many, feeling that they have simply exchanged one *patron* for another, perceive no change in their lives.[14] At one Phase I farm in July 1981, a journalist reports: "Asked how their lives now compared with their lives [before the reform], the peasants answered, 'the same.' "[15]

b. *Phase II*

As noted above, Phase II implementation has been postponed indefinitely. Since Phase II lands include areas of major coffee production, El Salvador's most important industry (15 percent of GDP and more than 50 percent of total exports), this phase is considered the heart of the agrarian program—thus its abandonment significantly reduces the reform's impact.

Administrative, managerial, technical and financial limitations, as well as resistance from coffee-growers and violence in general are among the factors blamed for the failure to execute this phase.[16] The government's willingness to implement Phase II has also been questioned:

Until Phase II is carried out El Salvador's agrarian reform will have ignored the most vital part of the agrarian sector. The failure to follow through seriously on Phase II, economically the most important phase, places in grave doubt the commitment of the Junta to agrarian reform.[17]

c. *Phase III*

Phase III is widely thought to have been introduced primarily as a political, not an economic measure, and it has been consequently evaluated by U.S. and Salvadoran leaders alike, almost exclusively in political terms. Peter Askin, director of the El Salvador AID office, said in July 1981:

It has not been a total economic success. But, up to this point it has been a political success. I'm firm on that. There does seem to be a direct correlation between the agrarian reforms and the peasants not having become more radicalized.[18]

Roy Prosterman, a key figure in the adoption of the program, also claims its political success:

Perhaps the greatest tribute to the reality and significance of the El Salvadoran land reform has been in the sharp attacks launched against it by both extremes: from the extreme right, because it takes away the major source of power and privilege of the oligarchs; and from the extreme left, because it takes away the base of recruitment and support among the peasantry that they require for a successful revolution.[19]

Perhaps because never designed primarily as a solution to an economic problem, the third phase so far has not had much economic impact. In fact, for the most part, it has not been implemented. Decree Law 207 potentially would require 125,000 provisional and definitive titles.[20] According to AID, as of August 1981, only 23,301 title applications had been filed, representing only a fraction of the intended beneficiaries, and only provisional titles have been issued so far. Statistics vary on the number of those, but by any of the figures quoted (AID reports 4,882 as of August 1981) only a fraction have been issued, usually in well-publicized ceremonies presided over by a Junta member.[21]

No definitive titles have been issued under Phase III as of August 1981. Without a definitive title there can be no security of ownership. An AID official reports:

In one case, I spoke with three men who were renting land along with some 40-odd other farmers. When asked if they would take legal action to get the rented plots for themselves, one of them answered: "What can we say? It's up to the *patron.* We can't do anything, we are low in stature (somos de baja categoria)." I found this general attitude everywhere among *arrendatarios* renting on medium-sized and large properties. When they are the owner of the land, there is little they feel they can do. When they are allowed to stay on, they are cautious. It is not likely that they will pursue their rights, granted in Decree 207, on their own.[22]

Their insecurity is further indicated by the fact that a substantial number of beneficiaries are still paying rent to former owners and that a significant percentage (as high as 17 percent) of others have been driven off the land by former landowners.[23]

In addition, it is reported that none of the former owners have received compensation for land confiscated under Phase III.

AID cited insufficient planning and resources for delays in issuing titles:

To transfer land ownership it is necessary to: (1) identify *"tillers"* who have the legal right to claim a particular *parcel* of land; (2) identify that parcel and prepare a *legal description;* (3) identify the current *owner;* (4) determine the land's *value;* (5) *negotiate* agreements or administratively resolve any *disputes;* (6) *record* the action into the cadastral system; (7) *register* this transaction in the land registry records; (8) issue a *provisional title;* (9) *publicize* these provisional transactions to assure that others who believe they have rights to the affected land have an *opportunity to contest;* (10) establish financial records to permit the beneficiary to make *amortization payments* and pay applicable taxes; (11) establish records to *compensate* former land owners, and (12) issue bonds and make cash *payments.*[24]

In addition, completing the entitlement application presents an insurmountable challenge to the large percentage of *campesinos* who are illiterate and who do not possess the legal proof of a rental agreement required by the application. Access to the application form, much less assistance in filling it out, is difficult. In April 1981, AID reported:

The activities most critical to success of the land transfer take place in the field and take place in the early stages of the implementation process. These are locating those lands subject to the reform, identifying eligible recipients, and issuing provisional title documents. To carry out these functions, FINATA . . . [the government's implementing office for the agrarian reform] has established 81 field offices throughout the country so far. The offices are organized into two person teams called Agrarian Committees who receive applications and match them up with cadastral map data for location and land description purposes. *So far there has been a minimum of farm site visits by Agrarian Committees; rather, farmer applicants have come to the FINATA offices to fill out and submit application forms.* [emphasis added][25]

The high level of violence in the Salvadoran countryside and curfew restriction deter applicants from traveling to FINATA offices. These factors probably account for the fact that so few of the intended beneficiaries under Phase III have filed claims.

There is also resistance to the plan by Salvadorans who see it as an American initiative insensitive to the needs and desires of El Salvador. In fact, Phase III's key architect was Roy Prosterman, who gained some prominence as a land reform specialist in Vietnam and who went to El Salvador as a consultant of the American Institute for Free Labor Development (AIFLD).[26] Prosterman, with U.S. embassy support, presented Phase III directly to the Junta, bypassing the appropriate Salvadoran ministries.

According to an AID assessment:

A sizable number of people in ISTA and MAG are suspicious of Decree 207 because it was designed virtually in its entirety by Americans, and slipped into legislation without their being consulted. This fact is known and resented. It is widely believed that "land-to-the-tiller" is a political move on the part of the U.S. Embassy and the State Department. Many believe it is a "symbolic" and "cosmetic" measure which was proposed because it would look good to certain American politicians, and not neces-

sarily because it would be beneficial or significant in the Salvadorean context. Whether or not this assessment is correct or
fair is another matter. It remains a fact that Decree 207 is
perceived in this light. And the technicians, of course, must put
their full support behind the reform if it is to be successfully
implemented.[27]

Like Decree 153, this plan does not include among its
beneficiaries the poorest of the *campesinos,* those landless
temporary workers who did not rent or sharecrop, a group
estimated to number 125,000 families or 35 percent of the
rural poor.

Moreover, rental properties in El Salvador are marginal
plots, the poorest farm land in the country. These lands
tend to be over-worked. Since Decree 207 virtually locks
campesinos into small plots of less than 7 hectares for 30
years, further depletion of the soil can be expected as the
same subsistence crops are grown year after year.

In addition, Salvadoran agricultural experts claim that
many of the owners dispossessed under the decree are
small land owners, including the elderly and widows, who
rely on rental income. Their needs are ignored by the
reform and reportedly, a number of renters are reluctant
to claim their rights under Phase III because of this.[28]

Thus, aside from granting a small percentage of provisional titles, Phase III has not been implemented, nor does
it seem that it will be in the near future.

PART II

THE HUMAN RIGHTS SITUATION IN EL SALVADOR

CHAPTER 3
THE RIGHT TO LIFE

The right to life is guaranteed in several international agreements ratified by the government of El Salvador as well as in the domestic laws of the country. Throughout the contemporary history of the country, there have been repeated and large-scale violations of this right by the government. The civilian death toll has risen dramatically in recent years with the escalation of the armed conflict. An estimated 1,000 persons were killed in 1979,[1] 9–10 thousand in 1980,[2] and over 9 thousand in the first half of 1981.[3] The Salvadoran Catholic Church, national and international human rights organizations, and refugee sources attribute the vast majority of these violations of the right to life to government forces and their agents.

Although President Jose Napoleon Duarte states that he is trying unsuccessfully to stop the killings,[4] to date no members of the military or security forces have been criminally punished for killing opponents of the government. Indeed, the figures the national police and the security forces use in tabulating politically motivated killings are so low—2,407 between October 15, 1979, and the end of July 1981,[5] about one-eighth of the total tabulated by the U.S. government—as to indicate that they do not recognize killings of government opponents outside combat as murder.

A. *Events prior to October 1979*

Within a month after the 1931 coup, which deposed El Salvador's last elected civilian President, the government killed thousands of unarmed peasants. This incident casts a pall over Salvadoran history. *La Matanza,* or "the Massacre," as the incident is known, was in retaliation to a violent 3-day peasant rebellion against low wages. All of those with Indian features and wearing peasant clothes around the western town of Izalco were rounded up and shot by government firing squads. Estimates of the number of men, women, and children killed range as high as 30,000.[6] Historian Thomas Anderson describes the event as follows:

As most of the rebels, except the leaders, were difficult to identify, arbitrary classifications were set up. All those who were found carrying machetes were guilty. All those of a strongly Indian cast of features, or who dressed in a scruffy, *campesino* costume, were considered guilty. To facilitate the roundup, all those who had not taken part in the uprising were invited to present themselves at the *comandancia* to receive clearance papers. When they arrived they were examined and those with the above mentioned attributes seized. Tied by the thumbs to those before and behind them, in the customary Salvadoran manner, groups of fifty were led to the back wall of the church of Asuncion in Izalco and against that massive wall were cut down by firing squads. In the plaza in front of the *comandancia,* other selected victims were made to dig a massive grave and then shot, according to one account, from machine guns mounted on trucks. In some cases, women and children refused to leave their menfolk and shared their fate.[7]

More recent events have resulted in fewer deaths but no less clear violations of the right to life.

On March 25, 1972, an unsuccessful military uprising, protesting the fraudulent elections in February of that year, left some 100 persons dead and another 200 wounded.[8] A wave of reprisals followed and presidential candidate Jose Napoleon Duarte and many other political and military leaders were detained and tortured.

In July 1975, students at the Santa Ana branch of the National University of El Salvador gathered in a peaceful, unarmed protest of the government's massive expenditures on the 1975 "Miss Universe" pageant held in San Salvador. National Guardsmen opened fire on approximately 2,000 student marchers, leaving many dead and wounded.[9] The Inter-American Commission on Human Rights (IACHR) of the OAS listed the names of 16 students killed in the incident and gave the following account of the event:

The shooting lasted some minutes, but because of the density of the demonstrators, those minutes were enough to spill much blood. They were out to kill. The repressors were in a kneeling position, which shows there was no armed response or any other response on the part of the demonstrators; the repressors acted as if they were facing a target in shooting practice.[10]

Protests over the irregularities in the 1978 elections brought on another massacre. Beginning on February 21, opposition supporters had gathered in a main plaza of San Salvador; by February 27, the crowd was estimated at several thousand. As in previous demonstrations, the government responded brutally. The IACHR reports:

At around 12:30 A.M. of February 28, the Plaza Libertad was surrounded by troops and police with tanks, armored vehicles and jeeps. The demonstrators, who at that point numbered around 6,000, were given ten minutes to disperse. Many left. The security forces then opened fire. Colonel [Ernesto] Claramount and some 1,500 to 2,000 individuals, including women and children, took refuge in the Church of El Rosario, alongside the Plaza. Gas grenades were then thrown inside the church and some of the people left, although there are 3 conflicting reports as to how many escaped. . . .

[The next] day there were massive arrests, hundreds of wounded and a number of dead. There are conflicting reports as to how many people died. Officially, the government acknowledged eight deaths; but some observers state that there were 40 to 60, while other sources estimate that there were between 100 and 300 deaths.[11]

Beginning in 1977, violations have included the summary execution of detainees and "disappearances."

Such violence against *campesinos* has been frequently conducted by rural-based paramilitary organizations with close links to security forces. The largest of these is the *Organizacion Democratica Nacionalista* (ORDEN). ORDEN was created in 1962 by the Ministry of Defense as a civilian security organization.[12] By the mid-1970s it is estimated to have had 80–100 thousand members[13] who carried weapons and were practically immune from criminal charges.[14] After protests by human rights groups against ORDEN's practices, it was officially banned in 1979.[15] The government, however, has never taken any concrete measures to dismantle it[16] and its death squads continue to function throughout El Salvador.

Amnesty International reported that, during 1977–78, its primary concern regarding El Salvador was the "increased number of detentions followed by 'disappearances,' as well as outright killings in the countryside."[17] On February 6, 1978, Amnesty submitted to the government of El Salvador "62 documented cases of unacknowledged detention, and 30 cases of apparent execution, all of them involving members of the official security forces, or of the Government paramilitary organization ORDEN."[18] Amnesty reported that "most of the bodies of the thirty dead showed signs of torture. Some had been decapitated, had had limbs amputated or were severely disfigured."[19]

Amnesty stated that the principal victims were members and leaders of agricultural workers' unions.[20] It also reported the murder and disappearance of a "considerable number" of Catholic religious and lay workers during this period.[21]

In its annual human rights report for 1978, the U.S. State Department also gave an account of the lawless killings by ORDEN:

A government-sponsored paramilitary mass political organization, ORDEN, which operates largely in rural areas, has used violence in its conflicts with anti-Government peasant organizations and has engaged in active opposition to dissent in rural areas. Clashes in the countryside with anti-Government peasant groups have resulted in deaths."[22]

The Inter-American Commission of Human Rights (IACHR) of the OAS, after a January 1978 on-site mission, concluded "that the conduct of the security corps and of the paramilitary organization known as ORDEN led to considerable loss of life."[23]

During 1978 many atrocities were also attributed directly to the military. One particularly shocking account was given by a British Parliamentary delegation which visited the country in December 1978. The delegation reported testimony that security forces had disposed of detainees after interrogation by detonating explosive devices that had been lashed to the victims' bodies.[24]

In 1979, the violence continued to escalate. In its annual human rights report for 1979, the U.S. State Department asserted that:

During the Romero government the security forces' use of excessive force resulted in needless deaths and injuries . . . There were numerous reports of people being found dead after being arrested by the security forces under the Romero government.[25]

The U.S. State Department and a number of human rights groups publicized another mass killing of demonstrators by police in May 1979.[26] The International Commission of Jurists (ICJ) describes the event as follows:

In May 1979, 23 demonstrators outside the Cathedral in San Salvador were fired upon by the police and died. Members of the Popular Revolutionary Bloc (BPR) occupied several foreign embassies to press for the release of three of their leaders held by the government. During one such occupation, fourteen persons were killed by the police outside the Venezuelan embassy. A day later, left-wing gunmen killed the education minister. The government then imposed the state of siege. In September 1979 the President's brother was slain."[27]

B. *Violations of the right to life since October 15, 1979*

Violations of the right to life did not abate after the October 1979 coup. Government forces continued to fire on unarmed demonstrators and to kill detainees. Moreover, many civilians simply disappeared.

To commemorate the 48th anniversary of the massacre of 1932, the *Coordinadora Revolucionaria de Masas* organized a massive demonstration in San Salvador on January 22, 1980. This demonstration, one of the largest in the country, was attacked by guards and sharpshooters on the rooftops of the National Palace. Estimates of the number of those killed range from 20 to 52.[28]

Another incident occurred on March 30, 1980, when security forces opened fire on a peaceful gathering for the funeral of the well-known human rights spokesman, Archbishop Romero. According to the eye-witness testimony of twenty-two church leaders, "the first shots came from the Presidential Palace."[29]

The declaration of a state of siege and the curfew are two developments since the 1979 coup which have been frequently cited as contributing to the bloodshed.

In March 1980, following the announcement of agrarian reform, a state of siege was declared. Constitutional rights were suspended. In the months following, violence reached an unprecedented level. By the end of the year approximately 200 deaths were recorded each week apart from those killed in armed clashes between guerrillas and government forces.[30]

Early in January 1981, the guerrillas launched a "general offensive" which led the government to declare martial law and impose a 7:00 P.M. to 5:00 A.M. curfew. Orders were given to the Salvadoran armed forces by the Ministry of Defense to shoot to kill.[31] As a result, hundreds of people have lost their lives at the hands of the security forces in violation of Salvadoran legislation and international commitments.

Socorro Juridico compiled a list of 168 people killed during the first month of the curfew between January 12 and February 18, 1981. Many of the victims were on their way home and were killed a few minutes after 7:00 P.M.; others were simply outside their homes; and still others were dragged from their homes and killed by security forces.[32]

Socorro Juridico estimates that between January and September 1981, 10,374 Salvadorans died as a result of political violence.[33]

The government of El Salvador and its supporters argue that those who were killed died in battle or at the hands of private groups not under the control of the government.

Human rights groups and the office of the Archbishop of San Salvador reject these claims and place responsibility for the majority of these killings on the government; they reject the claims that most deaths occur in combat and that the right-wing death squads are not under government control. At hearings in the spring of 1981 before the U.S. Senate Committee on Foreign Relations, Amnesty International makes the point this way:

> While these abuses have occurred against a background of civil warfare between government forces and guerrilla organizations (themselves guilty of serious abuses), evidence reaching Amnesty International indicates that the majority of victims of torture and death at the hands of the security forces have not generally been proven to have any direct involvement in armed insurrection. Most of the deaths have taken place after the victims had been seized from their homes or work places and were defenseless.
>
> During 1980, the government of El Salvador repeatedly claimed that independent "anti-communist" death squads beyond official control were responsible for these abductions and murders. This assertion, however, directly contradicts evidence compiled by Amnesty International from hundreds of individual cases attributing responsibility for serious violations of human rights to regular security forces. It would appear that by consistently attributing the detentions, tortures and assassinations of alleged members of the opposition to groups beyond official control, the government of El Salvador is seeking a means of evading responsibility for the actions of its own security forces.[34]

A number of deaths have been attributed to right-wing paramilitary groups. There have also been numerous allegations that the security forces of El Salvador continue to carry out operations with members of ORDEN and that, in addition, military personnel frequently operate in civilian dress. The much-feared ORDEN is a rural organization which was supported by the government prior to the 1979 coup and, though officially disbanded by decree, continues to operate with impunity.

In its 1980 Report, Amnesty International said:

Although a decree of 6 November ordered ORDEN to be dissolved, it continued to be a principal auxiliary of lawful security forces. No concrete measures were taken to dismantle the ORDEN organization nor to break the relationship between the police and military and ORDEN. No arms were confiscated from the tens of thousands of ORDEN members nor was any member reported arrested for abuses of human rights.[35]

Two episodes are described at some length because they provide striking detail which refutes the government claims that most deaths result from armed battles and that right-wing death squads are independent of the government. The first of these incidents involving the feared Treasury Police attracted international attention, including State Department comment. It is known as the Massacre of Monte Carmelo, in which more than 20 people were taken forcibly from their homes and shot on the night of April 7, 1981. Government officials claimed that the victims died in armed conflict with the police but Amnesty International gives this account:

On the night of 7 April 1981 when more than 20 people, including several youths were taken from their homes in San Nicolas de Soyapango, a suburb to the east of San Salvador, by a group of men, some of them in uniform, and were later found dead. On 9 April, Amnesty International called on the government of El Salvador to open an investigation into this incident (see AI document AMR 29/25/81 "Amnesty International appeals to El Salvador Government over Apparent Death List issued by Army.")

Initially, Salvadoran authorities claimed that the victims had died in an armed confrontation with the police, but residents of the area insisted that some of those who died had been shot on the spot, while others were taken from their homes by the Treasury Police, and their bodies were found later. Some of the bodies found elsewhere had their hands bound, a fact totally inconsistent with the official explanation that the victims had died in a shoot-out with the police. Later, however, both Salvadoran and U.S. officials (in the latter case, speaking on behalf of both the U.S. Embassy in San Salvador and the Department of State in Washington) said that "individual units" of this security force had apparently been involved, and U.S. officials stated that Salvadoran and U.S. officials were ccooperating to investigate the incident.[36]

The following testimony provides grim confirming details of the murder of two of the victims of Monte Carmelo:

At 2:30 on April 7 of this year my son, Luis Alonso Quintanilla Sanchez, and my husband, Luis Alonso Quintanilla Perdomo, were arrested at our home on the main street north, Guadalupe District, House No. 3, Apopa. The arrest was made by properly-uniformed Treasury Policemen, who came to the house in three pick-up trucks. The first was a white Toyota, and the other two were blue and red, respectively. There were approximately 30 Treasury Policemen. We were all asleep at the time. Since the house is still under construction, it does not have a door. In place of a door, we had put up a table, which was forcibly shoved aside when approximately 12 of them entered. The rest stayed outside the house. At the time of these events, I was with my eight children and my husband. We were all immobilized by all this since the Treasury Police entered noisily, screaming insults and threats. Once inside, they found another table used by the family and one of the Treasury Policemen yelled, "Get up, you son of a bitch, and come here and remove this table." The father of the children got up and said, "I'm coming." He took away the table and went back to bed. At that point a policeman approached his bed and shined a light on him and said: "Get up, you son of a bitch. Show me your papers. We are the armed forces." He got up, went to get his papers and said: "Here they are." The same policeman said: "Get out the weapons, son of a whore." Luis Alonso Quintanilla Perdomo replied: "I don't have weapons. If you want, search for them." Then a thin, white policeman sat on one of the dining room chairs and said to him: "You bastard, get them." He replied: "I don't have anything." The same thin, white policeman said to another policeman of the same physical description: "What do we do with this one, do we take him or do we leave him alone?" The other replied: "Let's take him, they're all guerrillas." Then I said to them, "Look, gentlemen, we don't have any weapons." And the same policeman who had forced my husband to get up said: "What are you talking about, everyone here is a guerrilla?" and even pointed to the children. They began to search the house, lifting mattresses, cushions and pillows and everything they found in their path. They even shined a light into the toilet looking for weapons. They went to my children's bedrooms. They did not find my son Jorge Alberto Quintanilla Sanchez. He was getting ready to leave by the backdoor, but before going he told one of his younger brothers that he was doing it so that everyone wouldn't be taken; in that way, only his father and his brother would be taken. But at the very moment he was saying goodbye, one of the policemen realized and yelled: "Hey, look, one of them is getting away." He then connected an apparatus that looked like a large searchlight and when an orange light lit up, the policeman released a burst of machinegun fire, aimed at my son. Since the boy had already left the house, when the policemen outside the house saw and heard the other policeman's weapons, they fired their machineguns. One could hear the boy calling: "Help!" One of the policemen outside yelled: "Kill the son of a bitch; don't let him get away." The others obeyed, and killed him. After this, one of the policemen said to Luis Alonso Quintanilla Sanchez Perdomo and his father Luis Alonso Quintanilla Perdomo: "Go on, get out of here; I don't want to kill anymore here." They shoved them outside and kicked Luis Alonso Jr. when he refused to walk. They also kicked his father when he said to the policeman: "Just let me put on my pants." All he had on were shorts and stockings. The policeman who had killed one of his children, Jorge Alberto Quintanilla Sanchez, said to him: "Why, just go that way."

When they had taken them, I left the house to give my husband his pants. Five agents had my husband, while 3 had my son, Luis Alonso. They were tying together their thumbs and their wrists. My son said to them: "Why are you taking me, I haven't done anything." The policeman who had murdered his brother said to him: "We're taking you in as a guerrilla." And the youth repeated: "I am not anything." The police did not reply and put him inside the white Toyota pick-up after having tied him up securely. When I came outside to give my husband his pants, one of the policemen grabbed me and told me: "If you don't want us to kill them here, you'd better go to bed." I obeyed and went back inside the house. Earlier he had warned us not to come outside because they were going to leave 2 policemen outside the house.

When I heard the vehicles start up, I saw that they headed in the direction of San Salvador. Inside the house, I and my six children cried and my youngest daughter told me not to cry, because she was afraid that they would come and kill everyone. She could see the policemen I mentioned earlier. So we decided to wait until after the curfew to look for the body of my son, Jorge Alberto. Shortly after 5 that morning, I went out to see whether my son was dead and found him with his skull crushed and his brains exposed. He had bullet wounds in the left cheek, nose, ear and right leg. They had robbed a watch he carried. I didn't know what had happened to my other son and my husband until 5:00 that afternoon when a friend had located their bodies at the El Recuerdo funeral home. The man that identified them had seen them in the San Nicolas District. Since the funeral home was in that area, I went to get them and the man in the funeral home told me that they were ripped to pieces, especially in the back. That same day, an item appeared in the Diario El Mundo, which stated that twenty-one bodies had appeared in the San Nicolas District, known as the Monte Carmelo de Soya-pango District, near a house whose address was not known; El Mundo went on to say that the individuals had died in a confrontation with the Treasury Police, who had uncovered a guerrilla cell. When the guerrillas saw the security forces, the confrontation occurred and it was there that the individuals in question died. This is false, since my husband and son, who were among the 21 bodies, had been taken away by the Treasury Police in the early morning hours that same day in Apopa, and taken under arrest to San Salvador, after those had killed my son Jorge Alberto Quintanilla Sanchez, at the scene of the arrest. According to witnesses and statements, the event reported in El Mundo and in an Official Bulletin of the Treasury Police did not occur in the manner reported; rather, just as my husband and son, those 21 individuals had been taken from their homes, moments before they were killed.[37]

The second episode demonstrates vividly connections between National Guard troops and armed civilians.

The following testimony given to *Socorro Juridico* describes the detention of two young Salvadorans by the National Guard. Photographs of the incident clearly show the prisoners being turned over to a group of armed civilians.

At approximately 9:30 A.M., October 3 of 1980, my son, Manuel Alfredo Velasquez Toledo, twenty-two, a student at UCA and single, was arrested by the National Guard because he had no identification papers. Also arrested with him was another youth whom I do not know. They put the two in an Armed Forces pick-up and took them off in the direction of the Central Headquarters of the National Guard. Upon learning of my son's arrest, I went to the National Guard to inquire for him and they told me that they had not participated in that operation and that they did not have him under arrest there. Then I decided to seek the services of the International Red Cross, the Human Rights Commission, the Legal Aid of the Archdiocese and the Archbishop of San Salvador. . . . We filed [a] writ (of *habeas corpus*) with the Supreme Court of Justice on October 10, but to date there has been no result. We also showed Mendez Castro photographs that show clearly my son and another youth being cap-

tured by agents of the National Guard, being put into a pick-up
and taken to the headquarters of the Guard . . . We left him some
photographs and these were shown to Colonel Eugenio Vides
Casanova, Director of the National Guard. When he saw the
photos, the colonel said that in fact the individuals making the
arrest had been agents of the National Guard and the pick-up
shown in one of the photographs is one of the vehicles the
National Guard uses. But he insisted that my son was not on the
list of prisoners that the Security Force carried. However, at the
National Guard they expressed great concern over the existence
of the photographs, because they said that this was going to hurt
that Institution's reputation.[38]

The testimony of the wife of the other young man captured in that operation states:

At around noon on October 3 of this year, my husband, Vinicio Humberto Bazzaglia, was arrested. He is twenty-four, a
student and a resident here. He was taken by National Guardsmen in the vicinity of the Family Banking Center, at a me-
chanic's shop, as he was passing by. The aforementioned Family
Banking Center is an Agency of the Commercial Agricultural
Bank, located on Cinco de Noviembre Street, in this capital. On
the date in question, there was gunfire. In connection with my
husband's arrest, not only did the owner of the aforementioned
shop make a statement, but a photograph also appeared in the
newspaper, *Hoy,* of October 5 of this year, which shows his
capture by members of the National Guard. Later, on October
11 of this year, I learned that a number of bodies had been found
in the Apopa Jurisdiction; I and other members of the family
went to that jurisdiction to inquire as to the names or descrip-
tions of the bodies that appeared on those dates. It was concluded that one of the bodies the tribunal investigated on
October 3, at 2:30 P.M., could be that of Mr. Vinicio Humberto
Bazzaglia. The body was immediately exhumed and it turned out
to be that of Vinicio Humberto Bazzaglia, who was identified by
myself and his brother. The examination found that he had a

bullet in the head, which was the direct cause of death. The body was removed and taken to the city's General Cemetery for burial. The place where the body was found when the Justice of the Peace examined it is in the hamlet of El Ranchon in the El Angel District of the Apopa jurisdiction; more specifically, it was alongside the street that goes from the Mariona District to a Cel Substation in the El Angel District. The exhumation was conducted in the Apopa Cemetery.[39]

Certain social sectors have been singled out for particularly harsh treatment, including *campesinos,* clergy, political leaders, children, teachers, human rights activists and workers, journalists, and trade union members. Some examples of violations directed at these groups follow:

1. *Campesinos*

Throughout El Salvador, *campesinos* suffer unspeakable brutality at the hands of the military and paramilitary forces. The exact number of *campesinos* slain in political violence is unknown, since many killings go unreported. In a *New York Times* account of the discovery in November 1981 of "scores of bodies and skeletons" in sugar fields three miles north of the capital, cane cutters stated they had often found bodies dumped in the fields but did not report the discoveries.[40]

There can be no doubt, however, that there have been and continue to be great numbers of politically motivated *campesino* deaths for which the government is responsible. The Legal Aid office of the Archdiocese of San Salvador, the *Socorro Juridico,* has documented thousands of such cases since the 1979 coup.

The testimony recorded by *Socorro Juridico* provides examples of the severe cruelty directed against the peasant population. The following testimony was obtained by the *Socorro Juridico* a few days after the events took place in the Department of Cabanas, northeast of San Salvador:

On Thursday, February 28, 1980, two truckloads of police and National Guardsmen in civilian dress arrived. With them were Napoleon Alvarenga Fuentes, Baudilio Galdamez and Saul Casco Noyola, Cinquera members of ORDEN. These three and other members of ORDEN are those who were in charge of leading the security forces and the Army to the homes of those people whom they believed belonged to some popular organization. That day they came to Cinquera at around 7:30 in the morning, and went to the home of Aida Escalante. They threatened all the members of the family. They tied her up and forced her into a truck. They took her in the direction of the district of San Nicolas. There they forcibly arrested Felix Rivera. Then they returned to the district of La Escopeta where they fired their weapons, searched two houses and stole a number of articles. They also took a number of sacks, put Aida and Felix in them, and then sat on them. They took them away to the National Guard station at Suchitoto, where Felix and Aida were tortured to death. I say they were brutally tortured because Aida's body did not have a single bullet wound, but her nose and her teeth were broken and her lip was missing.

. . . She had a hole in her head but I don't know how they did that; it was so large that a hand could fit in easily; they had removed her fingernails. Her fingers were shriveled. Her entire body had been soaked in some kind of acid. She also showed signs of having been raped . . . On Sunday, at around 5:00 A.M., six truckloads of soldiers, Guardsmen, police and members of ORDEN entered Cinquera. They got out and then went to El Cacao; there they took Isabel Barahona. At her home they murdered a young boy from Sitio del Nino who had arrived the day before to visit her. They took Isabel about one block from her home. A heavyset policeman grabbed her by the hair and swung her around three times. When she hit the ground they shot her three times. Then they went to the other side of the district and took a young girl by the name of Guadalupe Monge; from then they began to beat me. One of my daughters, Lucia Juarez, tried to defend me, but the Guardsmen grabbed her by the arms. One

Guardsman whose face was covered with a handkerchief slapped her in the face; she fainted and they took her to a grove of coffee trees, where they raped and murdered her with four machete strokes to the head. After killing her, they returned to my house and told me that we should stop causing problems; that because of us many Guardsmen had died. They left, but they returned shortly thereafter to burn the body and to order us to leave if we didn't want what happened to my daughter to happen to us. We left and headed for the mountains, where we spent the night. On the way, we saw that the Guardsmen and members of ORDEN were setting fire to a number of ranches. The next day we left for San Salvador.[41]

Another mass killing of peasants by the military occurred on May 14, 1980, on the banks of the Sumpul River. (This incident, resulting in the deaths of some 600 refugees, including many whole families, is discussed in detail in Chapter 11.)

Killing of *campesinos* has also been inextricably linked with the agrarian reform since its beginning. On March 17, 1980, after the reform went into effect, Amnesty International publicly urged the Government of El Salvador to call a halt to the campaign of murder and abduction of peasants which followed the announcement of agrarian reform. In June 1980, the *Union Comunal Salvadorena,* the *campesino* group cooperating with the junta in carrying out the agrarian reform, issued a strongly worded communique denouncing the execution of twelve of its members by the National Guard.

Government and church sources report that the reform's technicians and its beneficiaries alike have been the victims of human rights atrocities. As of September 15, 1981, 40 ISTA employees had been reported killed since the agrarian reform was initiated,[42] while *campesino* deaths number in the thousands.

The extent of military violence directed against the reform was dramatically symbolized when the President of ISTA and two top-level American AIFLD officials were assassinated by gunmen acting with the apparent protection of the authorities. On January 3, 1981, Rodolfo Viera, the first *campesino* President of ISTA, Mark Pearlman, AIFLD attorney, and Michael Hammer, AIFLD's regional director for Central America, were gunned down in the coffee shop of San Salvador's Sheraton Hotel.

2. *Clergy and religious workers*

Large numbers of Catholic religious and lay workers have been killed by the government in what appears to be general persecution of the Catholic Church (See Chapter 7). The efforts of the Archbishop of San Salvador, Oscar Arnulfo Romero, the *Socorro Juridico* and other church members to publicize human rights violations have led to severe reprisals against Church members.

Among the most notable killings was the assassination of Archbishop Romero in March 1980. His sermons regularly denounced human rights violations and advocated social reforms. The day before his death, Archbishop Romero delivered an impassioned appeal to the members of the Army and the security forces to stop the slaughter in the countryside and to "cease the repression." His homily was heard by hundreds of thousands of Salvadorans through the church radio station.[43]

The following day, on March 24, Archbishop Romero was shot to death while saying Mass in San Salvador. Although there were many witnesses, the assassin was never apprehended.

In an interview for this report,[44] one witness, Jorge Pinto, the exiled publisher of the San Salvador daily, *El Independiente,* stated that he believed that "the death of Monsignor Romero had been ordered from within the Chiefs of Staff [Estado Mayor]." He testified that someone who lived in the area where the events occurred said he saw three policemen giving protection to a youth with a rifle on the day the Monsignor died.

Judge Atilio Ramirez Amaya, responsible for the judicial investigation into the Archbishop's assassination, fled El Salvador after several death threats and an unsuccessful attempt on his life inside his home. In a statement prepared for this report, Judge Ramirez gave this account of the proceedings:

Monsignor Oscar Arnulfo Romero was murdered on the afternoon of Monday, March 24, with one good shot. I do not believe that the crime will be solved under the present circumstances. Above all, I believe that these proceedings will be unable to incriminate anyone.

The Criminal Investigations Section of the National Police intervenes in all cases involving violent deaths, even in cases of obvious suicide. They always arrive before the judicial authorities. However, in the murder of Monsignor Romero, they arrived almost four days after the event occurred and did not provide the Court any data or evidence of an investigation into the crime. On the 28th, I pointed out this failure to carry out the criminologist's obligations; I directed these remarks to the police experts who arrived at around noon, almost four days after the murder, to ask whether "they could be of any help." The same thing happened with respect to the Office of the Attorney General of the Republic; a special attorney arrived on the 28th, too, with instructions to appear in the proceedings. Because of such premeditated omissions on the part of the servants of justice, it is undoubtedly the case that from the very beginning, they were involved in a kind of conspiracy to cover up the murder.[45]

Roberto Cuellar, Executive Director of *Socorro Juridico* and an intimate friend and collaborator of Monsignor Romero, was also interviewed for this report. On July 5, 1980, the *Socorro Juridico* office in San Salvador was raided by the security forces. Among the files taken were those on the case of Archbishop Romero. The file included testimony implicating the military in the Archbishop's murder.[46]

Another widely publicized attack on the Church involved the murders of four American church women. The nuns, Ita Ford, Maura Clarke, Dorothy Kazel and the lay missionary Jean Donovan, were seized on December 2, 1980, after the latter two picked up the others at the international airport of El Salvador. Their bodies, bearing gun wounds and bruises, were found the next day at Santiago Nonualco, Department of La Paz.[47]

The murders of a number of other clergy, lay leaders and catechists have been reported by the *Socorro Juridico* and Amnesty International. These incidents include the murder of Italian priest Father Cosme Spezzotto on June 14, 1980; the murder of seminarian Jose Otsmaro Caceres while he was building a church in the District of Plantanares; the murder of Father Miguel Antonio Reyes Monico on October 6, 1980, after he was seized by the National Guard from his home; the disappearance of Father Marcial Serrano, after he was abducted by the National Guard on November 28, 1980; and the disappearance of Father Abrezo.[48]

3. *Political leaders*

Another large class of victims is composed of leaders of political opposition groups and supporters of peasant movements.

One particularly dramatic example is the brutal murder of six members of the executive committee of the broad-based Democratic Revolutionary Front (FDR) on November 27, 1980. The six leaders were kidnapped while preparing a news conference at the San Jose High School in San Salvador and their badly mutilated corpses were found later east of the capital. The abduction was carried out by heavily armed men in civilian dress while the school was surrounded by some 200 soldiers and police for

25 minutes.[49] According to the *Socorro Juridico,* the involvement of the government is also indicated by the fact that the vehicles used in the abduction were identified as belonging to official security organizations.[50]

4. *Children and youths*

Many victims are children and young people, including those too young to have had any involvement in combat. A few examples follow:

In the May 1980 Sumpul River massacre (see Chapter 11), hundreds of children were killed by Salvadoran troops. Based on eye-witness testimony, Amnesty reports:

ORDEN members gathered children and babies together, threw them into the air and slashed them to death with machetes. Some infants were reportedly decapitated and their bodies slit into pieces and thrown to the dogs; other children were reported to have drowned after Salvadoran soldiers threw them into the water.[51]

The *Socorro Juridico* and Amnesty International report that on July 9, 1980, members of ORDEN, protected by Army troops, staged a brutal attack in the Guadalupe Mogotes canton in San Pablo Tacachico. Twenty-two children were among those taken from their homes, lined up and executed by firing squads. Thirty-one members of the Mojica Santos family alone, including 15 children under 10 years old, were killed in the incident.[52]

In another incident, members of the military, along with several persons in civilian garb, attacked the Rodriguez family in the Canton of Santa Barbara, Tecoluca, on February 14, 1981. Five members of the family were killed, including two children under the age of 6.[53]

Throughout the country, many youths have been killed by security forces who apparently assume, on the basis of their age, that they are sympathetic to the opposition. On November 1, 1980, 62 young people between the ages of 14 and 22 in Soyapango were taken away be security forces in a systematic search of two villages. Two days later all of their bodies, bearing marks of torture, were found.[54]

On January 10, 1981, following the "general offensive" of guerrilla forces, 22 teenagers from Mejicanos were taken away by government troops; their mutilated corpses were later found.[55]

5. *Teachers and academics*

Teachers and academics form another group which has been subjected to brutal and systematic abuse. Attacks have been leveled against those involved in education, but seem particularly aimed against educators belonging to the union, *Associacion Nacional de Educadores Salvadoreños* (ANDES).[56]

In the first quarter of 1981, Amnesty reports that 22 teachers were killed, while others "disappeared."[57] According to the El Salvador Commission on Human Rights, ANDES reported the disappearance and subsequent murder of 12 teachers between June 1 and 18, 1981. ANDES also stated that, as of August 1980, 84 secondary school teachers had been murdered and, in the first half of the year, a total of 136 of its members had been killed.[58] Amnesty reported that 90 primary school teachers were assassinated between January and October 1980.[59]

One case was the murder of Vladimir Barrios, a teacher and leader of a school group in the La Parroquin suburb of Tecapa. According to *Socorro Juridico,*[60] in an operation coordinated by the National Guard, Mr. Barrios was gunned down in front of his pupils by heavily armed individuals who said they were members of the Death Squad. A schoolgirl, Blanca Lidia Orellana, was seriously injured.

Attacks have also been directed against universities. For example, on June 26, 1980, in the early morning hours a military operation was carried out in the slum area, *La Fosa,* adjacent to the National University of El Salvador. According to reports, several people were killed during the raid, and the attack spread to the University. During the operation, "the army and police forces surrounded the University for three hours and then entered the campus shooting. The result was about 27 dead, 15 wounded, and 200 arrested," according to the Annual Report for 1979–1980 of the Inter-American Commission on Human Rights.[61] The *Instituto Nacional General Isidro Menendez,* which is located next to the University was also occupied and a foreign camera crew witnessed and filmed the murder at the hands of the National Guard of a 14-year-old defenseless student who begged for mercy. The footage of the murder was shown in the U.S. as part of an NBC White Paper entitled, "The Castro Connection," aired in September 1980.

6. *Journalists and human rights monitors*

Journalists, both Salvadoran and foreign, have been subjected to persecution in El Salvador. (See Chapter 8.) A letter protesting these violations was signed by some 1,000 U.S. journalists and presented to the government of El Salvador on November 16, 1981. The letter, detailing the cases of journalists who were killed, tortured, or arrested or forced to leave El Salvador, stated:

Journalists have been attacked by a number of political factions, including the underground left and members of government security forces. But it is the ultra-right paramilitary groups that have been the most deadly. News reports show that these groups, which often identify themselves as "squadrons of death," are responsible for most of the incidents of violence against journalists. The groups are truly terrorist in nature. They have circulated anonymous hit lists. They have delivered anonymous death threats. They have claimed responsibility for the murder of at least two newsmen and countless news sources. They have dynamited radio transmitters, presses, and entire newsrooms.

No journalist expects nor desires special protection in order to do his job. Reporting in combat situations is never danger-free. But only a few of the journalist-victims in El Salvador have been killed or attacked while covering combat.

Listed among the disappeared are two journalists working for the American press Rene Tamsen (April 1, 1980) and John Sullivan (December 1980).

Other examples include the disappearances of eight staff members of the newspaper, *El Independiente,* after they were taken from their offices by security officials on January 15, 1981.[62] After this incident and the repeated attempts on the life of its editor, Jorge Pinto, *El Independiente* was forced to close. The managing editor and a photographer for *La Cronica del Pueblo* (the only other newspaper that had refused to practice self-censorship) were abducted in mid-1980. Their mutilated bodies were found the next day.[63]

Human rights monitors in El Salvador who have published information on government violations have themselves come under severe attack.[64]

In early October 1980, the press secretary of the El Salvador Commission of Human Rights, Maria Magdalena Henriquez, was abducted by two uniformed members of the police and subsequently found dead. Another Commission representative, Ramon Valladares Perez was killed a few weeks later. A number of relatives of Commission members have also been killed by government forces.

In April 1980, the names of a number of its staff appeared on a list of "traitors" issued by the military press office. Attacks have also been directed against the *Socorro Juridico.* Having been raided 17 times in one week, its offices were forced to close temporarily in December 1980. This list was viewed by the *Socorro Juridico,* Amnesty

International and other groups as giving official sanction to the killing of those human rights advocates.

In April 1981, the British relief agency OXFAM reported that 17 of its staff members were killed by the military or ORDEN in the last year. Another 300 individuals working indirectly on OXFAM projects were also killed.

The systematic persecution has forced many human rights advocates into exile.

C. *Enforced disappearances*

There have been large numbers of "disappearances" reported throughout El Salvador over the last five or six years.

Disappearances is the term applied to the politically motivated abduction of individuals by government security forces, or by paramilitary groups with the complicity or consent of the government. These are effectuated in a manner designed to avoid accountability by the government. Information on the whereabouts of victims is extremely difficult to obtain, since the government systematically either denies any knowledge of the disappearances or simply refuses to respond to inquiries. Legal remedies, therefore, are ineffective in cases of disappearances. Those abducted are subsequently subjected to imprisonment—often in secret detention centers—torture and/or death.[65]

In 1977 Amnesty International reported that "arrests followed by disappearance and probable murder of people in custody by security forces were its fundamental . . . concerns in El Salvador in the past year."[66] The following year Amnesty International again stated that in El Salvador "its primary concern [had] been the increasing number of detentions followed by disappearances. . . ."[67]

In 1978 the Inter-American Commission on Human Rights (IACHR) of the OAS also became concerned by the growing number of disappearances in that country. During its 1978 investigation in El Salvador, the IACHR delegation discovered five secret cells located in the third floor of the headquarters of the National Guard in San Salvador. The names and initials of several individuals who had disappeared after detention were carved into the doors of the cells. The authorities had denied knowledge of the whereabouts of these persons. The investigative mission found that:

> The security bodies have committed serious violations of the right to liberty, in making arbitrary arrests. They have maintained secret places of detention, where some persons, whose capture and imprisonment have been denied by the government, were deprived of liberty under extremely cruel and inhuman conditions.[68]

And, in a resolution concerning this case, the IACHR declared that:

> the Commission has in its possession unequivocal proof that Sergio V. Arriaza, Juan Jose Yanez, Lil Milagro Ramirez, Ricardo Arrieta, Carlos Antonio Madriz and Luis Bonilla (the persons whose initials were found on the doors) were detained and tortured by agents of the Government of El Salvador and there is fear for their personal security.[69]

In December 1978, eleven months after the IACHR investigation, the British Parliamentary Delegation which visited El Salvador also saw the clandestine cells in the National Guard headquarters. The Delegation concluded "that many disappeared people are detained in secret centres of the security forces."[70]

In its annual country report covering events in 1978, the U.S. State Department stated that "there were numerous reports of disappearances of persons and frequent appearances of corpses, sometimes in groups and often showing signs of torture." It cited the September 1978 list of the

Socorro Juridico, containing the names of 100 disappeared persons with dates of their reported capture by the security forces.

Disappearances continued to occur in large numbers throughout 1979. By October 15, 1979, the *Socorro Juridico* had documented some 200 cases of disappearances.[71] The U.N. Working Group on Enforced or Involuntary Disappearances received reports of 104 cases of disappearances for the period January to October 1979.[72]

One of the first decrees adopted by the Junta after the overthrow of President Romero, Decree No. 9 of November 6, 1979, established a special investigative commission on political prisoners and disappeared persons. The Commission was granted autonomy and full powers to carry out its task. It was composed of the Attorney General, a member appointed by the Supreme Court of Justice and "an honorable citizen" appointed by the Junta. It was given sixty days to carry out the investigation and submit "a detailed report" to the Junta.

The Commission ultimately failed to find alive one single person who had disappeared during the Romero or Molina regimes; however, it did find "a great number of bodies," some of which were identified as belonging to the disappeared. It also found "clandestine jails or places of torture," all of them empty, which were ordered to be closed or modified "in such a way as to make it impossible to use them as prisons."[73] The Commission commented: "All this brings us to the conclusion that we can presume that all the disappeared are dead." It added that "we have proof of the capture of many of them by various official security forces."

The Commission concluded that there had been an abuse of power by some officials under previous regimes "to such an extent that the most basic rights upheld in our Constitution, such as the rights of life and liberty, have been violated."[74]

Based on the evidence gathered, the Commission recommended that "both former presidents [Romero and Molina] . . . and the successive Directors General of the National Guard, Treasury Police and National Police" under the two presidents be prosecuted. The Special Commission placed at the disposal of the Junta and the courts the extensive evidence it had compiled.[75]

In spite of the report, the Junta has never brought charges against any of the officials mentioned, nor have the courts initiated an investigation to determine responsibility for the crimes. The Attorney General explained that the Commission never "submitted conclusive evidence regarding the responsibility [of Molina, Romero and the other military officers] for the disappearances and presumed death of the persons mentioned in the report of the Commission. . . ."[76]

While the Commission carried out its mandate, there were practically no cases of disappearances for political reasons.[77] Shortly after it had submitted its final report, however, cases of detentions followed by disappearance began occurring again. By the summer of 1980, the number of reported disappearances had increased dramatically; in August alone 88 cases were documented.[78]

The U.N. Working Group on Enforced or Involuntary Disappearances received 199 reports of arrests followed by disappearances in El Salvador during 1980. The Group also added that "the reports usually indicate the date and the place of the arrest, as well as the manner in which it occurred and the name of the branch of the armed forces which made it . . . [and that] the ages of the persons concerned range from eight months to 74 years."[79]

As to the places where disappeared persons may be held, the Working Group said:

For the period subsequent to the report of the Special Commission (created by Decree No. 9) little information has been received on places where disappeared persons might be held in El Salvador or on their fate. In a few cases the body of the disappeared person has been reported found, some time after the person's arrest. There is evidence, in addition to the information on the arrest itself, from which it can be inferred that prior to their deaths these persons had been detained somewhere for a period; the bodies bore marks showing that their hands had been bound and that they had been tortured. Furthermore, the Group is aware of the reports of the finding in El Salvador of numerous bodies, often mutilated beyond recognition which precluded their identification as missing persons.[80]

According to the reports on which the Working Group based its information, the arrests usually occurred at the home of the missing person, in the street or other public places. Most of the arrests were reported to have been made by members of government security forces and ORDEN.

From May 1, 1980, to April 30, 1981, Amnesty International launched 58 appeals on behalf of 472 people believed to have been detained or disappeared during that period.[81]

Socorro Juridico reports that from October 15, 1979, until March 27, 1981, a total of 602 persons have disappeared after detention in El Salvador.[82] This figure of 602 cases of documented disappearances over a 17-month period since the coup of October 15, 1979, must be contrasted with the total of 208 cases of disappearances reported for the seven years (1972–79) of the Molina and Romero administrations combined.

CHAPTER 4

THE RIGHT TO
HUMANE TREATMENT
AND
PHYSICAL INTEGRITY

The government of El Salvador has been no more punctilious in observing its obligations to protect the right to humane treatment and to enforce prohibitions against torture than it has in defending the right to life.

This chapter reports on the evidence of torture and degrading treatment under the current government in El Salvador prefaced by a brief summary of the pre-1979 coup situation.

A. *Events prior to October 1979*

A number of international groups and outside observers conducted reviews of the situation in El Salvador in the late 1970s; all concluded that the government was engaged in the systematic torture of its political opponents.[1] Following the 1979 coup the State Department summarized the situation as follows:

... . During the Romero period, there is no doubt that the security forces subjected prisoners to degrading treatment and punishment at stages of the judicial process from arrest to prison sentence.

. . . There were numerous credible allegations of torture by security forces during the Romero Government. Accusations against the National Guard and other security forces included denial of food and water, electric shock and sexual violation.[2]

Special committees of the Inter-American Commission on Human Rights (IACHR) and of the British Parliament visited El Salvador and gained access to secret detention cells in the Headquarters of the National Guard. They found "unequivocal proof" of torture. The visiting delegations also found evidence of torture by ORDEN and of atrocities committed by members of the National Guard and the Treasury police in rural areas. Amnesty International also discovered numerous cases of torture and of documented cases of mutilation of bodies in the countryside.

The Law for the Defense and Guarantee of Public Order of November 25, 1977, coupled with a "state of siege" decree promulgated on February 28, 1977, facilitated the abuse of the right to physical integrity. In their September 1978 analysis of the Law, the International Commission of Jurists stated:

In sum, the procedure established under this law invites an abuse of power on the part of the security forces . . . The amendment of the Code of Criminal Procedure to permit the use of extra-judicial confessions as a basis for decreeing provisional detention assures that the security forces will attempt to get such a declaration in almost every case . . .[3]

The state of siege also facilitated arbitrary detention, contributing to an increased likelihood of the use of physical and psychological duress against detainees while in unacknowledged custody, many of whom were later char-

acterized as "missing." The law was repealed in early
1979.

B. *Torture since October 15, 1979*

It is impossible to ascertain the exact number of persons
tortured or subjected to unlawful use of force since October 1979, but the weight of the evidence shows the problem to be of extraordinary dimensions. One difficulty in
determining the number tortured lies in the fact that the
right to physical integrity appears to be inextricably linked
to the right to life. A relatively small number of detained
persons are processed through the official judicial chan-
nels—others are tortured and then released. The great
majority of victims appear to have been dealt with in a
summary fashion in which torture routinely precedes execution. (See Chapter 3, The Right to Life.) Of the many
thousands of bodies which have appeared after detentions
and abductions by security personnel, a very high proportion show signs of torture including dismemberment,
beating, acid burns, flaying, scalping, castration, strangulation, sexual violation, and evisceration.

The torture and use of force does not appear to be aimed
at securing confessions, except in the case of some political
prisoners who are turned over to official detention centers.
In such cases Decree 507 issued by the Junta in December
1980 encourages torture by giving judges authority to impose preventive detention for as long as 180 days and by
changing the rules of admissibility of evidence to permit
various types of extrajudicial confessions. Article 11 of the
decree reads:

In addition to those established under regular law, the following shall be regarded as sufficient evidence to take the case to
plenary proceedings:

1) A confession made before a judge other than the one trying
the case;

2) A written extrajudicial confession; an oral extrajudicial confession verified by two witnesses, and a recording made in the manner established under regular law;

An oral confession shall be regarded as valid evidence even though it may have been given before each witness at differing places and times. The only requirement to make valid the declaration of witnesses to the confession shall be that the individuals witnessed the confession; that they are over eighteen years of age and that they state that the confession was given spontaneously.

The torture generally occurs before the prisoner is turned over to an official prison or released. Torture is less common after prisoners are officially detained. However, in most cases torture does not seem to be employed solely or even mainly for the purpose of extracting information and confessions. Rather, it routinely occurs before summary killings of suspected opposition sympathizers. The torture occurs in the open countryside, in barracks, and in headquarters and stations of the security forces. Groups who have investigated this phenomenon have remarked not only on the widespread nature of the torture, but also on the intensity of the brutality. A U.S. Public Health Commission of Inquiry noted in its 1980 report:

The brutality involved in the killings of health workers and patients and the accompanying torture suggest that this is a deliberate tactic aimed at striking terror into the hearts of others. Victims have been decapitated, emasculated or found with the initials "EM", which stands for Esquadron de la Muerte (Death Squad), in their flesh. Official forensic medical reports document these atrocities.[4]

Members of an ecumenical group organized by the American Friends Service Committee, and including the National Council of Churches and the U.S. Catholic Conference who visited El Salvador in March 1980, stated in their findings:

. . . The delegation was particularly shocked by the barbarity of the repression. We have heard testimony from eyewitnesses of rape, torture, mutilation, decapitation, garrotting, and the murder of unarmed and defenseless men, women, and children. The security forces burned fields and forests and destroyed bridges to prevent people from escaping the atrocities . . .

. . . It is our judgment that the repression is not only for the purpose of eliminating organized peasants or leadership of other sectors, but is particularly severe and barbaric in order to intimidate and terrorize actual or potential opposition. . . .[5]

Although these human rights abuses have occurred in the context of an open armed conflict between the government and guerrilla organizations, Amnesty International notes that those who are tortured are not generally captured in battle:

the victims of torture and death at the hands of security forces have not generally been shown to have any direct involvement in armed insurrection. Most of the deaths have occurred after the victims had been seized from their homes or work places and were defenseless. . . .[6]

The evidence of torture is presented in three sections: 1) violations of physical integrity prior to killing; 2) torture during short-term detention, interrogation, and release; and 3) torture prior to imprisonment.

1. *Torture and unlawful use of force prior to killings*

By mid-January 1980, an average of three tortured and mutilated corpses were appearing in El Salvador each day.[7] In the next two months, reports of torture in the countryside mounted sharply with 171 military operations carried out in various farming communities between January and March 1980. Most of the victims were summarily executed on the presumption of their association with peasant leagues, trade unions, or opposition movements, but other sectors of the population, including doctors, teachers and lawyers, were also affected. Then with the Agrarian Reform, and the simultaneous declaration of the state of siege, came increased allegations of summary killings preceded by torture. By June 1980, church sources documented the cases of 2,065 persons killed; many were tortured first. Such torture followed by death continued through 1981.

The Legal Aid office of the Office of the Archdiocese of San Salvador summarized one period as follows:

17 April 1980. Several hundred members of the paramilitary organization ORDEN, protected by the National Army and police of the National Guard, invaded in arms the Christian peasant communities of El Pajal, Upper Tehuiste, El Salto, San Lucas, Ulapa, Santa Lucia, Tepechame, in the San Vicente and Le Paz departmental districts in the east of the country. In Upper Tehuiste, the attackers murdered *campesino* Bernardo Guzman and another who could not be identified because of tortures. In Llano Grande, eleven police of the National Guard and members of ORDEN seized and subsequently decapitated *campesinos* Jose Orellana and Fidencio Alfaro. In the peasant hamlet of Alferez in the same departmental districts, the attackers seized an old woman Francisca Espinoza (77 years old) and decapitated her; the head was placed between the legs of the corpse.[8]

Eyewitness accounts provide clear evidence of torture followed by killing of individuals from all walks of life who are seized by security forces and not taken in combat. Some of the accounts are so horrible as to make repetition difficult. A brief sampling of the many reports available from numerous sources follows:

—The Secretary General of the Union Democratica Nacionalista (NSC) and his wife were seized by uniformed members of the national police in San Salvador. Their tortured bodies were found on a roadside forty miles outside the city.[9]

—Two doctors were abducted by armed men in civilian dress from a hospital in Cojutepeque while performing an operation. They were found later with clear signs of torture. One had had a depressed skull and was dead from strangulation. The other was unconscious and later died from a wound cutting the spinal cord.[10]

—Three buses with a contingent of national guardsmen came to Platanillo Canton in Quezaltepeque. One group went to the home of a woman with two small children and took her to the school where other prisoners were being held and where she was brutally tortured. An eyewitness described what took place as follows:

Mira Guevara was in her ninth month of pregnancy and the acts of torture forced the onset of labor. Even more suffering was caused when the head of the newborn appeared. The National Guardsmen then fired several bullets, destroying her face. They finished by breaking her hands and arms. Her body was left with four others who also were assassinated by national guardsmen.[11]

—Troops took 22 teenagers from Mejicanos. All were later found dead with marks of torture. Although an Army spokesman claimed that they died in a battle, a doctor who examined 17 of the bodies found that they had been shot after they were dead. Five of the young women were unidentifiable because their faces had been erased.[12]

—Members of ORDEN from Cinquera seized two women and took them away to a National Guard station where they were tortured to death. The next day a member of the National Police drove back with their bodies and threw them alongside the Quezalapa River. An individual who viewed the bodies described one as follows:

Aida's body did not have a single bullet wound, but her nose and her teeth were broken and her upper lip was missing. The blindfold that had been placed on her head when she was taken had a stick through it; they had turned the stick in order to tighten the blindfold. She had a hole in her head but I don't know how they did that; it was so large that a hand could fit in easily. They had also painted FPL on the blindfold. One leg was broken and they had removed her fingernails. Her fingers were shriveled. Her entire body had been soaked in some kind of acid. She also showed signs of having been raped.[13]

The victims' bodies are rarely given to relatives nor are they generally buried clandestinely, but are often displayed prominently, suggesting that the purpose of the mutilations and other tortures inflicted upon them are to intimidate and terrorize the population.

2. *Torture during short-term detention, during interrogation before release*

There are many instances since the 1979 coup of short-term detention by security forces where torture is routinely inflicted to extract information before the victim is released. Release is often accompanied by threats and warnings to leave the country. The tortures occur in the Central Headquarters of the National Guard, the Central Station of the Treasury Police, the Central Headquarters of the National Police in San Salvador and Police and National Guard Headquarters in other towns. The most frequent types of tortures inflicted are severe blows to all parts of the body, causing fractures and contusions, death threats, choking, electric shock to lips, mouth and genitals, hooding, drugging, submersion in water, cigarette burns, and simulated execution.

The victims, as noted previously, fall into a vast category of persons who were apprehended because of their presumed association with "oppositionist forces" including journalists, priests, workers and students.

What follows are excerpts from an account by an em-

ployee of a newspaper, *El Independiente,* taken by the
National Guard:

They took me to a room and began to ask me what my job was.
I told them I was a photographic technician and worked at *El
Independiente.* Then they began to hit me, saying I was from the
ERP and the FPL, clandestine organizations. . . . Then they said
they'd use a machine on me which would make me talk. They
put electrodes in my penis and my ear, and gave me electric
shocks. . . . They kicked me in the ribs and back. . . .

They said that if I worked at *El Independiente,* I must know
who the journalists were . . . Then they asked if I wanted to suffer
the same fate as the Mexican journalist. They asked me if I knew
a Demetrio. . . . He was the next journalist they were going to
kill. . . .

They carried on beating me, but I wouldn't change what I'd
said. So they asked if I'd like to try the "electric chair," the
"hood" and a number of other things they said they'd use on me
if I didn't collaborate. . . . Then they showed me photos of
journalists, asking if I knew them. They mentioned several foreign names, Italian and others I don't remember. They said the
same would happen to this Demetrio as had happened to his
priest, to the Monsignor and to the Mexican journalist. They
went on asking me questions all the time, until an electric shock
in the ear made me faint. . . .

Later, they hit me, threw me on the ground and put my head
in a bucket of water, holding me there until I couldn't stand it
any more. Afterwards, they took me back to where my colleague
was.[14]

There is no record of any investigations by the government of such allegations of torture.

3. *Torture before imprisonment*

The torture of those who are imprisoned rather than killed
generally occurs in the interim period after the arrest,
usually in police stations and National Guard barracks,

before prisoners are turned over to penitentaries. *Socorro Juridico,* in its compilation of 51 cases of political prisoners held in Santa Tecla Prison, documents the torture all of them suffered between their capture and consignment to Santa Tecla.[15] Prisoners were detained for periods ranging up to 90 days at National Police Stations and National Guard Headquarters where they endured electric shock, beatings, burning with cigarettes and acid, submersion in water, death threats, and partial garrottings. One prisoner captured by the National Police in April 1980 was held for four days, during which time his left leg was broken, a tooth was "wrenched out" and his forehead was fractured by rifle butt blows. Hooded, he was severely beaten and, with a revolver in his mouth, he was threatened with death. For two and a half months, he remained in Rosales Hospital receiving treatment for the injuries sustained during torture. He was later turned over to Santa Tecla Prison.[16]

The testimony of Professor Rafael Carias provides a vivid first-person account:

At around 11:00 P.M. on Saturday February 21, 1981, around 6 henchmen in civilian dress and 5 in uniform entered the area where I live. They remained in the street, but when they banged on the door, all that I could think of was the life of my two-year old son who was in his crib. When I opened the door the first thing they did was to hit me, throw me face down and tie my hands behind my back. They continued to kick me in the back and on the head. When my home was searched they removed my companion and the child. They blindfolded her and me and put us in a vehicle, along with certain articles such as the television set.

We were taken to the Office of the Mayor of San Marcos. There I was not mistreated. Two hours later we were taken to the El Zapote headquarters. There, at 7:00 A.M., I was taken away to a room used for torture. When they removed the blindfold, there were four executioners facing me. They beat me over my entire body. When they had finished, they lay me face-down on a wooden bench, handcuffed my wrists together underneath it and then bound up my entire body. They attached a wire to the toe of each foot. When the electricity was turned on, an executioner put a towel over my face so that I could not breathe; if I said something they would disconnect it. When that got them nowhere, the questions were accompanied by a blow to the stomach. This went on for more than two hours.

They untied me and took me to a sink with my feet and hands tied. They forcibly put me under water so that I would lose oxygen. For a few moments, I thought I was going to die, but I held fast to my convictions. This lasted another two hours. They removed me from the sink, put me face down, spread my legs apart and inserted a stick in my rectum. They laughed sarcastically during all of this. I was returned to the room used for torture and handcuffed to the same bench. They inserted a tooth brush in my rectum and turned it around. Since they didn't get what they wanted from me, they left me alone for some five minutes. This gave me time to meditate and to hold to my promise to suffer stoically.

When they returned, they had a bottle of acid and they told me that they would pour it on me, which they demonstrated with a piece of cloth. The executioners insisted that I was a high-ranking member of the organization. When they found that I could not be made to talk, they poured acid on my back for the first time. The pain was incredible. They continued to question me and when I did not reply, they used a ballpoint pen to mark my body and continued to pour acid on me.

Then they told me that they would pour acid in my eyes; one of them opened my left eye and when I saw that they were going to spill a small amount of liquid on me, I turned over to one side and struggled with them. They stopped pouring acid on me. Then a lieutenant came to interrogate me, but decided to take me to a cell. There in the cell I heard my small child cry and talk from time to time. That gave me strength because my young son, too, was experiencing the bestialities of the dictatorship, together with his mother.

At 6:00 P.M. they took me from the cell to the National Guard. There, the treatment I received was even more bestial, because upon learning that I was a professor, they tied me up like an object and kicked me in the chest, head and back. The electric shocks I received there were as follows: The first was done by applying electric shocks to the feet intermittently and for as long as five minutes, and then to the head, with the same frequency. Electric shocks on a metal bed, where I was tied and handcuffed to the bed; first they removed all my clothing and wet my entire body. This made the pain worse. All of these tortures were accompanied by questions from a certain female commander, as to whether I knew the places where we met, who was my chief, where did I keep the propaganda, etc.

The day the International Red Cross arrived they hid me. But the International Red Cross did not arrive in the morning, as the National Guard had expected, but in the afternoon instead. So it was that they found me."[17]

CHAPTER 5
THE RIGHT TO PERSONAL LIBERTY

In spite of the government's obligations under domestic and international law to protect personal liberty, the individual right to be free from arbitrary imprisonment is seriously undermined by recent enactments of the government of El Salvador, as well as by both open and covert actions of its security forces. This chapter assesses the present status of the right to personal liberty in El Salvador, again preceded by a summary of events before the coup of October 15, 1979.

A. *Events prior to October 1979*

The Romero government abused the right to personal liberty as it did other rights. In 1977 the Law for the Defense of Public Order and the state of siege only served to increase the instances of abuse by security forces, particularly in allowing them to conduct arbitrary and unacknowledged arrests.

Even after the Law was repealed in February 1979, many prisoners arrested under it remained in prison or were unaccounted for.[1]

B. *The right to liberty since October 15, 1979*

This section first describes changes in the law since 1979 as they further reduce the legal right to liberty. It then describes how the system has operated in fact, ignoring even those restraints that continue in force.

In spite of its announced intentions, the new government did not significantly improve respect for the right to personal liberty. As the situation of civil unrest worsened, in fact, the Junta dictated new laws restricting this right, and opened the door for arbitrary and abusive exercise of governmental authority.

1. *The legal protection of the right to liberty*

In this respect, three definite stages can be identified since October 1979, in the progression of the legal status of the right to protection from arbitrary arrest. The first stage runs from the establishment of the new government to the reinstitution of the state of siege on March 6, 1980. The second covers from March 1980 to December 3, 1980, when Decree No. 507 was enacted, in turn initiating the third and current stage.

a. *Phase I*

On October 16, the Junta, with Decree No. 3, granted "a general amnesty . . . to all those persons whose freedom was restricted for political crimes either with or without trial." The Junta also created a Special Investigative Committee of three members, charged with locating the whereabouts of political detainees who had "disappeared" after their arbitrary detention by security forces.[2]

This period was characterized by an attempt to restore the restraints and guarantees established by Salvadoran constitutional law, and to conduct arrests only by means of legal mechanisms which provide adequate safeguards against arbitrariness. However, this attempt was thwarted from the outset by those in the military and security forces who resisted such changes.

b. *Phase II*

The re-establishment of the state of siege, in accordance with Article 175 of the Constitution on March 5, 1980, marked the second stage.[3] The suspension of guarantees was presented as necessary to counteract disruption and social disturbance by those seeking to thwart the land reform program. While it was limited to thirty days, it has been extended for similar periods ever since.

The Junta declared all strikes and abandonment of posts by State employees illegal[4] and, under the threat of harsh penalties, made every official who has personnel under his authority responsible for reporting perceived abnormalities in the performance of services.[5] Later, the Junta declared a national emergency and placed a number of public service agencies under control of the Ministry of Defense and Public Security, headed by Col. Jose Guillermo Garcia.[6] As a result workers in those agencies were inducted into the Armed Forces.

These statutes provided the legal framework for the arbitrary arrest of workers involved in trade union activities in the public sector. Likewise, although the state of siege has nominally a limited effect in Salvadoran law, it in fact legitimizes actions by the security forces that include an increase in the number of unwarranted arrests and detentions prolonged beyond legal terms.

On May 22, 1980, the Junta issued two decrees that modified the Criminal Code and the Code of Criminal Procedures, respectively.[7] In increasing penalties for certain crimes and creating new ones, Decree No. 264 expanded considerably the legal definition of "terrorism" and severely punished many forms of peaceful demonstration and protest. Decree No. 265 banned release on bond or parole of those accused or convicted of a wide range of offenses, all of them related to political actions. These first attempts to widen the scope of permissible restrictions on freedom lend legitimacy to arbitrary decisions against the liberty of individuals.

c. *Phase III*

Initiating the third phase on December 3, 1980, the Junta issued a comprehensive package of legislation to deal with judicial proceedings arising out of its campaign against "subversive activities." This decree establishes permanent military courts with jurisdiction over all cases of offenses listed in Article 177 of the Constitution.[8] Military Judges impose sentences after an investigation by Military Investigatory Judges.

Some aspects of Decree 507 seem designed specifically to promote arbitrary or unwarranted restrictions on personal freedom. First, there is an extraordinarily long period of investigation (up to 195 days in total), during which the proceedings are conducted *ex parte.* In effect, this allows the Military Investigatory Judge as well to hold persons at his discretion, without cause, for over six months. Once the investigation is complete, the military judges can impose a sentence. However, alternatively the judge is authorized to impose "security measures" of up to 120 days' detention on suspects, even after finding no good cause for prosecution. This unusual authority to detain without cause results in detentions amounting to the terms of a short sentence, with no due process, opportunity for defense or appeal. But worse yet, it can be prolonged indefinitely even after the 120 days, by means of "measures of control" that the judge can impose, such as periodic appearances before the court, or the fixing of bond.

Traditional rules of evidence have been abandoned in favor of a system that allows greater flexibility to the judges both to find probable cause and to issue sentences against the suspects. Finally, release on parole is not authorized for those convicted under these procedures.

Thus, legislation sanctioned by the Salvadoran Junta has instituted a system of legalized arbitrariness that seriously constrains the right to personal liberty. Salvadoran lawyers have compared this law with Romero's *Ley de Defensa y Garantia del Orden Publico,* and found the latter "soft and benevolent" compared with Decree 507.[9]

As a response to the "general offensive" launched by the leftist organizations, the Armed Forces instituted "martial law" and a curfew throughout the country on January 10, 1981. There appears to be no legal authority to impose them, nor is there any legal instrument to determine their scope and effect. According to traditional military doctrine, however, it can be assumed that the Armed Forces are thereby authorized to make arrests, even if arbitrary and unwarranted, and to use deadly force against civilians found to be violating military orders, including the curfew.

2. *The right to personal liberty in fact*

In practice the government has failed even to observe the rights it has purported to grant to Salvadorans. Rather the government has conducted warrantless arrests and has prolonged detentions beyond reasonable terms to control its opposition. Although arbitrary deprivations of personal freedom are not the government's prime tactical measure against its opposition—government-sponsored killings and "disappearances" claim a far larger number of victims—there are enough cases to prove a deliberate and widespread pattern of violation of the right.

The Special Investigative Committee on Political Prisoners and Missing Persons, set up by Decree No. 9, was not able to find persons illegally in prison at the time of its investigation, but found ample evidence of such a practice in the administration deposed on October 15, 1979. It recommended bringing charges against military chiefs involved in them, and to modifying structures so that several police quarters could no longer be used as clandestine detention centers. It also recommended a clarification and expansion of the amnesty decree (No. 3, October 16, 1979), since it was not clearly producing the desired release of political prisoners. These recommendations apparently went unheeded.

Between January 5 and October 6, 1980, *Socorro Juridico* registered twelve incidents of illegal arrests of Catholic priests, nuns and lay workers, not counting those abductions that ended in the death of the victims.[10] In the course of one week in August, YSAX Radio, run by the Archdiocese of San Salvador, reported the arrest of student Roberto Funes Cartagena, 22 years old, by the National Police, of Mario Melendez Lopez, 16, held in the National Guard general headquarters, of Nelson Armando Gomez Castellon, 17, by combined forces, of student Jaime Silby, whose tortured and bullet-riddled corpse was found later, by the National Guard, and of U.S. citizen Sister Patricia Price, by the Treasury Police. Sr. Price was later released under pressure from the United States Embassy.[11]

In June 1980 alone, 33 persons—17 of them teenagers —were subject to arbitrary arrest by the security forces.[12] Between January 1980 and May 1981, at least 20 journalists were apprehended and tortured by government agents; three more "disappeared" after their abduction.[13] In the first three months of 1981, 424 non-combatants were reported to have been captured by security forces.[14]

The continued detention, since August 1980, of eleven leaders and activists of STECEL (the trade union representing the hydroelectric workers of Rio Lempa) demonstrates the government's disregard of the right to personal liberty. The government later arrested and still holds Hector Bernabe Recinos, Secretary General of FENASTRAS, a major labor federation of El Salvador, who had called for a general strike for the release of the STECEL workers. Although at the time of their arrest these unionists were subject to the Special Courts Martial procedure under the Code of Military Justice, it is unclear whether their continuing detention is by virtue of Decree 507. It should be noted that the application of Decree 507 to these persons would constitute a grave violation of the freedom from *ex post facto* laws guaranteed in the 1962 Constitution and in the human rights instruments ratified by El Salvador. After more than a year of detention—well in excess of the maximum investigatory periods provided for in the Code of Military Justice and in Decree 507—the legal situation of these unionists is still undefined and they have not been charged or tried under any law.[15]

The Armed Forces have announced that the STECEL files are missing, so that no legal action can be initiated against them. This has been interpreted as an excuse to maintain these defendants in indefinite arbitrary detention, thus avoiding the publicity of a public trial. Meanwhile, the prisoners' lawyers have been threatened and subjected to kidnapping attempts that have forced them to go into exile. Consequently, STECEL trade unionists are deprived of access to legal counsel.

Ninety-three political prisoners are held in the Santa Tecla Prison; all have been detained for more than 180 days; only six are facing charges before ordinary courts.[16] Thirty-seven have been visited by Military judges who induced them to plead guilty, but have not notified them of the charges against them. No one has informed the remaining 50 prisoners of their legal situation. One prisoner, a 25-year-old peasant, has been in prison now for over 1,000 days, the amnesty of October 1979 notwithstanding. His trial, before the 2nd circuit court of San Salvador, is paralyzed due to the lack of assistance by counsel.

3. *The failure of habeas corpus*

The Constitution of 1962 contains a detailed list of guarantees against arbitrary arrest. They are supported by well-developed statutory mechanisms that should normally be adequate to curb abuses of governmental authority. The Law of Constitutional Procedures contains three procedures to ensure the supremacy of the Constitution: a) a writ of declaration of unconstitutionality of laws, decrees and regulations; b) the writ of "amparo" for protection of all constitutional rights other than personal liberty; and c) the writ of *habeas corpus.* [17]

Habeas corpus has an elaborate but reasonably speedy procedure, as provided for in Art. 38 *et seq.* of the Law of Constitutional Procedures. It is submitted directly to the Supreme Court or, if in a jurisdiction other than the capital, to the Courts of Appeal. The Court is then to appoint an "executing judge" (an *ad hoc* auxiliary of the court), generally a lawyer, who is charged with visiting the detainee and submitting a report on the place of detention, the authority that ordered it and the cause. The "executing judge" is empowered to order the release of the prisoner if he finds insufficient cause for detention. If the prisoner is not produced for him, or his order of release is not obeyed, the "executing judge" can request from the Court the use of public force.

In many cases, however, the appointment of "executing judge" has fallen on young law students or graduates. According to testimony received by the authors from several reliable sources, including Salvadoran attorneys in exile, there have been numerous reported instances of security authorities ignoring their demands, and even jailing and mistreating the lawyers making civil demands. It would be an understatement to say that the Supreme Court justices have been less than forceful in obtaining police cooperation for the executing judges.

Eliseo Ortiz Ruiz, a Salvadoran lawyer summed up the situation concerning the filing of these writs in cases governed by law 507 in an interview for this report:

First, of all the majority of the cases are not processed because the Court takes a position that you file the writ and it's forgotten; in other words, it does not decide on the writs, to file them away. For example, missing persons, detainees, etc. are daily occurrences there; what occurs to the relatives immediately, almost automatically, is to file the writ of *habeas corpus.* Filing the writ is routine practice there. The executing judge is named and then he excuses himself. They prefer to be fined for failure to comply. If they appoint another executing judge, well, he simply makes some pretense of execution and either does not submit a report or submits an inconsequential report. If the Court receives a favorable report, what it does is file it and say that the Court is considering the matter. No decision is ever made. . . . Moreover, most people do not know how to go about filing the writ. The circumstances of the Human Rights Commission of El Salvador, of Legal Aid, etc. are quite precarious. There are no attorneys who want to defend political prisoners.

Moreover, since the legal profession has itself been targeted for repression, especially those lawyers who undertake the defense of political prisoners or the investigation of abuses of human rights, "executing judges" tend to be understandably reluctant to pursue fully their duties, particularly when they know that they cannot count on the necessary support of the Supreme Court.

In fairness to some individual, courageous lawyers, it must be noted that even under these dangerous circumstances, there have been a few instances of *habeas corpus* procedures conducted according to law. A noteworthy example is the case of Alejandro Molina Lara, Secretary General of the Fishing Industry Union (SIP), who was arrested during a search of the offices of FENASTRAS by combined military-police forces. His arrest was not initially acknowledged, and Mr. Molina Lara was listed as "disappeared." Because of the efforts of a conscientious Executing Judge, he was located in the basement of the National Police headquarters. The government then said that he would be tried under Decree 507. Because of the lack of any reasonable basis for this, the Executing Judge ruled that his arrest was illegal and ordered his release. Molina's captors ignored the order, and the Supreme Court had delayed, as of July 1981, any action to obtain his release.[18]

Overall, the intimidation and harassment of judges and lawyers has caused the remedy to become a dead letter. Now the security forces routinely respond to *habeas corpus* writs with a cursory statement that the person in question is under the authority of a Military Examining Judge under Decree No. 507. Although it is abundantly clear that insofar as the writ of *habeas corpus* is concerned, "there is no privileged authority, tribunal or exemption in this matter."[19] The executing judges and the courts do not go beyond this report, and refuse to inquire into the validity of the arrest or the observance of terms and other legal requirements.

CHAPTER 6

THE RIGHT TO
DUE PROCESS OF LAW
AND TO A FAIR TRIAL

Since the coup of October 15, 1979, the Revolutionary Governing Junta has promulgated over three hundred decrees, many of which have fundamentally altered El Salvador's Constitutionally mandated form of government, destroyed the independence of the judiciary, and indefinitely suspended the exercise of certain basic civil rights and liberties, particularly in the case of those persons whom the junta and its security forces regard as "subversives." It has systematically stripped away the rights under the 1962 Constitution and applicable laws. (The *normal* legal regime established under the 1962 Constitution is generally consistent with the minimum standards governing the rights to a fair trial and to due process of law set forth in various human rights and humanitarian law conventions that El Salvador has ratified.)

A. *Events prior to October 1979*

Perhaps the most flagrant attempt to "legally" abolish due process rights prior to the 1979 coup came with the enactment of the Law of Defense and Guarantee of Public Order.[1]

This law, enacted on November 25, 1977 and kept in force for 15 months, was described in 1979 by the State Department as "severely abridging civil liberties."[2]

The law defined eighteen categories of activity as crimes against the constitutional public order in such extremely broad and vague terms that it permitted their interpretation and application in a way that was used to harass and repress anyone who opposed the government of then President Romero.

The most important part of the law was Title III, which established a summary procedure for the trial of those accused of violating its provisions. In its 1978 Report on El Salvador, the Inter-American Commission on Human Rights (IACHR) of the OAS analyzed this section in the following way:

Those tried for these offenses are deprived of the fundamental procedural guarantees: in the first place, any presumption or indication on the participation of the person or persons charged in one of these offenses is sufficient for the Court to order his or their provisional arrest (Article 15). This may imply a serious limitation of individual freedom, since the persons charged with any of offenses punished by this law are not subject to release from prison (Article 6, final paragraph).

The right to appeal from the decisions of the Court that hears the case is also seriously limited in the case of trials governed by this law. In fact, the only decisions that may be appealed are the writ of dismissal, the writ of presentation to the full court, and the final verdict. Therefore, the decisions that provide for the arrest of the persons charged may not be appealed.

The standards that govern evidence also seem to be against the interests of persons who may be charged. Thus the law provides that there shall be admitted as means of evidence that should be considered by the Court the evident or notorious acts that may be in the public domain because massive information has been given about them (Article 21). In addition, the mere mention made by the person charged in his statement on the participation of a person in the commission of the offense may be the basis for proof, provided that his statement is corroborated by at least one other element of proof and when it is corroborated by more than one element of proof it may be considered as an element of presumption (Article 22). It is important to bear in mind that a mere indication is sufficient for ordering the provisional arrest, without release on bail and without appeal, of the person charged.[3]

In July 1978, the International Commission of Jurists sent Donald Fox on a mission to El Salvador to study the application of this law. The Report of the ICJ arrived at conclusions similar to those of the IACHR concerning the procedural aspects of this law.

In sum, the procedure established under this law invites an abuse of power on the part of the security forces and makes it exceedingly difficult for the judiciary to live up to its obligation to make an independent and critical evaluation of the proof in a criminal case. The amendment of the Code of Criminal Procedure to permit the use of extrajudicial confessions as a basis for decreeing provisional detention assures that the security forces will attempt to get such a declaration in almost every case. Once this decree is issued, the accused will be legally confined for a substantial period of time in any event. Permitting the court to take into consideration "notorious events" in order to evaluate the offenses, presumably to determine whether they are committed with an intent to introduce or support totalitarian doctrines, invites the court to be swayed by the extraneous and inflamed allegations made in the news media.

To depart from the well-considered rule in the Code of Criminal Procedure that does not countenance incrimination by an accomplice opens another path of abuse to the security forces. Providing a captured suspect an opportunity to obtain his release by inculpating someone else almost assures a widening ambit of consequences from most arrests.[4]

The ICJ Report also stated that "the nature of the procedure provided for by the law tends to put the judiciary in the control of the organizations of public security."

Due to considerable domestic and international condemnation, the Law of Defense and Guarantee of Public Order was finally repealed on February 27, 1979.

B. *The administration of justice since October 15, 1979*

Since October 15, 1979, the junta has introduced a series of measures that, over time, have profoundly changed the nature and administration of justice and have resulted in the virtual elimination of constitutional and internationally recognized guarantees of due process of law and of a fair trial in cases involving security offenses. Initially there were some token but unsuccessful efforts to restore the rule of law. During a transition period in 1980 military tribunals were vested with authority to try civilians for political crimes; however, no such trials were held. After December 1980 the basic rights of due process were stripped away. This section describes the current status of due process rights.

1. *Analysis of the provisions of Decree No. 507*

The promulgation on December 3, 1980 of Decree No. 507, which continues in effect today, drastically revised certain provisions in the Code of Military Justice applicable to persons accused of crimes enumerated in Article 177 of the Constitution and related laws i.e. so-called political crimes. (The Code of Military Justice as it existed prior to decree No. 507 is described in Appendix I.)

The Decree has five preambulatory paragraphs which, *inter alia,* affirm the right of all Salvadorans "to be pro-

tected in preserving and defending their life, honor, freedom . . . " (Par.I) and proclaim the need to enact new
standards "to restore effective trial and punishment of the
crimes referred to [in Article 177 of the Constitution],
thereby laying the ground for reestablishment of the rule
of law and the offender's rehabilitation" (Par.V). The specific provisions of the law are, however, utterly destructive
of those purposes.

Article I of the Decree provides that

> the present law is to govern the procedures that apply to in-
> dividuals *over the age of sixteen* who commit the crimes of
> treason, espionage, rebellion, sedition, and other crimes against
> the independence of the state. . . . [Emphasis added]

but, in the next paragraph states that *"any minor under
the age of sixteen who is found to be implicated in any of
the above crimes"* shall be subject to the *law's corrective
measures.* The application of military justice to children
of *any* age, including their "corrective detention for 120
days in 'special rehabilitation centers' " is in clear violation of Article 179 of the Constitution.

a. *The investigating period*

The procedures of the Code of Military Justice for initiating proceedings leading to a Special Courts Martial have
been revised by Articles 2 and 3 of the Decree. Article 2
vests military trial judges with jurisdiction to try civilians
for those crimes over which Special Courts Martials previously had exclusive competence under the C.M.J. The
Military investigating judge is no longer appointed by the
Minister of Defense, but by the Supreme Court of Justice,
at the proposal of the Defense Ministry. Moreover, these
investigating judges, rather than being appointed for *specific* cases, are made permanent and exercise nationwide
jurisdiction. They also have sole jurisdiction to begin investigative proceedings (Article 3).

Article 4 states that although the auxiliary organs must advise the military investigating judge of any arrest within *twenty-four* hours, they need not bring the arrested person before the judge until *fifteen days after the arrest.* This provision not only grossly violates Article 166 of the Constitution, but constitutes an open invitation to the security forces to arbitrarily detain, intimidate, torture, and extract, with impunity, extrajudicial confessions from the junta's critics and opponents.

In this regard, Article 5 of the Decree specifies that the auxilliary organ's "extrajudicial investigation . . . shall also serve as the basis for ordering provisional detention of the suspect, provided that those investigations establish that the suspect participated in the act." The other "test" set forth in Article 5 for ordering a suspect's provisional detention is "the existence of *any* information to give one cause to believe that the suspect was a participant in the crime." This test lacks any objective standard of proof and, thus, is subject to the judge's subjective determination. Article 5 also provides that within seventy-two hours of the time the suspect was brought before him, the investigating judge must order the prisoner's release or his provisional detention.

b. *Corrective detention*

Article 6 similarly departs from the traditional norms of legal proof in Salvadoran jurisprudence. It provides that

If by the time the seventy-two-hour period had ended the judge has found *no good cause to hold the suspect,* but by *studying the case* or by *any other means* has established the need to subject him to security measures, he shall so decide and *order his corrective detention for a period of no more than 120 days, at his discretion* [Emphasis added].

These detentions must be in special rehabilitation centers.

Once the term of corrective detention has been served, the

judge may take *such control measures as he deems pertinent,* so that the suspect must appear periodically before the court, under his jurisdiction and he may require bond (fianza de la haz) for fulfillment of this provision [Emphasis added].

Not only does this provision effectively "legalize" arbitrary detention of innocent persons, but it similarly authorizes the capricious imposition of a severe penal sanction without any objective proof of the victim's culpability.

c. *The secrecy and length of the investigation*

Article 7 states that the investigating phase shall be secret and may not exceed 180 days. During this period, ". . . neither the accused, nor the prosecution shall have the right to participate in the proceedings . . ." When his investigation is completed, the military investigating judge will refer the case to the Military Trial Judge, who will "examine it to determine whether it contains any gaps." If he finds any gaps or flaws, he will return the case to the investigating judge "to be corrected or to have any gaps filled." The military trial judge, "having received the case or having returned it, when necessary," will then decide whether to dismiss the case, i.e., free the prisoner, or take it to trial. *No* time limit is established within which the trial judge must make this particular determination.

d. *The prisoner's rights before and during trial*

It is only after the military trial judge orders the case set for trial that the prisoner is so notified and advised to appoint defense counsel. (The judge will appoint a public defender if the prisoner fails to name counsel within three days.) Further, it is only at the trial stage that the prisoner, his counsel, and the prosecution have the right to participate in the proceeding.

Under the terms of this Decree, a person now can be lawfully held *incommunicado* and without charge for at least 195 days. In fact, the prisoner's confinement under these conditions can extend considerably beyond 195 days since this figure excludes the time it may take the military trial judge to order a trial. The total secrecy of the investigatory proceeding and its length have no analogue in the Code of Criminal Procedure or the Code of Military Justice. Most importantly, during this critical pre-trial period, the prisoner is denied by law the most basic constitutional rights for ensuring a fair trial.

e. *Admissibility and standards of evidence*

Article 8 of the Decree provides that during the trial the parties may present and argue the evidence. However, the Decree has modified the normal rules governing the admissibility of evidence. Article 8 declares admissible the following "evidence" specified in Article 11:

(1) A confession made before a judge other than the one trying the case.

(2) A written extra judicial confession; an oral extra judicial confession verified by two witnesses, and a recording made in the manner established under regular law. An oral confession shall be regarded as valid evidence even though it may have been given before each witness at differing places and times. The only requirement to make valid the declaration of witnesses to the confession shall be that the individuals witnessed [heard] the confession; that they are over eighteen years of age and that they state that the confession was given spontaneously.

This provision provides an added inducement to the government's security forces and other auxillary organs to obtain a coerced confession during the *fifteen*-day period they are allowed to hold the prisoner under Article 4 of the Decree.

(3) Objects that are related to the crime discovered either in the possession of the accused or in the place where he is found; such items include arms, munitions, explosives, incendiary de-

vices, subversive propaganda or literature, military or terrorist plans, etc.; the record taken down by the arresting person or persons at the time of the arrest, if possible, shall suffice for this purpose.

Although this provision does not specify the requirements, if any, with which this "record" must conform to be considered as evidence, it does not seem to contemplate more than a written assertion, otherwise uncorroborated, that the objects were so discovered in lieu of their physical production at any time.

(4) For the purposes of Article 376 and 407 of the Penal Code, it shall be sufficient to establish that the accused belongs to organizations that have claimed responsibility for criminal actions or events publicized or, by using any association, issues statements that threaten public order or security or the State or incites to acts that can harm the national economy. Confirmation by any national or foreign communications medium shall be sufficient to establish that an accused belongs to one of the groups mentioned.

This provision permits proof of the accused's membership in an illicit association to be established by a mere allegation made in literally any news media. In this regard, a former Salvadoran judge, Atilio Ramirez Amaya, the second examining judge in the investigation of Archbishop Romero's murder, affirmed in a statement expressly prepared for this report that ". . . to manufacture evidence against someone, all that is needed is for Radio Nacional or the newspaper *Hoy* to say that that individual belongs to some popular group or organization. That is sufficient for conviction." This evidentiary standard is substantially similar to one contained in a provision of the 1977 Law of Defense and Guarantee of Public Order. That provision directed that one of the elements for determining whether an act had been committed intentionally was "the fact of acknowledging participation through mass media." In analyzing this provision in his 1978 Report to the ICJ, Donald Fox stated that "[a]knowledgement of participation through mass media presents an occasion for abuse as well as establishing a very remote and indirect link between an act and its real authors."[5] This observation is equally applicable to the provision in question.

The final source of evidence is "[d]ocuments that are private, although not yet acknowledged, that are corroborated by any other means of proof" (Article 11, para. 5).

The standard applied by the military judge in rendering a guilty verdict, is "when in the trial, there is sufficient evidence to convict the accused of participation in and culpability for the criminal offense" (Article 12). The Decree seriously limits the right to appeal the court's decisions. Article 10 specifically limits appeals to an order of dismissal, an order for plenary proceedings, and the final verdict. Thus, the person charged may *not* appeal *any* of the decisions that provided for his arrest. In addition, the Decree makes no provision for early or conditional release of those found guilty (Article 13). Finally, Article 16 stipulates that once the state of siege is lifted and constitutional guarantees restored, trials pending under this law will be continued in accordance therewith.

It is indeed difficult to envision a comparable measure in the guise of a law that is so exquisitely antithetical to the basic notions of justice and so transparent in purpose as is Decree No. 507. The Legal Aid Office of the Archdiocese of San Salvador has said:

We consider that Decree 507 is a *JURIDICAL MONSTROSITY* that on its face and as applied tramples on the basic rights of the accused and has become an effective instrument for the violent control of the Salvadoran people.[6]

In short, this measure emasculates, by design, the Constitution's prohibition against the suspension of the rights to due process of law and to a fair trial.

The declaration of unconstitutionality included in the Law of Constitutional Procedures—which can be petitioned directly to the Supreme Court without showing injury in fact—was recently used by *Socorro Juridico* to challenge Decree No. 507 and seek its repeal, not only because it contravenes the Constitution, but also "because it authorizes and legitimizes arbitrary detentions and cruel means of inquiry such as torture and drugs."[7] The Junta-appointed Supreme Court has never acted on this plea.

To compound the arbitrariness of the situation, as of September 7, 1981 not a single case of any person detained by virtue of Decree No. 507 has moved beyond the secret investigation phase. Thus, since this law became effective on December 3, 1980, none of the detainees has been actually tried or sentenced, but presumably all continue to be held *incommunicado,* without charge and right to legal counsel.

2. *Selective application of the law*

The junta has applied the law as to create a double standard of justice in El Salvador today. The junta's agents and sympathizers who commit violent crimes are rarely arrested and, if they are, they are brought before civilian judges who apply the ordinary penal code. On the other hand, the regime's critics and opponents invariably are subjected to the application of Decree No. 507. The regime's notorious failure to investigate violent crimes directed against its opponents is attested to by former Judge Ramirez Amaya in an interview for this report:

Criminal courts begin and end proceedings with the hypocritical phrase: "To investigate the death of an unknown person," In some cases the individual is named, as for example: "To investigate the death of Oscar Arnulfo Romero." And nothing more. At times the files contain a denunciation and a hurried medical-legal examination. That's all. The murders number in the thousands. The tribunals do not investigate the crimes materially. Those responsible for that investigation, in their capacity as "auxilary organs of the administration of justice" are, for the most part, the Office of the Director General of the National Guard, the Office of the Director General of the National Police, the Office of the Director General of the Treasury Police. This is ironic, but it is no joke.

He also states the following concerning the regime's efforts to investigate Archbishop Romero's murder:

The Criminal Investigations Section of the National Police intervenes in all cases involving violent deaths, even in cases of obvious suicide. They always arrive before the judicial authorities. However, in the murder of Monsignor Romero, they arrived almost four days after the event occurred and did not provide the Tribunal any data or evidence of an investigation into the crime. On the 28th, I pointed out this failure to carry out the criminalist's obligations; I directed these remarks to the police experts who arrived at around noon, almost four days after the murder, to ask whether "they could be of any help." The same thing happened with respect to the Office of the Attorney General of the Republic; a special attorney arrived on the 28th, too, with instructions to appear in the proceedings. Because of such premeditated omissions on the part of the servants of justice, it is undoubtedly the case that from the very beginning they were involved in a conspiracy to cover up the murder.

Everyone knew Monsignor Romero's position with respect to El Salvador's current situation. . . . [his] assassination can be understood only in that context. There are no accused in the legal proceedings that were initiated in the Fourth Criminal District of San Salvador. Those directly responsible for the assassination are among those who attempted to silence his constant denunciation of repression, institutional violence and social injustice. Monsignor Romero gave his solid support to popular organizations' projects for change. The murderers are among those who tried to silence that support.

After a-more-than nine-month investigation into the murders on December 2, 1980, of the four American churchwomen that has turned up evidence linking six National Guard members to these crimes, the government is still unwilling to institute proceedings against these persons.[8] Defense Minister Jose Guillermo Garcia was quoted as saying in late August 1981 that no trial was being offered because "we do not want, by being too hasty, to fall into lamentable errors."[9]

The legal proceedings against Ricardo Sol Meza aptly show how the judicial system treats the junta's supporters. According to an eyewitness, on January 3, 1980, Sol Meza, who belongs to two of the country's wealthiest families, murdered the head of El Salvador's land reform program and two American advisors in the Sheraton hotel. Although this witness identified Sol Meza as one of the assailants to government investigators shortly after these murders, he was not arrested until April 5, 1981. It took the government three weeks thereafter to get a judge, prosecutor, and other court officials courageous enough to begin the preliminary investigation. The judge, Hector Jiminez, ordered Sol Meza indefinitely held on charges of conspiracy to murder. However, on August 27, another judge ruled that there was insufficient evidence for denying Sol Meza bail. Sol Meza was ordered freed as a result of the *habeas corpus* petition filed by his lawyer. Similarly former Major Roberto D'Aubuisson, prosecuted in 1980 for sedition, was tried by ordinary courts.[10] There have only been three cases of investigations under these procedures of the violent actions by several right-wing secret organizations committed against members of the popular organizations, church officials and institutions and opponents of the government.[11]

3. *The loss of independence of the civilian judiciary*

In its 1978 Annual Report, the IACHR stated that "[i]t is obvious that in countries where the Judiciary is not completely independent, or where its independence may not be formally respected, [or where] . . . judges are subjected to pressures and threats from the executive authorities, there can be no effective domestic defense of human rights. . . . If, as often happens, there is no legislative branch, or if the legislators are docile instruments of the will of the executive, there is a total lack of domestic protection of human rights and fundamental liberties."[12] That the Commission's remarks are descriptive of the actual situation of the judiciary in El Salvador today and with it its inability to protect the rights to a fair trial and to due process of law from arbitrary abuse, was made clear in a report of the State Department:

El Salvador's judicial system does not function effectively when politically-motivated crimes are brought before it, and no serious attempts have been made to use the judiciary to control the political violence. No matter how strong the evidence against them, those of the right and left charged with crimes of violence, including leaders of terrorist groups, are regularly released by intimidated courts. The irrelevance of the judicial system has encouraged elements of the security forces to ignore it and to dispense their own brand of justice.[13]

When the Junta seized power and assumed both executive and legislative powers, it did not overtly deprive the civilian judiciary of its independence, but rather compromised it by removing all the sitting magistrates on the Supreme Court of Justice and replacing them with its own sympathetic appointees. Moreover, by its declaration of state of siege on March 6, 1980, the Junta in effect precluded the civilian judiciary from any meaningful role in the administration and review of the Special Courts Martial proceedings. The implementation of Decree No. 507 finally destroyed the judiciary's independence.

Perhaps the most telling evidence of the judiciary's loss of independence, indeed its utter irrelevance, is the fact that virtually every decree, including Decree No. 507, promulgated by the Junta that *prima facie* violates the 1962 Constitution recites in its last preambulatory clause the following language: ". . . and having heard the opinion of the Supreme Court of Justice, the revolutionary junta decrees, approves and enacts. . . ." Moreover, the Supreme Court has failed to act on the petition filed by the Legal Aid Office of the Archdiocese of San Salvador requesting it to rule on the constitutionality of Decree No. 507.

Various judges and defense attorneys have increasingly become the targets of officially condoned harassment and violence. The International Commission of Jurists (ICJ) reported that

[t]he judiciary has been made impotent by fear, while magistrates who have attempted to investigate crimes attributed to the security forces or right-wing groups have been immediately attacked, and several of them have been murdered.[14]

A case in point is the assassination attempt on March 26, 1980, against Judge Atilio Ramirez Amaya, who had to flee the country because of his participation in the investigation of the murder of Archbishop Romero. Judge Ramirez gave us the following statement concerning the attempt on his life:

I left El Salvador to save my life. They killed Monsignor Romero on the 24th. On the 25th and 26th I received death threats by telephone. On March 27, at 10:30 P.M., I was the victim of an of an attempt on my life. Two individuals came to the door of my home, posing as friends of a lawyer colleague. I told the maid that I would receive them in the living room and I went out to ask the reason for the visit. The two individuals were already sitting down, and after greeting them I asked how I could help them. One of them removed a small machine gun from a folder. Because of the threats, I had a pistol hidden behind my back. When I saw this individual take out the machine gun, I simply moved my arm and revealed the pistol. The maid ran and put herself between the individual with the machine gun and myself. They fired and wounded the maid. They fled, firing as they did. I, too, fired through a window, but I didn't hit anyone. For 40 minutes, more or less, I waited with my wife and my daughter until members of the family arrived, followed by friends and, finally, the police. I later learned that the police had been at a distance of some 200 meters from my house during the attack.[15]

The IACHR has confirmed that Judge Ramirez had accused Col. Jose Medrano, founder of ORDEN and former member of the National Guard, and Major Roberto D'Aubuisson, also a former National Guard member, of hiring Archbishop Romero's assassins.[16] However, as stated in Chapter 3 of this report, there is testimony that implicates a member of the Salvadoran military who is neither Medrano nor D'Aubuisson. The ICJ's Center for the Independence of Judges and Lawyers in a recent publication reports an even more "horrifying example of the practices of para-military groups which still operate with impunity in El Salvador." According to this report, "[f]ive relatives of a judge of San Salvador including two adolescents and a woman of twenty-eight were assassinated on 14 April 1981. Their heads were severed from their bodies and laid at the doorstep of the Judge's home."[17]

The situation of the dwindling number of lawyers who are willing to defend political prisoners appears to be no better than that of judges. As noted in the previous chapter, the attorneys who had agreed to represent the eleven

STECEL unionists arrested in August 1980 withdrew their representation after having received death threats and, in some instances, have been the objects of attempted kidnappings. In a lengthy interview with one of the preparers of this report, Eliseo Ortiz Ruiz, who defended a number of political prisoners before he left El Salvador, made the following pertinent statement:

First of all, in El Salvador there would be no one who would agree to serve as defense attorney at the present time. First, because those who would agree to serve as defense counsel, as I said, would be those whom the regime would tolerate because they are at the service of the ruling class; attorneys associated with the regime would serve as defense counsel for the business ventures. . . . Most "defense" attorneys have left the country and I am one of them. So, there are two barriers. . . . The first is a legal barrier; with that law [Decree No. 507], no matter how brilliant the attorney is, it doesn't matter, since he cannot intervene. The second barrier is that if they intervene they face a problem: repression, threats, and persecution. In my particular case they searched my office, they wanted to apprehend me, they searched the house. . . . [When asked why, he replied: "Because I served as defense counsel for political prisoners."]

Socorro Juridico, the Archdiocese's Legal Aid office which has been critical of the junta's laws and the conduct of its security forces, has been the target of repeated government repression. The IACHR's 1979–80 Annual Report contains the following description of one incident:

At 7:00 A.M. on July 3, 1980, 120 national security agents riding in three small tanks and military vehicles with gunnery pieces forcefully entered the Legal Aid Office of the Archbishopric, where there is also a primary and secondary Jesuit school. The agents made a complete search of the office and confiscated records compiled by Legal Aid dating back to 1975. The military operation lasted virtually all day. According to charges received by the Inter-American Commission on Human Rights, the agents carried away a large number of legal documents concerning consultations on labor, penal and civil matters. They confiscated photographs of . . . the directors and members of Legal Aid.[18]

CHAPTER 7

THE RIGHT TO FREEDOM OF CONSCIENCE AND RELIGION

The Catholic faith is of central importance to the lives of a great majority of the people of El Salvador. Freedom of religious belief—the ability to live one's life as a Christian —therefore takes on special importance in a study of human rights in that country. Because there is substantial dispute about the proper role of the church in El Salvador this issue is discussed briefly before describing the extensive violations of freedom of religion before and after the 1979 coup.

A. *The role of the Church and pastoral mission in El Salvador*

Over the past decade, the Catholic Church in El Salvador has become known throughout Latin America for its dynamic implementation of recent teachings of the Catholic faith emphasizing support of the poor and the need for social change. The Archbishop of Washington, Msgr. James A. Hickey (who visited the Cleveland Diocese Mission Team in El Salvador frequently during his six-year tenure as Bishop of Cleveland) described this role in testi-

mony before a House of Reepresentatives Inter-American
Affairs Subcommittee, March 5, 1981:

As a Catholic bishop, I wish to stress that a specific dimension
of the El Salvador situation requires attention: the role of the
Church. Here again historical perspective is crucial. To understand the role that the Church in El Salvador is playing today,
we must see its pastoral decision to give special attention to the
poor. This it did in the light of the teachings of the Second
Vatican Council, of the Medellin (1968) and Puebla (1979) Conferences of the Latin American Bishops and of the teachings of
Pope John Paul II. The changing posture of the Church in Latin
America in the last fifteen years, from a socially conservative
position to that of the leading voice for reform and social change,
can be traced to the experience and teaching of Vatican II. It was
the Council which called the Church to stand as the sign and
safeguard of the dignity of the human person. . . . Through the
Medellin Conference and the Puebla Conference it outlined a
pastoral plan of evangelization which includes the defense of
human dignity and the promotion of human rights as essential
elements.

The Church in El Salvador exemplifies this larger movement
of the Church in Latin America. Under the pastoral leadership
of Archbishop Romero and of Bishop Rivera y Damas, it has
followed the imperative of the Puebla Conference, "to make an
option for the poor," and it has brought it about that the Church
is intimately joined to the struggle of the people of El Salvador
for social justice and social reform. Catechists, members of the
communidades de base (Christian family groups) together with
other laity and clergy have taken to heart the Gospel message
and have tried to live it genuinely in all facets of their lives. From
a truly spiritual perspective they have tried to introduce Christian principles to farming, business and government. For attempting this renewed Christianization of their country, they
have been called communists, subversives; and they have suffered persecution, even death for the Gospel. An archbishop,

eleven priests, thousands of lay people and now four American missionaries are dead in that effort.

At the same time, in fulfilling this ministry, the Church of El Salvador has drawn support from the words of Pope John Paul II. . . . Equally applicable is the forceful statement of the Holy father that, "Even in exceptional situations that may at times arise, one can never justify any violation of the fundamental dignity of the human person or of the basic rights that safeguard this dignity." The Church's ministry in El Salvador and throughout Latin America since Medellin has been at the service of human dignity and human rights. It is my conviction that one cannot understand the role of the Church in El Salvador today apart from these themes. Furthermore, one cannot understand the situation in El Salvador apart from the Church and its ministry.[1]

The Salvadoran church received worldwide attention during the life of Archbishop Oscar A. Romero and at the time of his assassination in March 1980. However, the path taken by the church predated the naming of Msgr. Romero as Archbishop. In the preface to a church publication dated June 1977, then Auxiliary Bishop of San Salvador, Msgr. Arturo Rivera y Damas, described the ongoing process of evangelization of the poor of El Salvador:

Under the experienced guidance first of Msgr. Chavez y Gonzalez, and then his worthy successor, Msgr. Oscar A. Romero, the Church of San Salvador had undertaken the road marked out by the Second Vatican Council and Medellin, renewing its pastoral task from the perspective of the urban and rural poor. The priority task of evangelization—to which the struggle for justice and full development of the human being are inextricably linked —led to the emergence of adult Christian faith communities throughout the Archdiocese, their consciousness working as yeast, their tangible outreach taking the form of personal and communitarian conversion. Along with individual sin, people came to discover the sin of our society as a challenge to their faith; and as a necessary consequence, a new presence of the church emerged. This church, the "Universal Sacrament of Salvation" that restores dignity and gives a voice to the outcasts and the peasants, to those whose voice and dignity was unrecognized, this church was not to be tolerated. And an end had to be put to it, not only in the Archdiocese—considered the main target —but also in the most vital sectors of the other dioceses. And the persecution began at all levels.[2]

The two Bishops, Rivera and Hickey, raise the same important questions of what the church is in El Salvador, what constitutes legitimate pastoral mission, and what may be the consequences of an institutional commitment to the poor in such a country. These three points are central to an understanding of restrictions on religious freedom in El Salvador, a situation which, since 1976, constitutes systematic persecution of the church.

The hierarchy of the Catholic church in El Salvador is comprised of the Archbishop of San Salvador (at present, vacant, with Bishop Rivera y Damas acting as Apostolic Administrator); the Papal Delegate or Nuncio; the Bishops Conference (with representatives from the Archdiocese of San Salvador and the four remaining dioceses); and offices under the head of the church, Bishop Rivera y Damas. According to church teachings referred to earlier, "the church" includes large numbers of catechists, layworkers, members of Christian base communities and the Archdiocese Legal Aid Office alongside the church hierarchy, priests and members of religious orders. In this predominant view,

The Church is in the first place the *people* of God, before any other distinction between hierarchy and the faithful. The Church is sacrament, *sign*, in a double sense: sign of all humanity in the road to the Father, and sign of the historical presence of Christ among men. The Church is the *assembly* convoked around the summoning word of God and to which response is made in the liturgy, and it is *community* in which faith is lived and the praxis of love lived . . . and it proclaims as its own duty a heightening solidarity with the poor, leading it to take on their problems and struggles as its own (cfr. Medellin, Poverty, No. 10).[3]

Not all within the Catholic church hierarchy in El Salvador subscribe to this view of the "role of the church," nor to this broad definition of what constitutes "church." However, the positions taken by three successive heads of the Salvadoran church, Bishops Chavez y Gonzalez, Romero, and Rivera, and others in the church hierarchy as well as the broader Catholic Community, make it possible to talk of an institutional position of the church in El Salvador, which coexists with a different analysis and practice on the part of other Bishops and their followers. It is the promoters of this institutional position who have been the object of persecution.

B. *Events prior to October 1979*

Following its January 1978 trip to El Salvador, the OAS Inter-American Commission on Human Rights (IACHR) concluded that:

As a result of the activities that the Catholic Church is carrying on because it considers that they are an integral part of its mission, priests, members of religious orders of both sexes, and lay persons who cooperate actively with the church have been the object of systematic persecution by the authorities and organizations that enjoy the favor of the government.[4]

The OAS report brought to international attention a situation that had been carefully analyzed and documented by the Salvadoran church over the previous year and a half. In June 1977, the Inter-Diocesan Social Secretariat, in its series "The Church and Human Rights," published a 103-page booklet, "Persecution of the Church in El Salvador."

For the period January 1976 to June 1977, the report lists the following acts of persecution against the church:

10 bomb explosions; 2 searches; 1 ransacking and desecration of the Blessed Sacrament; 1 threat to close the church radio; 7 prohibitions for priests wanting to enter El Salvador; 3 priests tortured and 2 mistreated; 3 priests arrested; 2 priests and 4 laypersons assassinated; 3 priests forced to leave the country due to death threats; a defamation campaign; threats to expell an order of women religious; 15 parishes without priests.[5]

In 1978, reports by Amnesty International[6] and U.S. Rep. Drinan[7] corroborated many of the IACHR findings. The U.S. State Department Annual Reports on Human Rights for the year 1978 said:

The Constitution prohibits political activity by the Church or clergy. The Government continued throughout 1978 to denounce those Church statements and activities which it considered anti-government and unconstitutional. The number of physical threats against the so-called progressive elements of the Roman Catholic hierarchy by right-wing groups decreased in 1978. The Church made credible charges that some lay workers in rural areas continued to be intimidated, beaten and harassed as "subversives" by local police authorities and Government supporters.[8]

For 1979, the State Department reported:

Other radio stations joined the Archdiocese station in offering access for opposition views. Unorthodox political messages also had begun to be permitted on commercial TV. . . . Most protests of infringement of freedom of religion have come from the activist wing of the Catholic Church. There are frequent allegations of open or disguised Government harassment and persecution of lay leaders, nuns and priests. Three priests were killed in 1979, one in front of the altar of his church, presumably by right-wing terrorists. Several foreign-born nuns and priests were expelled during the year by the Romero Government. Smaller religions and sects have apparently not been the target of similar treatment. . . . In practice, freedom of association has been somewhat inhibited by excessively technical or otherwise inadequate legislation. The activist wing of the Catholic Church made frequent allegations of open or disguised government harassment.[9]

In the period preceding the 1979 coup, six priests were killed in El Salvador. An American pastor, Rev. Jorge Lara-Braud, was in El Salvador visiting Archbishop Romero at the time of the assassination of Fr. Octavio Ortiz on January 20, 1979.

On this day, 20 January at 6 A.M. while I was asleep at the Christian retreat house, "El Despertar," a property of the San Salvador Archdiocese located in San Antonio Abad, many uniformed members of the National Guard and National Police entered the retreat house violently, shooting their weapons. A large, olive-green vehicle, an armored military truck, and a jeep entered the patio, occupying the central courtyard. I was at the retreat . . . with 10 other young persons, for a gathering of Christian instruction for 28 young men, aged 12 to 20 years. . . . No one had any weapons of any kind. Before I was captured by uniformed members of the National Police, I discovered that precisely in front of the office, at the entryway, Fr. Octavio was lying in a pool of blood, with blood still flowing from his head. The police agents took me . . . to the central headquarters of the National Guard, where both of us were interrogated and where I gave witness to that which I stated in the given document. At the Headquarters, while standing there frightened, following the hurried reading of a document, I signed that document, whose contents now—with this present testimony given freely and without coercion—I categorically deny. . . .[10]

C. *Freedom of religion since October 15, 1979*

Thus, during the three years preceding the October 1979 coup, there was a pattern of severe restrictions on religious belief.

The Armed Forces Proclamation of October 1979 promised to break with the practices of past governments and to respect human rights, including freedom of religious belief. On October 16, 1979, Archbishop Romero issued a "Pastoral Message for the New Situation in the Country." In the section directed to the people of El Salvador, he called for prudence, urging people to wait before making judgments or taking action. He ended by saying:

Our message is not only a call for prudence; it is also a promise: the Church is once again committing itself to disinterested service in favor of the people. The new situation in which we find ourselves in no way changes our will for service. It was just that sincere desire to serve and to defend the people which led the Church to come into conflict with the previous Government. Therefore, this conflict can only be resolved when we have a government that is truly at the service of the people. . . . Our words are now directed to the New Government emerging from the military insurrection that deposed the previous regime. We have carefully studied the messages which express the official thinking of the new Government. In those messages, we find good will, clarity of ideas, and clear consciousness of responsibility. Nevertheless, we want to make very clear that this Government will only win the confidence and collaboration of the people when it is able to show that the beautiful promises included in the Proclamation made known this morning are not dead words but rather are true hope that a new era has begun in our country. For our part—in our capacity as pastor of the Church—we are disposed to dialogue and to collaborate with the new government. We only set one condition: that both the Government and the Church be conscious of the fact that we exist to serve the people, each in our own way.[11]

The documentation available on human rights violations for the period October 15 to December 31, 1979, contains few incidents of restrictions on freedom of religious belief.

But from January 1980 to the present, the documentation shows a renewed and systematic persecution of the church.[12]

On March 1, 1981, the Archdiocese Legal Aid Office issued a report on persecution against the church by government security forces for two periods: (I) January 5 to October 10, 1979; and (II) October 11, 1979, to February 17, 1981. For the first period, the documentation indicates: 25 assassinations; 14 bombings; 18 threats; 21 detentions; 41 machine-gunnings; 15 acts of robbery; 3 persons wounded; and 33 searches. For the second period, the documentation indicates: 11 assassinations; 5 bombings; 40 threats; 25 detentions; 2 machine-gunnings; 15 robberies; 19 searches; 1 seven-day militarization of a church; 1 seven-day militarization of a seminary; 1 fifteen-day militarization of Archdiocese refugee centers.[13]

Among the most frequently violated rights of churchpersons are: (a) the right to life; (b) the right to humane treatment; (c) the right of thought, assembly, and association.

As mentioned, the most notorious violation of the right to life was the assassination on March 24, 1979, of the Archbishop of San Salvador, Msgr. Oscar Arnulfo Romero. Two weeks before his assassination, on March 9th, a valise was found inside the Basilica of the Sacred Heart containing 72 sticks of dynamite, with a fuse set to ignite at 5 P.M., the hour at which Msgr. Romero was to celebrate a mass for Mario Zamora, a Christian Democrat party leader who had been assassinated. (See Chapter 3 for details on the assassination of Archbishop Romero.)

The assassination of four North American women on December 2, 1980, was the first instance in which Americans and religious women were victims of persecution against the church in El Salvador. Sr. Melinda Roper, President of the Congregation of Maryknoll Sisters, said, "I believe that the deaths of the four women cannot be separated from the general pattern of persecution of the church in El Salvador and from the deaths of thousands of innocent Salvadorans." (See Chapter 3 for details on the assassination of the four North American women.)

While less known outside the country the assassination of numerous other Salvadorans working with the Church has been documented by the Archdiocese Legal Aid Office from January to June 1980.[14] At least two priests were murdered by security forces, one after being picked up by security forces at his home and the other after being detained by the National Guard after mass. The deaths of more than 20 other catechists, seminarians and other Church workers was also documented and attributed to ORDEN, the Army and security forces. More than 40 people were seized in Church buildings by security forces and later found dead.

Priests and religious workers have also been seized, tortured and then released. Government forces have also raided churches, parish residences and other church properties.

The generalized and systematic restrictions on religious freedom were characterized by three Salvadoran church leaders in 1980. Msgr. Romero, in referring to the search of the priests' house in Zacamil in his March 16 speech, said:

Given this situation, under the instructions of the Archbishop, with these letters we denounce this action [in Zacamil] which violates the freedom of religious belief and the inviolability of the home. This confirms for us that the Church continues to be persecuted in its ministries. We believe that even in a time of state of siege there are other more civilized ways to treat the Catholic Church, which has support of the immense majority of the Salvadorans.[15]

On October 19, a close friend of the slain Archbishop, Fr. Fabian Amaya, director of the Office of Social Communications characterized the attacks by ORDEN and the Security Forces on the CARITAS warehouse and parish church in Aguilares, as "clear, cruel and arbitrary persecution against the Church."[16] This communique demanded:

(a) That the oft-proclaimed promises of the Government Junta to work to benefit the people and to respect human rights be fulfilled;

(b) That the Government Junta, which has power over the High Command of the Armed Forces, order the Security Forces —uniformed or not—to respect both in daytime and at night, the right of *campesinos* to organize, just as the Security Forces respect the right to organize of organizations such as ANEP, ASI, etc.;

(c) That the material and intellectual authors of so much crime, cruelty and sadism be punished, since the authors are known; and

(d) That the Pastoral Work of the Church be permitted and that it be allowed to complete its mission.[17]

Fr. Amaya later received death threats and the following March, along with nine other priests, was placed on a list which includes 138 persons considered by the Armed Forces to be "subversives."[18]

In December 1980, following the assassination of the four North American women, Bishop Rivera y Damas charged in a December 5, 1980 communique, that

these criminal acts of persecution against the Church are the culmination of four years of persecution, which has grown in frequency and cruelty during 1980, a period that coincides with the new political leadership of the country by the military and the Christian Democratic Party. . . . The Church is persecuted because it speaks the truth, truth which irritates the powerful.

The Church is persecuted because it has taken a preferential option for the country's poor, who for centuries have been oppressed by unjust structures and who today continue being oppressed with a virulence bordering on the unbelievable. . . . Only an immediate end to the repression and persecution could demonstrate the clear will to stop such acts; only this could exonerate the Junta, at least to some degree, from its responsibility. And only an immediate end to the repression and persecution would give credibility to the repeated offers of dialogue for bringing peace to the country. In any other case, all possibilities for finding a true peace in the country through non-violent means will be strangled.[19]

Restrictions on religious freedom were not limited to the Catholic church but were also encountered by those working with the Baptist faith in El Salvador. In March 11, 1981 testimony before the Subcommittee on Inter-American Affairs, Robert Tiller, speaking for the American Baptist Churches in the U.S.A., reported that

our denomination has a close relationship with the indigenous Baptist organization, the Associacion Bautista de El Salvador. . . . One of the truly frightening facts of life for Christians in El Salvador today is that they are persecuted, kidnapped, tortured and killed solely because they are Christians. . . . You have heard and read about the horrible reign of tortures and death brought down upon the Roman Catholic Community of El Salvador, both Americans and Salvadorans alike. . . . But the Roman Catholic community is not the only subject for indignities, detention and martyrdom. The Baptist Association, tiny and not very powerful, has also been the subject of organized, government-sponsored terrorism. . . . As recently as one year ago, we had five American missionaries there, part of an active, long-term cooperative ministry. Within the past year, all five of these missionaries have left El Salvador. The escalating violence and terrorism were not the only factors in their leaving, but they were very important factors. One missionary couple is taking additional language work and is planning to return to El Salvador when the violence has somewhat abated. The other three received threats of murder and were urged to leave by the Salvadoran people with whom they worked. They reluctantly decided that this was the best course of action.[20]

CHAPTER 8

THE RIGHT TO FREEDOM OF THOUGHT AND EXPRESSION

This chapter discusses the present status of freedom of thought and expression in El Salvador, prefaced by a brief summary of its status prior to the 1979 coup.

A. *Events prior to October 1979*

Limitations on freedom of expression, whether by legal restrictions, direct governmental military intervention, or threat, were a feature of Salvadoran life in varying degrees for a substantial period before the 1979 coup. Abuses and violations of this fundamental right often take on a more subtle form than the violation of other rights: the mere warning of swift and harsh consequences often successfully generates self-censorship. In November 1978, the Inter-American Commission on Human Rights (IACHR) of the OAS noted:

The Special Committee received complaints about censorship or threats to the press such as threats by governments' authorities —although not carried out—of closing the periodical of the Salvadoran Catholic Diocese, *Orientation,* and its radio station,

YSAX, unless they submitted to strict censorship . . . and the closing, during the State of Siege, on March 3, 1977, of the newspaper *La Cronica,* an influential paper of small circulation respected by Salvadorian public opinion. When the State of Siege was lifted (July 1977), the closing of *La Cronica* was lifted, and it has been published since then. This newspaper has protested editorially against the restrictions imposed on the freedom of the press through the effect of Section 15 of Article I of Decree No. 407.[1]

However, the greatest restriction on freedom of the press and expression at this time was the "Law for the Defense and Guarantee of Public Order," enacted November 25, 1977. Although the purpose stated in the preamble was to supply the necessary legal buttresses to enforce the last paragraph of Article 160 of the Constitution prohibiting "propaganda advocating anarchistic or anti-democratic doctrines," its effect was to severely restrict the actions of human rights monitors, trade unions, opposition groups, and rural peasant leagues. The law imposed penalties on

those who propagate, encourage, or use their personal status or circumstances, either by the spoken or written word or by any means, doctrines aimed at destroying the social order, or the political and juridical organization that the Constitution establishes. [Article 1, No. 7]

Those who propagate by the spoken or written word, or by any other means, within the country, or send abroad, tendentious or false news or information designed to disrupt the constitutional or legal order, the tranquility or security of the country, the economic or monetary system, or the stability of public values and property; those who publish such news and information in the mass communication media; and those citizens of El Salvador who, while abroad, disseminate news and information of that kind. [Article 1, No. 15][2]

Not surprisingly, the International Commission of Jurists described this law as "a serious attack on freedom of expression particularly that of the press . . ."[3] IACHR, in its 1978 Report on El Salvador, pointed out that "the practical result of these standards is the imposition, in practice, of self-censorship. . . ."[4] The IACHR Commission heard from Salvadoran trade union leaders that the mass media was noticeably reluctant to accept union press releases unless subjected to prior censorship as a result of the law's promulgation. Consequently, unions were compelled to disseminate their information via pamphlets and fliers, thus exposing those circulating them to the risk of arrest for the distribution of subversive literature. The Law was also seen as a source of intimidation by those Salvadoran organizations monitoring the situation of human rights who wished to provide information to national and international bodies and foreign news organizations.

Under the mounting domestic and international pressure, the Law was repealed in early 1979. Yet while greater criticism was nominally permitted after its repeal, and *El Independiente* and newspapers from the National and Catholic Universities published less constrained commentary, threats and bombings of newspapers continued to influence the decision to print. In early 1976, *La Cronica* was machine-gunned twice. On June 5, its editor received an anonymous telephone call stating that he had been "judged, found guilty and sentenced to death.[5]" The next day a bomb whose packaging indicated armed forces participation, exploded outside his home. On July 14, 1979, the offices and printing plant of the newspaper were burnt to the ground by incendiary bombs. Jose Napoleon Gonzalez, the editor, reported that since 1975, he had been repeatedly approached by government agents urging him to change his editorial policy and representatives of economic interests offering substantial financial inducement to do so.[6]

B. *Freedom of thought and expression since October 15, 1979*

This section details changes in the law since 1979 before describing the right to free association in fact under the present government.

1. *Legal steps and public statements by the government affecting freedom of expression*

The Armed Forces Proclamation of October 15, 1979, promised "to guarantee the observance of human rights . . . by stimulating free expression of thought, in accordance with ethical standards."[7]

However, on March 6, 1980, simultaneous with its Agrarian Reform Decree, the Revolutionary Governing Junta promulgated Decree 155 ordering a State of Siege, which suspended the guarantees of articles 158 and 159 of the Constitution, dealing with freedom of expression. The IACHR noted in its 1979–1980 Report:

The state of siege clearly gives the government control over mass media through censorship, restricted access to sources or other means of control generally accepted under emergency conditions. . . . But since the state of siege was declared, the Commission has been receiving reports of incidents that could not be justified by the decree suspending constitutional guarantees and which are a violation of the right to freedom of opinion and expression and also simply evident violations of other fundamental rights covered in the aforementioned Inter-American instruments, the observance and promotion of which was undertaken by the Salvadoran Government.[8]

Included in the rules of evidence sufficient to take cases to plenary proceedings under the Decree law were "objects related to the crime discovered in the possession of the accused or in the place where he is found: such items include subversive propaganda or literature. . . ." This directly contradicted paragraph 4 of article 158 of the Constitution. Decree Law 155, which has been renewed every thirty days since its promulgation, in conjunction with the rules of evidence set forth in Decree 507, constitutes a severe impediment to freedom of opinion and expression.

Decree 43, of August 21, 1980, militarized a number of public services including the National Telecommunications Administration (ANTEL), resulting in all affiliated workers and employees being considered enlisted in the armed forces and thus under the direction of the Minister of Defense and Public Security. ANTEL supervises the use of airwaves by Salvadoran radio stations, as well as monitoring telephone lines.

Decree 603, of February 26, 1981, ratified the closing of the University of El Salvador, and announced the appointment of a general manager of the University, while suspending all staff salaries as long as the University remained closed. The Constitutional rights to academic freedom and education, and the autonomy guaranteed the University by the Constitution are practically obviated by this measure.

In addition to formal decrees, the armed forces have issued a number of public communiques which have had a chilling effect on freedom of expression and opinion. On March 29, 1981, an armed forces communique listed the names of those persons whom the military believed responsible for "the chaos created in our country." The communique published in *La Prensa Grafica* referred to those listed as "bandits and terrorist criminals," "Cuban, pro-Soviet extremists," and "psychopaths." It said the 139 persons named were traitors "responsible for the terrorism in El Salvador and disgracing our country in the eyes of the international community. . . ."[9] Among the names are members of the first and second Juntas, the ex-Minister of Foreign Affairs, ex-President of the Central Bank, ex-

Presidential Chief-of-Staff, ex-Minister of Education, university professors, lawyers and human rights monitors. In February 1980, Christian Democrat Mario Zamora Rivas had been shot dead in his home by armed men, after a February 23 televised speech by former Major Roberto D'Aubuisson who urged security personnel to go beyond the law to combat subversion and named Zamora as one of many "subversives." The Armed Forces' list was identical, even to the same non-alphabetical order, as one published May 11, 1980, by the seven most active paramilitary deaths squads vowing to "eliminate physically" "these traitor communists."

On April 3, 1981, the Press Committee of the Armed Froces of El Salvador (COPREFA) announced "drastic measures" against foreign journalists who continue to "distort" the image of the Salvadoran Government and people.[10]

2. *Freedom of expression in fact*

According to the Legal Aid Office of the Archdiocese, since January 1980, seventeen news offices and radio stations have been bombed or machine-gunned, twelve journalists have been killed and three have disappeared.[11] Of the twelve, seven were killed by soldiers of the Salvadoran army, one by the National Guard, three by combined military forces.

A number of journalists also have been killed when covering combat situations. At present, no independent newspapers are in operation. The last two, *El Independiente* and *La Cronica del Pueblo,* had closed by January 1981 after numerous bombings, threats, military interventions and assaults on employees. The two major newspapers of El Salvador presently being published, *El Diario de Hoy* and *La Prensa Grafica,* support the government, particularly the armed forces.

The government continues to threaten those who seek

to exercise freedom of expression. Some representative cases follow:

—On March 11, 1980, Demetrio Olaciregui, a Panamanian citizen and UPI correspondent in San Salvador, received a letter from Defense Minister Col. Jose Guillermo Garcia several days after the reporter's analysis of the agrarian reform had been published. Garcia wrote, "if you persist with information that threatens the security of the state, we will be obligated to see that the law is complied with. . . ." Two days later, as Olaciregui was leaving the Immigration Ministry where he had been summoned to discuss his visa, three men placed a pistol at his temple and forced him into a waiting van. After being beaten and kicked, he was driven 140 miles to the border where he was left.

—On April 1, two journalists from the Dutch television network were shot and wounded by an army patrol in San Salvador. Frank Diamond and Rhud Van der Heyden stated: "We were leaving a restaurant when a patrol stopped us. We identified ourselves, were questioned and later after being allowed to continue, we were shot from behind."[12] The Netherlands newsmen said they were asked if they had brought instructions from Nicaragua for the Salvadoran leftist organizations. They denied this.

—On June 27, the premises of *El Independiente,* the only remaining independent newspaper, were destroyed. There had been two previous attacks, one of which killed a messenger standing in the doorway. In the course of two months, editor Jorge Pinto was the target of three assassination attempts. "Once my car had 36 bullet holes, another time 32, and again 42 . . ." said Pinto in an interview from exile.[13] Pinto described the harassment of his paper:

On January 22, 1980, there was an enormous demonstration; that was before the bomb. At that time *El Independiente* published that guardsmen had fired on the demonstration. Then, I received a summons from the Attorney General of the Republic. When that happens, I don't take one witness, I take twenty—the person who wrote the article and the date she used to write it, and a secretary from the newspaper who was trapped inside the Cathedral because of the gunfire. Legally we established that those who fired on the demonstration were guardsmen, guards of the National Palace, guardsmen from various parts. Then they summoned me for criminal proceedings, since the case had already been passed on by the Attorney General's Office. Again, I mobilized my 20 witnesses. They burried the case. But then came the bombs.[14]

On January 15, 1981, army tanks and trucks surrounded the offices of *El Independiente* and occupied Pinto's home. Pinto said later:

Members of the Guard grabbed my three-year-old son in my home; they told my wife: "We are going to take him, we have to kill him because he is the seed and we have an order to stamp out the seed." But she used a number of resources at that time and established that it was not her son. Then they finally left him. I had just left the newspaper five minutes before the militarization and when I telephoned, everything had already happened.[15]

Several days earlier, eight employees of *El Independiente* were arrested. Two are still imprisoned, the others were released six months later, never having been charged. Pinto offered to exchange himself for his imprisoned employees. They were told "since that son-of-a-bitch is making statements, you're not getting out."[16]

—The newspaper *La Cronica del Pueblo* closed down permanently after its editor and photographer were abducted and found dismembered July 11, 1980.

—Several days later correspondent Ian Mates of UPI Television and Michele Taverna, special correspondent of the Italian daily *Corriere dela Sera,* were detained by plainclothes agents of the National Guard in Coatepeque, sixty-five kilometers west of San Salvador. Thumbs bound behind their backs, they were interrogated for several hours in a Santa Ana police station before being released.[17]

—Near the end of August, two workers from *El Independiente* were detained by the National Guard. In a later press conference they said their captors showed them pictures of six foreign journalists "who are condemned to the same fate as the Mexican correspondent." One of the detained workers stated: "They put electrodes in my penis and ear, and gave me electric shocks. . . . They asked me if I knew Demetrio. . . . He was the next journalist they were going to kill.[18]

—On November 25, Nina Bundgaard, of the Danish monthly *Politisk Ruvy,* was detained outside of San Salvador. Five days later, she was handed over to a Danish official at the San Salvador airport and officially expelled from the country. She testified:

I was detained on 25 November 1980, at about 4:30 P.M. in the Colonia Santa Lucia, Llogango, near the Air Force base . . . They blindfolded me. . . . They took me to the Air Force base. In the truck they said it was a shame that "such a pretty girl with such a beautiful future . . . ," as if they were going to kill me. . . .

The following day . . . three plainclothed men took me away in a heavily armed civilian truck, the kind that the National Guard use . . . They took my fingerprints, photographed me, blindfolded me . . . took my watch, hair grips, and handcuffed my wrists behind my back. . . . An officer began to interrogate me. He accused me of being a leader of the San Vicente guerrillas, and many other things I don't remember. They said Mauricio (a friend arrested at the same time, and still unaccounted for) had said that I'd come to the country as a member of a solidarity group. They asked me why I'd got mixed up in El

Salvador's affairs. They demanded . . . the names of my comrades. . . .

(In the afternoon) they interrogated me for an hour. They asked about my family, about which socialist countries I had visited. . . . I told them I'd been in Sweden and Norway. They asked me about my friends, my work as a journalist, my solidarity work (which I denied). . . .

In the cell there was a toilet, shower and mattresses infested with fleas. It was very dirty. All the guards who passed the little window in the door threatened me. They said that now I'd see what they did with foreigners who interfere in Salvadoran affairs. I told them I was a journalist. They said that everyone who gets mixed up with communists is beyond the law. . . .[19]

That the harassment of the press presently continues to be as extensive as this list indicates, demonstrates the severe impairment of freedom of expression. As a result of both the physical elimination or expulsion of individuals (by direct interventions of security personnel and the cooperating paramilitary squads) and the psychological impact of so many fulfilled threats, accurate news coverage has become increasingly diluted and stifled. In June 1981, the International Commission of Jurists said:

The right to the free expression of ideas and opinions, and the rights of assembly and association are severely restricted by the state of civil war that exists and by the state of siege, augmented in January 1981 by a curfew. Several journals, publications and radio stations have been forced to interrupt their activities, due not so much to the official censorship as to the attacks made on their premises with explosives, and the threats to, assaults upon and even murder of journalists.[20]

The International Executive Board of the Newspaper Guild said "the government has failed to provide the most elementary protection to foreign journalists . . ." and continued by saying that blame for such acts "cannot be laid entirely at the door of paramilitary death squads . . . The government itself has arrested the editor of the official publication of the Catholic archdiocese and has closed the last independent newspaper, *El Independiente*."[21]

The Committee to Protect Journalists, said the goals of the intimidation were:

to inhibit news coverage and to punish journalists for what they write, photograph or broadcast. Those responsible appear to operate without fear of government arrest or sanction. Despite protests by journalists, the Salvadoran government has completed no known investigation of any facts of terrorism against the press.[22]

"It's terror and it's constant," said Associated Press correspondent Gordon Mott in San Salvador.[23] When asked whether the targeting of the press had been effective in stifling news coverage in El Salvador, Alan Riding of the *New York Times,* whose name has appeared on death-lists and no longer covers the country, replied "it's been effective in stifling me."[24]

Jorge Pinto, editor of *El Independiente,* wrote in the *New York Times* of the government's responsibility for the attacks:

These attacks on the news media were not made by so-called death squads operating independently of the military. My country is small and its capital is small. Everyone knows everyone else. Those 40 workers had no doubt that those placing the dynamite were members of the armed forces. I myself do not believe in the existence of any death squads. They are nothing more nor less than the military itself.[25]

Security forces have also systematically attacked teachers:

—On January 27, 1980, Alvaro Rafael Rodriguez Olmedo, a teacher, aged 40, was detained by the National Guard in Canton Quitazol, Tejutla. In the presence of his mother, the house was ransacked, and Rodriguez was taken into the street, where he was severely beaten, then shot. He died in the hospital the same day.[26]

—On April 19, 1980, in Tecapan, Ozatlan, Usulutan, teacher Mauricio Vladimir Hernandez, aged 26, was murdered by National Guardsmen in the presence of 40 seven-year-old students.[27]

On the same day, Angel Erasmo Figueroa, aged 24, a teacher at the National University, was shot in Armenia, Sonsonate, by National Guardsmen under unclear circumstances. While Professor Figueroa was anesthetized, after undergoing surgery at the San Rafael Hospital in Santa Tecla, National Guard Troops surrounded the hospital, and five Guardsmen entered the operating theater and machine-gunned him to death as he lay unconscious on the operating table.[28]

Following a two-day national strike, combined military forces of the Army and National Guard attacked the National University in San Salvador. While some 5,000 students were inside, on June 26, 1980, between 22 and 40 were killed, and according to the Superior Council of the Catholic University (UCA), many students, professors and employees of the National University were abused, beaten, and forced to submit to strip searches.[29] Officers reportedly led troops in the ransacking of offices, destruction of office equipment, and book burnings, resulting in damage in excess of $8 million. The University remains closed.

While planning for the scheduled reopening of the University, as promised by President Duarte for the beginning of March, on February 10, 1981, 21 senior university officials, including eight deans, were arrested. On February 26, 1981, Decree 603 provided for the governmental intervention in Universities, the suspension of salaries and the governmental appointment of a "general manager."

The Legal Aid Office of the Archdiocese has stated:

There is a conjugation of resources whose objectives are to destroy educational work. The massive assassination of teachers, the closing of educational centers that are then converted into military garrisons, the assassination of the Rector of the National University, Felix Ulloa, and the unjust detention of members of the Superior University Council cannot be interpreted in any other way.[30]

CHAPTER 9
THE RIGHTS OF ASSEMBLY AND ASSOCIATION

Despite formal protections, the rights of association and assembly have been severely curtailed in El Salvador by emergency legislation and by actions of government authorities unwilling to tolerate activities which challenge the Government's programs. Archbishop Oscar Romero commented on this discrepancy between law and practice in his Third Pastoral letter in which he observed:

Unfortunately there is an enormous difference between legal declarations and the reality in our country. Various political, trade union workers, peasants, cultural and other associations do exist here. Some of these enjoy legal recognition, others do not. Some of them—with or without legal recognition—are able to function freely, others are not. However, we do not now want to concentrate on the legal aspect of formal recognition. We are more interested in looking at the freedom in practice of any human group to exercise its natural right of association and the support and coordination it can expect from an authority genuinely concerned with the common good "to enable it to achieve its own fulfillment in a relatively thorough and ready way."[1]

This chapter examines the current situation in El Salvador with respect to these rights, focusing on the problems of trade unions, political parties, the church, human rights organizations, students and educators.

A. *Events prior to October 1979*

Since General Maximiliano Hernandez Martinez ruled El Salvador in the early 1930's, the military has controlled the country in a manner which has precluded free association by those perceived to be effective opponents of the Government. Following the peasant revolt and massacre in 1932, all organizations of agricultural laborers were banned, and none were formed again until the late 1960's. Though the Salvadoran constitution has guaranteed the right to strike and the legality of unions for more than twenty years, such status has yet to be extended to agricultural workers. According to one commentator:

It is alleged that the law does not implement the rights that do exist and that only two strikes have been recognized as legal in the last twenty-five years. It is clear that official toleration of concerted effort by agricultural workers is markedly less than that extended to industrial workers.[2]

As peasant unions began to organize more effectively in the 1960's and early 1970's, government action against them and their supporters correspondingly became more brutal. By the mid-1970's this violence had escalated substantially in scale and geographic scope. A 1978 report by the International Commission of Jurists concluded that: "It is from late 1976 that the detention, torture, disappearance and murder of peasant leaders began to be reported with alarming frequency."[3]

It was against this background that in October and November of 1977, a number of industrial organizations undertook measures to demand higher wages. Two *campesino* organizations, the *Federacion Cristiana de Cam-*

pesinos Salvadorenos (FECCAS) and the *Union de Trabajadores del Campo* (UTC) were centrally involved in these actions, particularly efforts to raise wages for the cutting of sugar cane and the production of coffee and cotton.

Both of these unions, along with the National Teachers Union (ANDES) and others, belonged to a larger, politically active labor coalition called *Bloque Popular Revolucionario* (BPR). In the summer of 1977, the BPR occupied the offices of the Ministry of Labor in order to force a hearing on these issues.[4]

Partially in response to these actions, on November 24, 1977, the Ministries of Defense and Public Security and Justice proposed the "Law for the Defense and Guarantee of Public Order."[5] Passed by the National Assembly on November 25, 1977, this provision greatly limited union rights by making public meetings and all strikes illegal. It also provided up to five years imprisonment for persons "taking advantage of their status or personal condition" to threaten order, a warning to the clergy to limit their activities and associations.[6] From November 1977, when the law was passed, until July 1978, 716 people were detained under its provisions.[7] In the face of widespread condemnation the Public Order law was repealed in February 1979.

In describing the pattern of disappearances that occurred in 1979 prior to the coup, Amnesty International noted:

Most of the victims of "disappearance" and murder were individuals believed to be linked to the three opposition movements, all largely trade union based, the *Bloque Popular Revolucionario* (BPR), Popular Revolutionary Bloc; the *Ligas Populares 28 de Febrero* (LP-28), Popular Leagues of 28 February; the *Frente de Accion Popular Unificada* (FAPU), Popular Front of Unified Action. Moves to crush the opposition movements were met by increasingly militant activity. Left-wing guerrilla organizations also stepped up anti-government activity, including killings.

Throughout the final months of the Romero administration and even now up to the time of this writing the Salvadoran authorities refused to recognize the mass political organizations FAPU, BPR and LP-28 as lawful political organizations, or to negotiate with their leaders. By October 1979, after months of street demonstrations and increasingly militant protest actions by the opposition, including bloody actions by guerrilla groups, polarization between government and opposition was extreme.[8]

B. *Freedom of association after October 15, 1979*

Although the Proclamation issued following the coup guaranteed "the establishment of (political) parties of all ideologies" and recognized "the right to unionize, in all labor sectors,"[9] attacks on unionists continued to take place almost from the outset. One day after the coup, government security forces forcibly ousted striking workers from several factories in San Salvador. Eighteen workers were killed, another seventy-eight were arrested and detained, and many of them tortured.[10] According to Amnesty International: "Within a week the new government was responsible for more than 100 killings of demonstrators and striking workers who had been occupying farms and factories."[11] One worker who was released during the first week described his treatment by Salvadoran authorities: "My head was beaten. I received blows in the testicles. My body was burned with cigarettes, they put ants on me, they wounded me with machetes and I was bound for twelve hours."[12]

On October 22, 1979, a political demonstration organized by the *Frente de Accion Popular Unificada* (FAPU) was attacked by snipers, killing five people. A demonstration on October 29 left 30 civilians dead, all killed by government troops.[13]

By mid-November the junta announced that at least 50 members of the National Guard were being dismissed as a result of these and similar incidents, in what the government promised was a first step to restore order and control of the security forces.[14]

Despite this apparent reform, violence continued throughout the last two months of 1979, particularly in the heavily populated coffee growing areas of Chalatenango, San Salvador and Morazan departments where unions of rural workers, including FECCAS and UTC, were strongest.

Following promulgation of the agrarian reform program on March 9, 1980, security forces continued to direct their actions toward *campesinos* in these areas where these opposition labor groups were well-organized. Amnesty International reported that by March 16 in several small towns in Cuscatlan, more than 600 people had fled their homes and "at least 80 have been detained and killed in Cuscatlan since the land reform was decreed, including 26 children."[15] Amnesty concluded:

There appears to be no doubt whatsoever that members of the major *campesino* groupings, all of them affiliates of oppositionist political coalitions, are being systematically persecuted in areas to be affected by the agrarian reform.[16]

Throughout the latter half of 1980 peasant leaders and organizers continued to be special targets of government security forces. (See Chapter 2 on Agrarian Reform.) The case of Maribel Santana, a member of the *Union Comunal Salvadorena* (UCS) cooperative in Sonsonate, who was dragged out of her plantation and shot and killed, is typical of these incidents. In another incident involving the UCS during this period, twelve union members were machine-gunned to death in the early morning outside of their cooperative.[17]

In yet another incident a squad of more than 20 uniformed National Guardsmen drove to a government agricultural cooperative in an armored car. According to one report, they carried with them a list of the cooperative leaders considered to be subversive. "Twelve of the leaders —the local directors who are supposed to carry out government-related reforms—were killed and the 160 families living there fled in terror."[18]

Details of the suppression of freedom of association are best illustrated by examining the government actions against unions, including suppression of teachers' unions, and efforts to destroy human rights organizations.

1. *Government action against unions—the promulgation of new legislation*

On June 24, 1980, a national strike was called by the newly formed FDR in opposition to the junta's policies and rule. On the same day the government enacted Decree No. 296 which prohibited strikes or collective abandonment of posts by officials and employees of the state and its decentralized agencies. Decree 296 calls for the immediate dismissal of those who organize any such work stoppage. Other employees who fail to obey a supervisor's order to go back to work are subject to suspension without pay and dismissal for the second offense. Under the terms of this provision, harsh penalties may also be imposed against any officials or employees who have personnel under their authority who fail to abide by the law. These penalties may be imposed administratively without regard to the existing civil service laws and are not appealable.

Two months after the enactment of this provision the intensity of the confrontation between the unions and the government further escalated. On August 21, El Salvador was blacked out for 24 hours during a strike by 1,500 members of the Union of Electricity Workers at the Rio Lempa power station (*Sindicato de Trabajadores de la Electricidad de la Central Electrica del Rio Lempa,* STE-

CEL). Government authorities ended it by arresting at least 15 leaders of STECEL who were taken to the Santa Tecla Prison.[19] Also arrested was Hector Bernabe Recinos, the Secretary General of the National Federation of Salvadoran Workers Union (*Federacion Nacional de Sindicatos de Trabajadores Salvadorenos,* FENASTRAS).

In describing the initial hours after their arrest, Recinos explained that he and the STECEL leaders were taken to the National Guard headquarters:

where we were subjected to psychological torture. (The National Guardsmen) threatened to chop us into little pieces and do the same to our children and wives. During our interrogation sessions a number of unionists were brutally tortured. . . .

During our stay of 60 days at the barracks, we could hear the cries of companeros being tortured night after night. To drown out the cries, we would turn up our radios full volume. We saw our companeros with bruises and blood over their bodies. At all hours of the night we would hear cars leaving . . . probably taking the dead in order to dump their bodies somewhere in the streets, or taking prisoners to kill them elsewhere. . . .[20]

These union leaders were detained and assigned to the jurisdiction of a military tribunal. All are subject to those decrees promulgated immediately after the STECEL strike incident.

On August 21, 1980, the date of the power outage, the government promulgated Decree No. 43 which declared the country to be in a state of emergency, and, accordingly, militarized automatically several autonomous government agencies including: the National Administration for Aqueducts and Sewage (ANDA); the National Telecommunications Administration (ANTEL); the Hydroelectric Executive Commission for the Lempa River (CEL); and the Autonomous Executive Commission of the Port Authority (CEPA). Under the terms of this provision, all employees of these agencies were automatically enlisted in the armed forces, accountable directly to the Minister of Defense and Public Security.[21]

Decree No. 44, August 22, 1980, dissolved STECEL, and froze the union's assets. The decree specifically charges the union with interrupting electric power service in various parts of the country "through violence or by the use of force or coercion against workers there."

A third decree (No. 366) in response to this incident, released on August 22, 1980, empowers the Executive to dissolve any "professional associations established in the state agencies and autonomous or semi-autonomous agencies," that are deemed to be interrupting essential public services, engaging in acts of sabotage or acting in a way "designed to subvert public order and support political activities." Under Decree 366, the determination as to what constitutes a violation of these provisions rests solely with the executive power.

This Decree appears to violate both Article 191 of the Constitution, which protects the juridical personality of these associations, and of Articles 619–626 of the Labor Code of El Salvador which establish specific procedures for the dissolution of unions.

In an interview in March 1981, Americo Duran of the Committee of United Trade Unions (CUS) analyzed the effect of these new provisions:

Under the present junta, the situation for the workers has become much worse because of government decrees against their rights. Decree 296 deprived public and municipal workers of their rights. Decree 366 denied the legality of the electrical and sanitation workers' unions. Then with Decree 44, military centers were set up inside the electrical works. Most recently, the workers' rights to collective bargaining and to strike were denied with Decree 507. These measures have pushed our country to a state of siege; the workers are under military law. The trade union movement conceived of in peacetime is very different than one being carried out in wartime.[22]

Violence in El Salvador has continued throughout the first eight months of 1981, and has continued to focus on trade unionists. Though neither public demonstrations or meetings now take place in El Salvador, security forces continue to search out those deemed to be opponents of the regime. Thus, for example, in January 1981 Alejandro Molina Lara, the Secretary General of the Fishing Industry Union (SIP) was abducted by government security forces as they searched the offices of FENASTRAS. Though the Salvadoran government subsequently said that Molina had disappeared, a *habeas corpus* petition filed on his behalf revealed that he was being detained, illegally, in the basement of the National Police headquarters. His case was initially sent to the Supreme Court of Justice which ruled that his detention was illegal, and that he should be released. That order has thus far been ignored and his case is before a military tribunal. Molina is now being held at La Esperanza Penitentiary in the district of Mariona.

On July 5, 1981, members of the Oil and Lard Products Labor Union *(Sindicato de Trabajadores de Aceite y Grasas)* and members of the local union at the "El Dorado" factory were detained by treasury police. A communique issued by the treasury police said that these people had "forcefully occupied" the El Dorado facility, one of the most important holdings of the de Sola family. Members of the union assert that in fact when they were arrested they were meeting with the management of the factory, discussing working conditions.

The Salvadoran teachers union *(Asociacion Nacional de Educadores Salvadorenos—ANDES—21 de Junio)*, its leaders and members have not been overlooked in this crackdown. Following raids on the unions headquarters, one leader of the teachers association, Professor Lionel Menendez, was shot and wounded in May 1980. He was subsequently abducted from the operating theatre at Rosales Hospital in San Salvador and has since disappeared. Eyewitnesses report that the hospital had been surrounded by vehicles belonging to the National Guard as well as agents of the National Police. One leader of that union described the escalation of violence against teachers since the mid-1970's:

Between 1970 and 1975, Government repression took the form of taking and dispersing militant teachers to remote areas, taking prisoners and an occasional assassination or prisoner disappearance. By 1975 one hundred percent of the primary and ninety percent of the secondary school teachers were organized. Beginning in 1976, state violence began to escalate. The original trade union focus on immediate economic issues began to shift, the organization began to be politicized. Under the General Molina regime (1972–1977) 150 teachers disappeared and 36 were killed; under General Romero (1977 to October 1979) 96 were killed; under the current junta 181 school teachers were killed between October 15 and July 31. There are 22,000 teachers in total.[23]

At least 19 primary and secondary schools were raided and a large number of professors and teachers were subjected to physical harassment and killed between January and August 1980. The level of violence escalated yet more sharply in early 1981. Amnesty notes that "Between January and mid-March 1981, 156 teachers are reported to have been killed in El Salvador."[24] One prominent victim of this violence was Felix Ulloa, the Rector of the National University in El Salvador and International President of the World University Service who, according to Amnesty International, was killed by machine-gun fire on October 28, 1980. The report of a delegation from the Archdiocese of San Francisco who interviewed Sr. Ulloa during July or August notes that:

According to Felix Ulloa, the repression against the university is in response to the university's historical role as a public forum where free discussion of ideas is both encouraged and pursued. The Democratic Revolutionary Front (FDR) announced its formation on the university campus.[25]

As an understandable result, many teachers have gone into exile. Amnesty International estimates that 85% of the schools in the Eastern Departments of La Union, San Miguel and Usulutan have been forced to close.[26]

2. Suppression of human rights groups

Government efforts to deny freedom of association have not been confined to political leaders of labor unions and their members. Another group that has faced particularly harsh treatment by government security forces are those organizations that have reported on violations of human rights. Because of the importance of such groups in resisting suppression of other rights the government's attacks on them are described in detail.

The *Socorro Juridico,* the legal aid office of the Archbishop of San Salvador, has been under continuous government attack. Established in 1975, *Socorro Juridico* has provided legal assistance to victims and family members of those whose rights have been violated. It also has served as a documentation center, issuing frequent reports on the current human rights situation in the country.

On July 3, 1980, Security Force personnel arrived at *Socorro Juridico*'s offices, located in the Jesuit-run San Jose school, in three small tanks and military vehicles with gunnery pieces. They forcibly entered and searched the offices and confiscated records dating back to 1975. The raid was sharply criticized by a number of organizations including the U.S. Catholic Conference which termed it "a most reprehensible and cowardly act."[27] In a letter to the Inter-American Commission on Human Rights,

Bishop Thomas C. Kelly, the USCC's General Secretary, noted that:

While the act itself cannot be compared in terms of human suffering with the escalating number of reported atrocities committed, in the main, against simple peasants and workers, it does strike at the heart of the very system of laws and guarantees which all modern societies, including that of El Salvador, purport to provide for their citizens.[28]

Describing his own personal experience, Roberto Cuellar, the Director of *Socorro Juridico,* explained:

From 1979 onward I had to cut myself off from my family. Armed civilians came to my home seeking me out. They found only my wife and two children. We had already sensed that something might happen because of my work in this.[29]

Cuellar describes how the harassment escalated in April 1980 following the murder of Archbishop Romero:

Armed men in civilian clothes came to my home twice in search of me. My family moved on a number occasions (but the security forces) managed to find them in the home of one of my wife's relatives. They came to the house. . . . I believe it was between May 10 and 12, more or less, and said that if they didn't find Roberto Cuellar they were going to kill the two children and my wife. The next day, in front of the house, they arrived with three coffins: a large coffin and two small coffins. They said that this coffin was for the señora and the two small coffins were for the children: "For the teacher," my wife is a teacher, "and for the two children."[30]

In describing the July 5 raid of *Socorro Juridico*'s offices, Cuellar charges that:

The Legal Aid papers taken also included lists of the unions that we at legal aid had served, lists of union members. Some of them have either disappeared or been murdered. I recall the case of two or three individuals, among them the Secretary General of the Lido Factory Union, Maximiliano Montoya, who was on the lists that we had at the Legal Aid of the Archdiocese. Other people (also) might have been murdered. The Army took those papers, because those that took over Legal Aid of the Archdiocese were members of the Army. There is no doubt about that whatever. . . .[31]

Five months later in December the Archdiocese of San Salvador was forced to close *Socorro Juridico* temporarily after its offices had been raided 17 times in one week by the National Police. Though the offices were later reopened, its members have continued to face frequent incidents of harassment by government agents, and its director, Roberto Cuellar, has been forced to leave the country.

On March 30, a communique from COPREFA (Armed Forces Press Committee) accused members of *Socorro Juridico* of being "traitors." This time they were on a list with various leaders of the church, universities, unions, political parties and another human rights organization, the Salvadoran Commission on Human Rights.

Harassment against the Commission on Human Rights dates to April 13, 1979, when its vice chairman was wounded by machine gun fire. In May, and again in June, 1979 the Commission's chairman was arrested by government police because he was representing political prisoners as defense counsel.[32]

On March 13, 1980, the Commission's office was destroyed by a bomb and its files confiscated by uniformed members of the National Police. At this time individual members of the Commission received telephone and written death threats which were never investigated by authorities.[33]

In September 1980, a bomb again destroyed the Commission's offices. Following the blast, partially clothed, decapitated, burned bodies were placed in the doorway to the Commission's offices.[34] On October 3, Maria Magdalena Henriquez, Press Secretary of the Commission, was abducted while shopping with her son in San Salvador. Several witnesses said she was taken by two heavily armed men who were members of the National Police.[35] Shortly after, her body was found in a shallow grave near the port of La Libertad, some twenty miles from San Salvador. She had been shot four times in the head and twice in the chest.[36] Sra. Henriquez had been active in submitting writs of *habeas corpus* to the courts in cases where people have "disappeared."

The government's response to this case is both revealing and typical. Despite corroborated eyewitness testimony that she was abducted by government security force personnel, an official government spokesman has stated that the government "was not implicated" in this matter.[37] To date no further action has been taken and no one has been arrested or tried for this crime.

Three weeks after Sra. Henriquez' arrest, on October 25, Ramon Valladares, an administrator with the Commission, was also abducted and killed. The Commission charges that his murder was also carried out by the National Police.[38]

In January 1981, the Commission's telephone line was cut and surveillance of its office by National Guardsmen and Army personnel was increased. On January 15, the Commission received a communique from COPREFA (The Armed Forces Press Committee) accusing its members of being "traitors." In the week previous to raids on Medrano and Villas, Salvadoran President Duarte accused the Commission of being "unpatriotic," and called for the creation of a "true human rights committee, with honorable and neutral individuals, to safeguard and defend the Salvadoran people, and not the FDR."[39]

Four days later, on January 24, Victor Medrano, the

information and administrative secretary of the Commission, was abducted from his home by members of the National Police and taken to their central barracks. Using his keys, government agents searched the Commission's office confiscating a number of items. Medrano was held by the police for 17 days before he was finally released.[40]

On January 28 at 9:40 P.M., uniformed members of the security forces and army violently raided the house of Lic. Marianella Garcia Villas, President of the Commission. Though she was not home, police arrested seven people who were staying in her house, including three children. All were questioned as to her whereabouts, and when they were unable to provide this information, all were reportedly beaten, including the three children, Carolina Concepcion, age 7, Sandra Guadalupe, age 5, and Angelica Perez, age 13. All seven people subsequently were taken into custody and the Garcia home was ransacked. In February 1981, two other members of the Commission, Tomas Antonio Leyva and Armando Paz Turcios, were also abducted and beaten.[41]

CHAPTER 10
POLITICAL
RIGHTS

This chapter discusses the operation of the political system including the role of political parties and elections.

A. *Events prior to October 1979*

El Salvador has not enjoyed a fair election for the last 50 years. In 1931, the government of Pio Romero Bosque held elections that were won by Arturo Araujo. The Communist Party was not allowed to participate. Araujo's victory was acknowledged and he was allowed to take office, but on December 2, 1931, his vice president and Minister of Defense, General Maximiliano Hernandez Martinez took over in a coup that inaugurated 50 years of military rule. In power for 13 years, Martinez banned all political and trade union organizations, and amended the Constitution to allow re-election.

On May 8, 1944, General Martinez was ousted and elections were announced. Before they were held, on October 21, 1944, the Chief of Police, Col. Osmin Aguirre y Salinas staged a *coup d'etat,* during which the civilian candidate was wounded and then forced into exile. A

fraudulent election brought General Salvador Castane
Castro into power. He ruled for four years, under a conti
uous state of siege, until a group of younger office
deposed him in 1948, installing a Revolutionary Coun
of Government. In 1950 one of its members, Col. Osc
Osorio, took over the presidency and founded a new of
cial party, *Partido Revolucionario de Unificacion Deme
cratica* (PRUD).

At this time, trade unions and political parties wer
legal but the government conducted clandestine and selec
tive repression, generally in the form of killings of oppo
nents. For the elections of 1956, the major oppositior
party, *Partido de Accion Renovadora* (PAR) and its candidate, Edmundo Canesa, were officially disqualified. When
the rest of the opposition candidates withdrew in protest,
the elections were won, with no opposition, by the official
candidate, Col. Jose Maria Lemus. Towards the end of
Lemus' rule, a major opposition party, *Partido Revolucionario Abril y Mayo* (PRAM), was denied recognition and
Canesa was attacked and fatally wounded. Lemus was
driven from office by a *coup* in October 1960, and replaced
by a Junta of three civilians and three members of the
Armed Forces.

Because of the Junta's attempt to re-establish democratic freedoms, and hold open elections with the participation of parties that had been proscribed until then, it
was itself toppled by another *coup* on January 25, 1961.
The Junta was replaced by a civilian-military Directorate,
one of whose members, Col. Julio A. Rivera, resigned in
order to run for president. The official party was re-organized under the name of *Partido de Conciliacion Nacional*
(PCN) and under its auspices Rivera won the elections of
1962, running unopposed.

During Rivera's presidency, the opposition parties re-
organized and made a strong showing in elections for
legislative seats and municipalities. In the presidential

elections of 1967, the PCN candidate, Col. Fidel Sanchez Henandez ran against three opponents and won. The *Partido Accion Renovadora* (PAR), one of the opposition parties that had made an impressive show of strength, was banned immediately after the election.

After five years of increasingly repressive rule, the PCN candidate, Col. Arturo Armando Molina, was faced with a unified opposition coalition, the *Union Nacional Opositora* (UNO), whose candidates were Jose Napoleon Duarte for president and Guillermo Ungo for vice president.

Early unofficial returns pointed to Duarte and Ungo as winners. The government then suspended radio announcements of the election results, and two days later declared Molina the winner. Col. Benjamin Mejia staged a coup, pledging to respect the popular vote, but with the help of Guatemalan and Honduran forces, Sanchez Hernandez was able to defeat the coup attempt, complete his term and inaugurate Molina. Mejia, Duarte and other leaders went into exile.

Molina's rule was marked by increased repression, with massacres of student and peasant demonstrators. His Minister of Defense, Gen. Carlos Romero, became the PCN candidate in 1977, running against Col. Ernesto Claramount, the UNO candidate. The official count gave Romero the victory, amidst widespread claims of massive fraud. The UNO coalition offered the U.S. Congress evidence of corruption in the conduct of the election, showing that the government had rigged the voter's register by duplicating and adding fictitious names, intimidated and assaulted voters with the help of ORDEN members and military personnel, denied UNO representatives access to polling booths and prevented them from overseeing the count. The operation had been coordinated by mobile units using a radio link-up and a crude code. The UNO candidates led a popular demonstration that lasted several days, demanding annulment of the elections. After several days in which thousand of persons peacefully occupied the main square in San Salvador, the Army cordoned off the square and opened fire on the demonstrators. Col. Claramount and other leades were forced into exile and a state of siege was again declared.

The opposition boycotted the 1978 elections for legislative seats and municipal governments, because of the lack of governmental guarantees of fairness and of a political climate conducive to carry out a campaign.

The Department of State has repeatedly acknowledged the fraudulent nature of Salvadoran elections. In a message to Congress of February 8, 1979, it said:

Recent elections in El Salvador have been marred by fraud. The present government of General Carlos Humberto Romero came to power following the elections of February 1977, in which fraud was again an issue.

The same report, commenting on the freedom to participate in the political process, added that ". . . administrative improprieties, government manipulation and fraud have impaired this freedom."[1]

In a subsequent report to Congress, the Department of State summarized El Salvador's recent history in this fashion:

Authoritarian military governments allied with a wealthy elite have been the trademarks of Salvadoran politics. A democratic facade has been maintained over the years through regularly scheduled elections resulting in the periodic changing of Presidents, Legislative Assembly members, and municipal administrations. Since the early 1970s, the results of the elections inevitably have been challenged as fraudulent, and although personnel have changed, the character of the governing coalition and its *modus operandi* have not. As a result, the Government party controlled all but four of the fifty-four Legislative Assembly seats and all two hundred sixty-one mayoralites at the time of the October 15 coup.

Legally, participation in the political system is open to all citizens. However, the functioning of the opposition political parties allegedly had been inhibited through repression, harassment, and collusion that have prevented effective recruitment, organization, and campaigning, including denial of access to the media. The new government has pledged to open the political process.[2]

In its 1981 Report, the State Department says that "El Salvador has long been dominated by powerful elites who ruled through the security forces . . . Faced with increasing demands for social change in the 1970's, traditional ruling groups continued their dominance by employing electoral fraud and repression."

The Inter-American Commission on Human Rights of the Organization of American States, after the "in situ" investigation of its Special Committee, from January 6 to 18, 1978, concluded that:

There is widespread skepticism among the citizenry regarding the right to vote and to participate in government. In particular, the political parties of the opposition, in this connection, come to have no confidence in the possibility of having full and honest elections, not only in the light of their experiences during the course of recent elections, but also because of the structure of the electoral system and of the obstacles the parties encounter in trying to organize in the interior of the country. For all these reasons, the Commission considers that electoral rights are not effective under the present circumstances.[3]

B. *Political rights since October 15, 1979*

This extreme abuse of the democratic process, and the resulting lack of confidence in it by a majority of the Salvadoran electorate, were among the major factors that led the officers to overthrow Romero in October 15, 1979 and establish the present regime. The Proclamation of the Armed Forces of that day said that "the successive governments (were) themselves the product of scandalous election frauds" and that this, among others, was the "basic cause of the economic and social chaos and of the generalized violence at the present time, which can only be overcome by the coming to power of a government that guarantees the enforcement of a truly democratic system." The new Junta pledged "to guarantee the observance of human rights by: (a) creating an atmosphere appropriate to holding free elections within a reasonable period of time, (b) allowing the establishment of parties of all ideologies, so as to strengthen the democratic system and (c) stimulating free expression of thought, in accordance with ethical standards."[4]

The Junta and Cabinet installed on October 15, 1979 reflected the attempt to involve democratic parties and sectors in the government. The governing coalition, therefore, included representatives of the Christian Democratic Party and of the *Movimiento Nacional Revolucionario* (MNR), a social-democratic party headed by Guillermo Ungo, as well as other politicians and groups who had been part of the opposition to the Romero regime.

The uneasy coalition lasted less than three months, for in December the military commanders, apparently reacting against an attempt by younger, moderate officers to form a council, announced to the assembled Junta and Cabinet that they would not obey the Junta but would only follow orders from Col. Jose Guillermo Garcia, the Minister of Defense.[5] In early January, most of the civilian members resigned and the military struck a deal with the Christian Democrats, in which Hector Dada Hirezi and Jose Antonio Morales Ehrlich were brought into the Junta. Dada's subsequent resignation from the government and the party shortly after the killing of Mario Zamora Rivas showed that the Christian Democratic Party (PDC) was irrevocably split over the issue of continued support for the process initiated in October 1979.[6] Since then, civilian participation in the government has been reduced to Duarte, Morales Ehrlich and R. Avalos Navarrete and its political base today does not extend beyond the fraction of the PDC that Duarte leads.

The Junta continues to confront varying degrees of opposition from conservative circles. The PCN has recently issued political statements, and seems to be reorganizing for the 1982 electoral campaign.[7] During the summer of 1981, a few minor parties surfaced, apparently as a result of the announcement of elections. They are the *Movimiento Democratico Salvadoreno,* the *Partido de Orientacion Popular* and a party calling itself the "authentic" MNR, formed primarily by former MNR members still occupying lower positions in the government. The three are expected to form a moderate coalition to oppose the PDC and PCN. Some of their leaders, like Ivo Priamo Alvarenga and Rene Fortin Magana, as well as some representatives of the business sector, are expected to join the Junta in the near future, either joining the Christian Democrats or actually replacing them.[8]

The opposition to the Junta has re-organized since October 1979. The "popular organizations" represented in the *Revolucionaria de Masas* (CRM) have been joined by many prominent moderate leaders, including Ungo, Dada Hirezi and several others who held Junta or cabinet positions after October 1979. They have formed the *Frente Democratico Revolucionario* (FDR), an umbrella coalition of opposition political parties and independent organizations. The several guerrilla organizations, in turn, have themselves become united under the name of *Frente Farabundo Marti de Liberacion Nacional* (FMLN). The FDR and FMLN agreed to coordinate their actions, and a Political-Diplomatic Commission of the FDR-FMLN has become the visible head abroad of the opposition to the government.

The denials by the government of the right to political participation of a large number of citizens are best exemplified by the publication, in March 1981, of a long list of "traitors" held responsible for the current situation in the country. The list includes the best-known opposition politicians like Guillermo Ungo, Roman Mayorga Quiros, Hector Dada Hirezi, Fabio Castillo, Alberto Arene, and Roberto Lara Velado. It also includes prominent citizens like Hector B. Recinos, one of the country's highest trade union official; Father Inocencio Alas; Professor Ignacio Ellacuria, Rector of the Catholic University; journalist José Napoleon Gonzalez and attorney Roberto Cuellar, of the Legal Aid Office of the Archdiocese. The majority of the remaining names are those of grass-roots leaders in different organizations, all of them potentially important in an electoral campaign, because of their support in such sectors as peasants and workers. The list is particularly relevant in light of the killing by government forces in November 1980 of major leaders of the FDR who had been similarly identified.

In the midst of this political situation, the government has announced elections, to be held in March 1982 to choose delegates to a constituent assembly, to be followed by Presidential and legislative elections in 1983. On March 5, 1981, the Junta enacted Decree No. 603 which repealed the 1961 electoral law, appointed three principal and three alternate members to fill the vacant positions of the Central Election Council, and entrusted it with the task of preparing a new draft election law, to be submitted to the Junta for consideration.

The Council proceeded immediately to seek assistance in drafting the new draft electoral law. On May 6, the Council met with the Board of the *Federacion de Abogados de El Salvador* (Salvadoran Bar Association) and requested a list of jurists to help draft the necessary legal instruments. On May 11, the Bar declined to submit such a list, on the following grounds:

- the state of siege and martial law continue in effect.
- public credibility and confidence are deeply affected by the unilateral configuration of the provisional government, since the majority of the members of the Junta belong to a single party.
- the composition of the Central Electoral Council is "strongly influenced by the party in power." (At least two of the Council members belong to President Duarte's Christian Democratic Party.).
- the generalized climate of violence that dominates El Salvador.[9]

The Council nevertheless submitted to the Junta a draft Provisional Law for the Formation and Registration of Political Parties that was strongly criticized by the FDR because it required the formation of a new party identifying at least 3,000 of its members as well as supplying their addresses, too obvious a risk in the present climate.[10] The law was enacted on July 10, 1981 after the Central Electoral Council had accused the Junta of "not giving due importance to the electoral process scheduled for March of the coming year."[11] The original time-table had called for the Law of Political Parties to be in effect by May 25.

Jorge Bustamante, chairman of the Council, said on May 21 that no elections could be held in El Salvador as long as the government maintained the state of seige and martial law in effect. Public meetings, publications of paid advertisements in newspapers and political tours should be permitted, he said.[12] In July, U.S. Ambassador Deane Hinton also expressed hope that the government would restore constitutional guarantees before the elections.[13] As of mid-September 1981, neither the state of seige, nor martial law nor the curfew had been lifted and no announcement had been made as to when they would.

The electoral law setting specific conditions for elections, establishing a timetable and actually providing for the holding of an electoral campaign, is being drafted, but no announcement has been made as to when it will be enacted.

At the same time that the provisional law of political parties was made public, on July 10, 1981, the Junta announced the automatic recognition of four parties, the Party of National Conciliation (PCN), the Christian Democratic Party (PDC), the National Revolutionary Movement (MNR) and the National Democratic Union (UDN), the latter two members of the opposition coalition, FDR. Later however, the leadership of the latter two parties rejected this recognition and denounced it as a ploy to provoke a split in the opposition.[14]

According to the chairman of the Electoral Council, the FDR would be allowed to participate if it becomes a political party, puts down its arms and publicly states that it has broken away from, and does not support, any guerrilla group. Col. Gutierrez, however, has said that the FDR cannot participate "because it is not a political party but the democratic facade of the guerrillas."[15] In July an unidentified Cabinet minister told *The New York Times* correspondent Raymond Bonner that the army would not allow Ungo to be a candidate in new elections.[16]

CHAPTER 11

REFUGEES AND
DISPLACED PERSONS

At least 350,000 persons, mainly peasant families, have been forced to abandon their homes and seek refuge in neighboring countries or in less dangerous areas of El Salvador. Some have left the armed conflict; others have been indiscriminately killed by security forces and the military. More than half have fled the country. In June 1981, the U.N. High Commission for Refugees estimated there were more than 200,000 Salvadoran refugees in neighboring Central American states and Mexico.[1] A later UNHCR Background Paper for Embassies conceded the number may be as high as 301,000.[2] The International Committee of the Red Cross placed the figures for displaced persons within El Salvador at 150,000 in June 1981.[3] Salvadoran Green Cross estimates bring the figure to 175,000.[4]

A. *Conditions producing refugees*

Church sources and human rights observers have linked a surge of refugees in mid-March 1980 to the initial implementation of the agrarian reform. National Guard units and Army troops ostensibly deployed to guarantee the implementation of agrarian reform measures were allegedly involved in the disappearance, torture and execution of hundreds of rural inhabitants of villages where the population included membership in opposition labor organizations in Morazan, Cuscatlan, Chalatenango and San Salvador Departments. Amnesty International reported "that Army, National Guard and ORDEN forces virtually wiped out several hamlets in Cuscatlan on 13 March, killing four persons outright, and detaining and causing thirty others to 'disappear'. By 16 March, reports obtained from the estimated 600 *campesinos* that have fled Cuscatlan to seek refuge in San Salvador say that at least 80 *campesinos* have been detained and killed in Cuscatlan since the land reform was decreed, including twenty-eight children."[5]

A March 1981 report of the International Committee of the Red Cross links "huge numbers of people" fleeing their villages to mid-1980 "large scale military operations in the northeast. . . . The inhabitants of remote hamlets moved into villages abandoned by people who themselves had fled to other villages or towns."[6]

The testimonies regarding summary execution, torture, rape and aerial bombardment of the non-combatant population suggest that counterinsurgency measures have largely obscured the crucial distinction between persons actively taking part in the hostilities and the unarmed civilian population. In fact, the counter-insurgency campaign's objectives appear to require the displacement of large numbers of inhabitants. The military strategy of the security forces of El Salvador appears to seek to deny guerrilla organizations rural bases by "depopulating villages in the region . . . to isolate the guerrillas and create problems of logistics and food supply."[7] The Canadian group's report and journalists' accounts suggest that this strategy has led to the slaughtering of livestock, theft of food, the razing of villages, crop-burning and direct assault upon the civilian population. A Canadian news-weekly, *Maclean's,* noted:

But the guerrilleros themselves are elusive, and all too often it is the organizations' non-militant union or peasant supporters who bear the brunt. In the countryside, the military's tactic has been to root out the guerrillas' logistical base, as well as their strongholds—routinely killing suspected sympathizers, burning houses, slaughtering farm animals and making off with provisions, leaving the survivors little choice other than to leave.[8]

On January 17–18, 1981 Rep. Barbara Milkulski (D-MD) talked with refugees from El Salvador along the Honduras-El Salvador border. Congresswoman Milkulski was accompanied by officials from UNHCR and interpreter.

Interview—Woman No. 2: Maria, Age 45:

She says that she would like to tell us the following: That many of her family were killed, so many were killed that she doesn't even remember their names. She would first like to speak about her brothers and sisters. She mentions about five that were killed. She says that six, two sisters and four cousins, all women were killed and found naked. One of those women was pregnant. These women have left children. One left two, the other left three orphans. They have not accounted for all of them. About 7 months ago, they killed one of her family and the child was an infant and is now in a hospital in a nearby town close to death. The army threw the baby in the river when they found them, and they took them into the woods and later they were found. She personally saw children around the age of 8 being raped, and then they would take their bayonets and made mincemeat of them. With their guns they would shoot at their faces.[9]

B. *Refugees in El Salvador*
1. *Physical conditions in the camps*

Socorro Juridico has classified internal refugees in three categories.[10] The first is the 80 percent or more already discussed who flee military conflict in their native areas, and go to other rural zones. Relief assistance is extended to them by the Government of El Salvador, voluntary agencies and humanitarian relief institutions such as the ICRC, the Green Cross, and the Salvadoran Red Cross. Efforts at humanitarian assistance are often impeded by official restrictions on entry to the troubled areas by relief agencies except for the Red Cross. Population movements of these dimensions create severe supply difficulties and serious medical problems as hygiene and nutrition in over-crowded villages deteriorate. The Catholic Relief Service calls hunger a "critical" problem, and says "food supplies in many areas are totally inadequate and deliveries are often impeded.

In another category of refugees are the 10,000 to 15,000 families formally evacuated by the Armed Forces before military operations. *Socorro Juridico* suggests that these refugees, because of family links with "army elements and security forces, including members of the pro-government paramilitary organization, ORDEN," occupy a priviliged position among refugees, and enjoy a rare degree of protection by government, military and civilian authorities. Press reports on the four refugee camps in the city of Berlin, fifty miles from San Salvador, suggest that these refugees receive favored treatment because they are viewed as supportive of the government, and are free to work outside the camps.[11]

In the third category are the approximately 5,000 refugees in and around San Salvador in some ten camps and sites provided by the Archdiocese of San Salvador, and who are attended to by that institution, Caritas, and ASE-SAH, among others. The first wave of these refugees, 800 within two weeks, arrived simultaneously with the promulgation of the Agrarian Reform decree (March 7, 1980) having fled military operations in Cuscatlan, Cabanas, and Chalatenango. Between March 1980 and November 1980, the Archdiocese gained approval to open ten sites to accommodate the waves of refugees, most of whom arrived without possessions and suffering physical and psychological trauma as a result of their displacement.[12]

Living conditions in these refugee camps have been variously described by church sources and journalists as subhuman and squalid.[13] The Public Health Commission of Inquiry from the U.S. went to El Salvador in July 1980 and reported that:

In the refugee site visited by the Commission, food, water, bedding and medical care were in critically short supply. Outbreaks of diarrhea, especially in the children, were compounded, by inadequate water supplies and sanitary facilities. Children with distended bellies and lice were seen. The refugees slept in an open yard exposed to the elements, or beneath a veranda.

The fear of the refugees and their grief were palpable . . . they dared not leave the sites provided by the churches for fear of further retaliation by military forces. They were therefore unable to seek out needed medical services.[14]

2. *Violations of refugee rights*

Despite clear obligations set forth in the Geneva Conventions to respect the neutral humanitarian work of medical and relief personnel, there is abundant evidence that an attitude of official indifference severely impedes relief and health work among refugees. The Public Health Commission, with the support of the American Public Health Commission, the Physicians Forum and the American Friends Service Committee, conducted an on-site inquiry in 1980, on the issue of abuses of medical neutrality. The Commission of Inquiry concluded in its public report that the relevant articles of the Geneva Conventions were being "recklessly disregarded" noting that:

The Government of El Salvador maintains strict vigilance over the importation of medicines, surgical equipment, and other supplies. As a consequence, relief organizations have expressed concern about obtaining necessary medicinals. Some health practitioners are unable to obtain ordinary equipment and supplies.

. . . the outcome—no doubt intended—of this pattern of killings and torture [of health workers and patients] on the part of military and paramilitary groups is that health workers are afraid to render services to patients who are, or could conceivably be considered, "oppositionists," even if this means merely being a member of one of the numerous, *legal* popular organizations. The risk of swift, brutal and fatal reprisal means that most health care professionals will necessarily have second thoughts about which patients they will treat. They are, moreover, aware that the government has not taken effective steps to identify or prosecute the killers.[15]

Elizabeth Enloe, Program Coordinator for Latin America, and the Caribbean for Church World Services noted:

Those who carry out this humanitarian program do so at great personal risk. Anyone who appears to be in opposition to the government or the military is in jeopardy, and relief workers who are reaching out to those suffering the consequences of political violence might be considered by some to be aiding and abetting the opposition.[16]

The serious health and psychological problems suffered by the refugees are compounded by high levels of fear and a sense of precariousness generated by assaults and incursions by security forces. Clause 7 of United Nations *Resolution 2675* notes "places or areas designated for the sole protection of civilians such as hospitals and similar refuges, should not be the object of military operations".[17] Common Article 3 of the *Geneva Conventions* stipulates that:

. . . persons taking no active part in the hostilities, including members of the armed forces who have laid down their arms and those placed *hors de combat* by sickness or wounds shall be in all circumstances be treated humanely. . . . (Article 3).[18]

Statements made by Salvadoran authorities as well as repeated acts of harassment suggest that the Government believes that refugees constitute a military or security issue rather than a relief problem. Between August 20, 1980, and March 17, 1981, *Socorro Juridico* documented sixty-seven separate instances of killings, detentions, robberies, encirclements, threats, searches and military occupations of refugee centers by National Police, Army, Treasury Police, civilian agents or combined forces. The following instances, documented by the Archdiocese, provide some examples:[19]

—November 19, 1980—Civilian agents operating with members of the Army entered the refugee center of San Jose de La Montana, robbing, threatening and assaulting several refugees.

—December 31, 1980—Soldiers from the San Carlos Barracks detained refugee, Marcial Cruz, 18, of Cojutepeque, in the refugee camp of Domus Maria, Mejicanos. The detained man was later seen in the San Carlos Barracks by the Chancellor of the Archdiocese, P. Rafael Urrutia. Military authorities urged the priest "not to worry". Cruz' mutilated cadaver was discovered on January 9, with two others.

—February 16–17, 1981—Truckloads of soldiers entered the refugee center of Domus Maria, Mejicanos, three separate times, beating two refugees, robbing medicine and food, and issuing death threats.

—According to a number of reports, on July 4, 1981, combined Army and National Guard units evicted more than 2,000 refugees from La Bermuda, a refugee camp eighteen miles northeast of San Salvador and forcibly relocated a portion of them six miles north, in Suchitoto Penitentiary. Some military authorities said the 2,000 refugees were being moved for their own safety and to better living conditions. Others said the refugees were evicted because they were "relatives of the guerrillas" and because the Army needed the area as a base camp for search-and-destroy missions in the surrounding area.[20] Press reports based on the interviews with refugees, indicate that the army had entered the camp on several prior occasions. The Green Cross and journalists report that up to 100 people were forcibly removed from the camps.[21]

A foreign news photographer (name withheld) related the following incident:

It was late March of this year [1981]. I drove to La Bermuda, which is about twelve kilometers from Suchitoto. As I was arriving, there was a raid. Army troops from Suchitoto had come into the camp and an informer with a hood was pointing out individuals, who were immediately taken out. (There were two entrances, and people were being removed via both.) The Army personnel told me I couldn't take photos, but I did anyway. I followed some Army personnel out to the road with some of their detainees including this girl in the photo. She was about sixteen and was weeping. The Army personnel took her and several others into some bushes, and then I heard shooting, a lot, and the atmosphere became very tense. . . . My sixth sense told me to get out, so I did. The Green Cross later confirmed that bodies had been found there, a group of civilians. . . .[22]

Colonel Adolfo Cotto, an armed forces spokesman, told the press that "from a military point of view, (the forced evacuation) makes sense, so we can have control over these people day and night."[23] The National Guard Commander in Suchitoto who supervised the transfer, said he was acting upon orders from the Ministry of Defense. He added:

We give [the refugees] support and medical attention and show them movies to orient them and we supervise their activity constantly. . . . There are people in that camp who have been very closely connected to the guerrillas, and the Suchitoto community is afraid they might try something funny.[24]

More than 1,000 refugees are now crowded into penitentiary cells at Suchitoto, under the eye of military police in prison watch-towers. According to testimony by refugees, they wanted to remain in Le Bermuda where they had recently planted corn and vegetables. One said, "now we are like prisoners here, as if we had committed a great crime." After evacuating La Bermuda, the Army burned all the buildings there.[25] Health conditions at Suchitoto are reportedly very poor. A New York Times account described several children as "having worms and their stomachs were grotesquely swollen. Their glassy eyes were filled with pus. They looked like most of the 300 or so children here."[26]

C. *External Refugees*

The U.N. High Commissioner for Refugees (UNHCR) estimated last June that there are between 181,000 and 301,000 Salvadoran refugees in the countries stretching from Panama to Mexico.[27] The commission provided a breakdown as follows:

Country:	No. of Refugees:
Belize	7,000
Costa Rica	10,000
Cuba	—
Dominican Republic	—
Guatemala	50,000/100,000
Honduras	33,000
Mexico	70,000/140,000
Nicaragua	20,000
Panama	1,000

According to *UNHCR INFORMATION*, Rep. No. 1., of June 1981 the UNHCR is assisting some 60,000 of these refugees, in response to requests of the governments of the countries concerned.

The UNHCR argues that

... in situations of large-scale influx it is frequently impracticable to resort to an individual determination of refugee status due to the large numbers involved and also to the frequent necessity to provide assistance and protection on an emergency basis. In order to overcome these various difficulties recourse has frequently been had to what is known as *'prima facie* group determination'. This is based on the assumption that in view of the conditions prevailing in the country of origin, all members of the group should, in the absence of clear indications to the contrary, be regarded as refugees.

As regards persons who have left Salvador after the outbreak of the Civil War early in 1980, we considered that the above-mentioned conditions are indeed fulfilled. Concerning Salvadorians who have left their country prior to the outbreak of the Civil War, it is possible that a number of them may be exposed to serious danger in the event of their returning to their country of origin, a matter which would need to be examined in the light of the circumstances of the particular case.[28]

In 1980, the UNHCR spent $2.5 million for Salvadoran refugees. On June 25, 1981, it appealed for $9.8 million to finance the increased needs of the assistance program.[29]

Given the dimensions of the current refugee influx into the region, governments are "noticeably reticent in dealing with the problem."[30] In some cases, the chief concern is the economic and social tensions generated by waves of impoverished persons. In others, political concerns arising from the nature of the Salvadoran conflict play a significant role. The circumstances of refugees in neighboring countries vary considerably, the situation in Honduras being the most acute, according to extensive reports.

1. *Salvadoran refugees in Honduras*

Estimates of Salvadoran refugees in Honduras range from 33,000 to 70,000, the majority of them located in scattered towns near the Salvadoran border in the Departments of

Lempira, Ocotepeque, Intibuca, and La Paz.[31] Most are from peasant families, 40 percent are children, 40 percent women, and 20 percent men, according to UNHCR.[32] In press interviews, 80 percent of the refugees said they fled the National Guard and 20 percent said they left because of the generalized conflict.

After the arduous circumstances of the flight to the border and the previous physical and psychological trauma endured by the refugees in their own cantons, many of them also encountered violent joint efforts by Salvadoran and Honduran soldiers to prevent them from entering Honduran territory. The situation of Salvadoran refugees in the border areas is related to official military objectives as the refugee area in Honduras lies across from the region of El Salvador where counter-insurgency operations and military confrontations have been heaviest. The Salvadoran army has sought to secure the border to prevent suspected guerrillas from crossing it freely. In a cease-fire agreement after the 1969 Honduran-Salvadoran war, a six-kilometer area along the border was made a neutral zone under Organization of American States supervision. On October 31, 1980 El Salvador and Honduras signed a peace treaty which did not resolve issues of border demarcation and left 35 percent of the border under dispute. This allowed Salvadoran forces to enter parts of the previously restricted area.[33]

Defense Minister Jose Guillermo Garcia told the *New York Times* last June that "at least 15 percent, or 4,500 of the refugees along the border are considered to be subversive." He conceded that some were "real refugees," but insisted that "a large sector (exists) that appears to be refugees and are simply terrorists, who go precisely to find refuge, and then return, commit their misdeeds, and go back."[34]

Numerous testimonies document instances of what appears to be a policy to prevent entrance into Honduran territory of Salvadoran refugees. Two major incidents at the Sumpul and Lempa Rivers provide examples.

a. *The Sumpul River*

On May 14, 1980, thousands of Salvadoran *campesinos* fled from a military operation apparently intended to flush out guerrillas in the area, and sought refuge in the nearby territory of Honduras. As they were crossing the river, they were attacked by two Salvadoran helicopters, troops and members of ORDEN, killing at least 600 peasants, including many women and children.

The massacre only received attention after the clergy of the city of Santa Rosa de Copan, Honduras, denounced the deaths on June 19. The relevant parts of the declaration signed by Monsignor Jose Carranza y Chavez and all the priests and clergy of the diocese, follow:

The Facts:

"Since last January, a good number of Salvadorans, the majority children, women and old people have sought refuge in our country. During their exodus they have been systematically harassed by the Salvadoran National Guard.

"A prime example of this harassment and cruelty, occurred on the 14th of May of this year. The previous day a number of trucks and other vehicles of the Honduran Army arrived in Guarita overflowing with soldiers. The soldiers, without pausing in the town, descended 14 kms. to the vicinity of the river Sumpul, demarcation line between Honduras and El Salvador, cordonning off the left bank near the Honduran villages of Santa Lucia and San Jose. Over megaphones pointing towards Salvadoran territory, they shouted out that it was forbidden to cross the border. On the opposite bank at about seven in the morning, in the Salvadoran hamlet of 'La Arada' and its vicinity the massacre began. At least two helicopters, the Salvadoran National Guard, soldiers and the paramilitary organization ORDEN, began firing at the defenseless people. Women tortured before the final coup de grace, nursing babies thrown into the air for target practice, were some of the incidents of the criminal slaughter. Salvadorans who crossed the river were returned by Honduran soldiers to the area of the massacre. By mid-afternoon the genocide had ended leaving a minimum of 600 dead.

"A few days before, according to the Honduran press, in the city of Ocotepeque bordering Guatemala and El Salvador, a secret meeting of high military officers of the three countries took place. News of it was announced publicly shortly thereafter.

"At least 600 unburied corpses were prey for dogs and buzzards for several days. Others were lost in the waters of the river. A Honduran fisherman found the bodies of five little children in his fish trap. Rio Sumpul became contaminated from the village of Santa Lucia on."[35]

Both the Salvadoran and the Honduran governments denied the allegations. Honduras called the contention that Honduran armed forces "participated in an operation in conjunction with the Salvadoran Army to massacre peasants absolutely false and irresponsible."

Nevertheless there are numerous testimonies of survivors and eye-witnesses.[36]

Hugh McCullum, editor of the Canadian publication, the United Church *Observer,* interviewed Salvadoran President Jose Napoleon Duarte about the Sumpul River. President Duarte reportedly admitted that an "action did take place in the area of Rio Sumpul" and that "about 300 were killed, all of them 'Communist guerrillas'."[37]

b. *Deaths on the Lempa River*

On March 17, 1981, another large group of Salvadoran *campesinos* again fleeing the area of fighting tried to reach Honduras by crossing the Lempa River.

On March 18, 1981, an estimated 4,500 to 8,000 Salvadoran refugees, mostly women and children fleeing military confrontation in Cabanas Province, attempted to cross the Lempa River into Honduran territory. According to eyewitness testimony by survivors, doctors, priests, and relief personnel present at the scene, the Salvadoran Air Force dropped bombs and helicopters strafed them as the army fired mortars and machine gun rounds, leaving twenty to thirty dead and one hundred eighty-nine missing. Two priests assert that twenty male Salvadoran refugees were killed by Honduran troops on the Honduran side, shot, beaten to death, or killed by machetes.[38]

Eyewitnesses say the helicopters' altitudes were sufficiently low such that it was inconceivable the pilots could have been unaware that they were firing upon unarmed civilians and particularly children.

Despite the reports, the Salvadoran Embassy in Washington said no helicopter attacked noncombatants in the Lempa River.

Having not yet ratified the United Nations Convention on the Status of Refugees and its 1978 Protocol, the Government of Honduras created the National Commission of Refugees. Established on January 21, 1981 it was designed to act as liaison between the UNHCR and international relief agencies as well as to coordinate national relief activities.

Conditions in the refugee camps remain a matter of grave concern. The refugees suffer from a variety of serious health problems—malnutrition, dehydration, diarrhea, respiratory, skin and eye diseases. An incomplete census conducted in late April 1981 in Colomoncagua by Caritas workers noted that 400 children out of 4,214 persons suffered from serious malnutrition.[39]

Relief services say the main causes are lack of food with sufficient protein for children and lactating mothers, exacerbated by deplorable health and austere housing conditions, severe overcrowding, and insufficient shelter from cold and rain. A church official said in September 1980 that refugees were "sleeping in plastic-lined 'housettes' with roofs only some three feet in height, that *campesinos* generally used for the protection of pigs."

Numerous accounts point to a pattern of murder, harassment, assault, abduction and forcible return to El Salvador by Salvadoran security forces operating in Honduras, members of ORDEN operating with apparent impunity in Honduras and Honduran army personnel.

A UNHCR spokesman confirmed reports that in January, Salvadoran Air Force planes conducted air raids over the Honduran border while numerous house-to-house searches were made in Honduran villages by armed men, some in civilian dress and others in Salvadoran military uniforms.

Amnesty International and human rights observers have documented various cases of refoulement. In Tegucigalpa, Honduras, on April 22, 1981, fourteen Salvadoran refugees and two Hondurans were arrested, eleven of whom have now "disappeared." According to *El Tiempo,* four of the detainees, children between the ages of five and eleven were returned to relatives in El Salvador. Among those detained was Nora Trinidad Gomez de Barillas, who had been Archbishop Oscar Romero's secretary. The grandmother of one child was also deported to El Salvador.

The Honduran newspaper *El Tiempo* reported on May 25, 1981, that Concepcion Navarro (fifty) and four Salvadoran children were handed over to the Salvadoran police at El Amatillo on the border of the Salvadoran Department La Union, by Immigration Inspector Oscar Flores and police officer Evelin Rosa. Ricardo Melgar Cisneros, of the *Oficina de Migracion de El Salvador,* said the reason for their transfer back to El Salvador, was that they had been abandoned in Honduras.[40]

The information to date suggests that protection from killings, harassment, assault, and arbitrary detention remains a vital concern for refugees in Honduras. Charles

Henry Bazoche, Director of the Honduras Office of the UNHCR said in a recent interview that he has protested to the Honduran Government regarding army brutality charging that last March, refugees were killed after being taken from a camp by Honduran Army officials and turned over to Salvadoran soldiers. While he said that army incursions into the camps have "somewhat lessened but it remains a major concern of ours, the major problem remaining is the turning back of refugees at the border."

2. *Salvadoran Refugees in the United States*

Although it is difficult to ascertain the precise number of Salvadorans in the U.S., most government and non-government agencies estimate the number to be 500,000 as of 1979.[41] Between 25,000 and 60,000 are believed to have arrived in the last year, mostly illegally, according to INS figures, although the Salvadoran Refugee Defense Committee in San Diego estimates 100,000. Since January 1980, 12,828 Salvadorans were apprehended by the U.S. Immigration and Naturalization Service.[42] While only 2,378 of these Salvadorans were formally deported, according to the INS, the majority of the remaining were persuaded or induced to leave voluntarily—at their own expense but without formal deportation proceedings. Some immigration lawyers working on Salvadoran cases see a consistent INS pattern of inducing Salvadorans to leave the country voluntarily and not apply for asylum by various methods including threats of prolonged detention and the posting of high bail. Civil liberties organizations, religious and ethnic organizations, legal aid groups, immigration law groups, and a number of Members of Congress have pressed the State Department to grant "extended voluntary departure" to Salvadorans in this country who have expressed fear of returning to El Salvador. This short term measure permits the beneficiary to work in the country of reception, without conferring permanent status. It is permitted for persons who are under a "temporary inability to return . . . to their home country because of civil war or catastrophic circumstances there. . . ."⁴³

Richard Fairbanks, Assistant Secretary of State for Congressional Relations in a written response to Congressman Michael D. Barnes, Chairman of the Subcommittee on Inter-American Affairs (which held hearings on the issue) clarified present U.S. policy on this issue as of April 8, 1981.

The Department at this time is not in a position to recommend to the INS the granting of voluntary departure status for Salvadorans now illegally in the U.S. The Department, however, will resume April 15 the case-by-case review of Salvadoran political asylum requests and will provide the INS with "advisory opinions" on pending cases which were suspended on January 17.

While civil strife and violence in El Salvador continue at distressing levels, conditions there do not warrant the granting of blanket voluntary departure status to all Salvadorans now in the United States. While fighting in some areas has been severe, El Salvador has not suffered the same level of widespread fighting, destruction, and breakdown of public service and order as did Nicaragua, Lebanon, or Uganda, for whose citizens voluntary departure was recommended by the Department and granted by INS. Public order and public services, while under a serious attack, are still maintained, especially in San Salvador and the larger cities. Moreover, Salvadorans now present in the U.S., estimated at 500,000 who were not involved in political or military activities before their departure, would not, upon their return, be in greater danger than other non-combatants in El Salvador. We cannot accept the thesis that the majority of Salvadorans now in the United States departed their country only to seek safe haven. Those legitimate refugees who actually have fled turmoil in El Salvador are now located for the most part in neighboring countries, principally Honduras.⁴⁴

Immigration lawyers respond that the decision to *not* grant voluntary departure status to Salvadorans is a radical departure from U.S. immigration policy to date. In the past, they say, it has been routinely implemented in similar circumstances, as in the cases of Nicaragua, Ethiopia and Lebanon. Lawyers and human rights observers have also pointed out that the dimensions of the problem in human terms outweigh the fact that "public order and public services . . . are still maintained" in a situation where the government will not guarantee the right to life in many cases.

PART III

THE
U.S.
ROLE

CHAPTER 12

U.S. INVOLVEMENT IN EL SALVADOR

Since the coup of October 15, 1979, the United States has become deeply involved at a diplomatic, economic, and military level in the affairs of El Salvador. U.S. officials in Washington and at the U.S. Embassy in San Salvador have taken an active role in promoting reforms, encouraging a professionalization of the Salvadoran Army and security forces, and supporting a political process to lead to national elections scheduled for March 1982. The United States has also endeavored to gain the support of major U.S. European and Latin American allies for its policy in that Central American nation.

U.S. economic aid since the coup has totalled over $300 million (including proposals for Fiscal Year 1982),[1] more than the amount provided to any other Latin American nation. Security assistance—arms sales, grants, and training—for Fiscal Year 1980 through Fiscal Year 1982 is more than four times what it was for the entire period between 1950 and 1979.[2]

Of all the aspects of U.S. involvement in El Salvador since the October coup, however, perhaps none has been so controversial as the sending of military aid and U.S. military personnel to that country. Debate in the Congress, the press, and the U.S. public has focused on the human rights record of the military forces receiving such aid, on the effect of such aid on the balance of power between the armed forces and civilians in the government in El Salvador, and on parallels to the early days of U.S. involvement in Southeast Asia. Last March, a Gallup poll revealed that only two percent of the U.S. public supported the sending of U.S. troops to El Salvador, and that less than one in five appeared to favor providing economic assistance, military supplies, or military advisers.[3]

Both economic and military aid, to the extent that they fulfill their intended purpose, have an impact on the status of human rights in El Salvador. This report, however, focuses on human rights abuses committed by the Salvadoran Army and security forces. Because U.S. military aid and training are being provided to the same units alleged to be engaged in violations of human rights, it is the military aspects of U.S. involvement in El Salvador that have the greatest bearing on human rights. Therefore, the following section will concentrate on the nature and extent of U.S. military involvement in El Salvador, as well as the extent to which U.S. assistance and training can be directly linked to such human rights abuses.

A. *U.S. involvement prior to October 1979*

U.S. military involvement in El Salvador began after World War II, when the United States initiated training and assistance programs in pursuit of a hemispheric policy of guarding against external Soviet attack. In the mid-1940's the United States sent its first military mission to El Salvador, and began its first equipment grants under the Military Assistance Program (MAP).[4] U.S. assistance remained extremely modest, however, totalling only $16.7 million in grants, credit, and training in the post-war decades between Fiscal Years 1950 and 1979.[5] During that time the U.S. trained 1,971 Salvadoran officers, including at least seventeen in Urban Counter-insurgency, fourteen in Military Intelligence, one hundred eight in Basic Combat and Counterinsurgency, and one hundred twenty-four in Basic Officer Preparation.[6]

After the Cuban revolution in 1959, the U.S. security focus in the hemisphere shifted to one of guarding against internal subversion by increasing support for police and paramilitary units such as the National Guard and National Police. In order to upgrade El Salvador's internal security apparatus, the Untied States instituted in 1957 a Public Safety Program "to develop the managerial and operational skills and effectiveness of its civil police forces."[7] Between 1957 and the program's termination in 1974, the Office of Public Safety spent a total of $2.1 million to train 448 Salvadoran police, and provide rifles, carbines, riot control gear, communications equipment, and transport vehicles.[8]

Between 1957 and 1963, the Public Safety program was directed mainly at the National Police; from 1963 on, the program's emphasis shifted to improving the training, investigations, riot control, communications, and other police skills of the National Guard.[9] At the height of U.S. involvement between 1963 and 1965, five U.S. advisers were stationed in El Salvador to oversee training and program management. A special U.S. investigations adviser worked with intelligence units of the National Police, National Guard, and Immigration.[10]

When Congress terminated the OPS program in 1974 after allegations that U.S. support was contributing to the repressive practices of many Third World police, U.S. A.I.D. analysts concluded that " . . . the National Police . . . has advanced from a nondescript, *cuartel*-bound group of poorly trained men to a well-disciplined, well-trained, and respected uniformed corps. It has good riot control capability, good investigative capability, good records, and fair communications and mobility. It handles routine law enforcement well."[11] An earlier report said that U.S. public safety advisers had "efficiently trained the National Guard and National Police in basic tactics so that authorities have been successful in handling any politically-motivated demonstrations in recent years."[12]

Graduates of OPS training, including those brought to the United States for studies at the International Police Academy in Washington, D.C., occupied key positions in the Salvadoran security establishment. The assistant to the head of the Intelligence Division of the National Police was an IPA graduate; at various times, the top positions in the Treasury Police, the Customs Police, and the Immigration service were U.S.-trained, as were the second and third-in-command in other security agencies.[13]

Public safety advisers reorganized the Police school, prepared a standard textbook for the Treasury Police, and trained and equipped special riot control units in the National Police and National Guard. OPS created within the National Police a bomb-handling squad ". . . responsible for investigating terrorist activities . . ." established a central police records bureau, and installed a teletype system linking El Salvador, Nicaragua, Honduras, Guatemala, Costa Rica, and Panama.[14] Included in the teletype system were files on "suspected subversives."[15] In the late 1960's, U.S. intelligence agents also provided aid to a special intelligence unit headed by Col. Jose Alberto Medrano, the founder of ORDEN, a paramiliary spy network, then having some 30,000 informants.[16]

In 1977, the first year of the Carter Administration, El Salvador rejected U.S. military aid in protest over U.S. criticism of the human rights practices of the incumbent Romero government. The act was largely symbolic, however, because U.S. military aid had been suspended in

1976 after Salvadoran Army Chief of Staff Manuel Alfonso Rodriguez was convicted in New York for trying to sell 10,000 machine guns to the U.S. mafia.[17]

B. *U.S. military aid to El Salvador since October 1979*

U.S. military aid to the first civilian-military junta in El Salvador (October 15, 1979–January 3, 1980) was extremely limited. On November 4, 1979, the United States shipped $205,000 worth of riot control equipment, (steel helmets, flak jackets, and tear gas) to El Salvador, along with a team of four Army advisers to train Salvadoran troops in riot control.[18] The sale was justified on the grounds that training in non-lethal methods of crowd control was essential if human rights abuses by the security forces (i.e., opening fire on unarmed demonstrators) were to be reduced.

On November 4, 1979, Archbishop of San Salvador Oscar Arnulfo Romero declared that:

It seems to me that the best way the U.S. can help El Salvador at this time is to condition its aid to purification of the security forces, a satisfactory resolution of the problem of the disappeared, and punishment of those guilty. If it doesn't set these prerequisites, the military assistance the U.S. might give would only be strengthening those who oppress the people, even if it is providing tear gas and protective jackets. This will mean more confident repression of the people.[19]

Later, in a letter to President Carter, Archbishop Romero referred to the November sale charging that "the security forces, with better personal protection and effectiveness, have repressed the people even more violently, using deadly weapons."[20]

The only other U.S. aid provided during the first junta was a $300,000 "re-programming" of International Military Education and Training (IMET) funds, for use in training Salvadoran officers in U.S. military schools, or in

funding the activities of U.S. Mobile Training Teams in El
Salvador.[21]

The first major debate on U.S. military assistance to El
Salvador began in February, 1980, following a *Washington Post* report that the Carter Administration was considering sending three twelve-man Mobile Training Teams
to El Salvador to train troops in communications, logistics, and intelligence, as well as up to $7 million in arms
credits to purchase equipment.[22] The announcement provoked an immediate response from Archbishop Romero,
who wrote to President Carter on February 17, 1980 saying that "the contribution of your government, instead of
favoring greater justice and peace in El Salvador, undoubtedly will sharpen the repression."[23]

The Secretary General of Amnesty International, Martin Ennals, also wrote to then-Deputy Secretary of State
Warren Christopher on February 29, 1980:

as all security forces in El Salvador are combating this unrest,
and are in varying degrees implicated in abuses—including torture and summary executions—we believe that assistance
proposals for these forces should be very carefully examined to
determine whether they might encourage further violations of
human rights. . . . It has been pointed out that the provision by
the United States of some U.S. $200,000 worth of materials and
training in November, 1979 for the control of political demonstrations or riots, coincided with a massive loss of life when street
demonstrations were attacked by authorities, a practice which
continues in El Salvador.[24]

Congress became involved in a major debate over military aid to El Salvador in March, 1980, after the Carter
Administration requested a "re-programming" of $5.7
million for non-lethal military equipment including transport vehicles, communications gear, and night vision devices.[25] During hearings before the House Appropriations
Subcommittee on Foreign Operations, Administration

witnesses maintained that the military aid would "strengthen the Army's key role in reforms" and enable troops to "resist violence of the radical right and left groups opposed to the reforms."[26] Opponents of the aid argued that "political power no longer lies with the young officers responsible for the coup, but with old-line military leaders in government positions who practice a policy of reform with repression."[27] The $5.7 million was approved by the subcommittee in April by a vote of 5–3.

At approximately the same time, Congress began consideration of the 1981 military aid requests. The Carter Administration proposed $5 million for El Salvador in Foreign Military Sales credits to purchase "patrol boats, helicopters, jeeps, parachutes, aircraft engines, megaphones, trucks, and radios," as well as $498,000 in International Military Education and Training grants "to expose officers to U.S. military doctrine and practice as well as provide them training in internal security."[28] (The aid became available to be spent on October 1, 1980, the beginning of FY 1981). The U.S. Department of Defense also indicated to Congress that licenses would be issued to private U.S. companies to sell arms to El Salvador, "mostly for carbines, handguns, and rifles."[29]

Amnesty International again expressed its "dismay" over the FY 1981 requests in a letter to Secretary of State Edmund Muskie on June 25, 1980. The letter indicated that:

Amnesty opposes security transfers where it is reasonable to believe they will contribute directly to human rights violations. . . . In the Salvadoran context, this includes torture, arbitrary imprisonment and summary execution on a massive scale.

The letter also noted that:

it is indeed reasonable to expect that assistance intended to improve the operational capabilities of the Salvadoran security system, including training and material assistance, will contribute to worsen the human rights situation in that country.[30]

In the summer of 1980, U.S. officials decided to proceed with the training of up to 300 Salvadoran officers at U.S. schools in Panama; one three-week course, entitled "Human Rights Aspects in Internal Defense and Development," was especially designed for the Salvadorans. According to Lt. Gen. Wallace Nutting, head of the U.S. Southern Command, "the Salvadoran forces need to improve their proficiency in a technical, professional sense." He described the Human Rights course as an effort to teach "how to be nice to people while you force them to do what you want them to do. How to assert force without being brutal."[31]

Panama's President Aristides Royo strongly criticized U.S. use of the Canal Zone to teach anti-guerrilla tactics to the Salvadoran Army. "Any training that is intended to repress a country cannot be accepted morally or politically," he said.[32]

From the beginning of FY 1980 until May 24, 1981, the United States trained three hundred twenty-seven Salvadoran officers, including forty-one in "Operations," one hundred forty in "Professional/Specialization," thirty-three in "Communications," and one hundred one in "Maintenance."[33]

On December 15, 1980, the UN General Assembly passed a resolution on "the situation of human rights and fundamental freedoms in El Salvador" which called on governments to "refrain from the supply of arms and other military assistance to El Salvador" because of "the death of thousands of persons and the climate of repression and insecurity prevailing in the country, which favors terrorism by paramilitary groups. . . ."[34] The resolution passed 70-12, with 55 abstentions. The United States abstained.

On December 2, 1980, when four U.S. churchwomen were abducted in El Salvador while traveling from the airport to the capital city, and later murdered, the State Department expressed its "shock and dismay" as well as its concern over "reports of involvement of the Salvadoran security forces."[35] On December 5th, the United States put a "hold" on all economic and military assistance commitments. The "hold" however, did not affect the activities of U.S. military personnel in El Salvador at that time (see below), or the training of Salvadoran officers underway in the United States and in Panama; it meant essentially that unspent portions of FY 1981 aid would not be committed.

The Carter Administration reinstated economic aid on December 17th, citing progress in the investigation of the murders.[36] Military aid was reinstated on January 14, shortly after the beginning of a major military offensive by Salvadoran opposition guerrillas. The State Department announced that "leftist guerrillas over the past weekend (have) . . . demonstrated that they are better armed and constitute a military threat. Captured weapons and documents confirmed that the guerrillas have received a substantial supply of arms from abroad."[37] The Carter Administration also announced the lease of two U.S. UH-1H Bell helicopters to the Salvadoran armed forces.[38]

Then, on January 17, the Carter Administration invoked special executive authority (Section 506A of the Foreign Assistance Act of 1961) to send $5 million in additional emergency military aid to El Salvador, this time for overtly lethal weapons—grenade launchers, M-16's, ammunition, etc. The State Department said "we must support the Salvadoran government in its struggle against left-wing terrorism supported covertly with arms, ammunition, training, and political and military advice by Cuba and other communist nations."[39] In addition to the $5 million in emergency aid, the U.S. leased another four helicopters to El Salvador.[40]

The Reagan Administration dramtically increased military assistance to El Salvador. In February, 1981, it issued a voluminous "White Paper" on "Communist Support of the Salvadoran Insurgency."

The White Paper summarized the Reagan Administration's view of the situation as follows:

This special report presents definitive evidence of the clandestine military support given by the Soviet Union, Cuba, and their Communist allies to Marxist-Leninist guerrillas now fighting to overthrow the established Government of El Salvador. The evidence, drawn from captured guerrilla documents and war material and corroborated by intelligence reports, underscores the central role played by Cuba and other Communist countries beginning in 1979 in the political unification, military direction, and arming of insurgent forces in El Salvador.

From the documents it is possible to reconstruct chronologically the key stages in the growth of the Communist involvement:

- The direct tutelary role played by Fidel Castro and the Cuban Government in late 1979 and early 1980 in bringing the diverse Salvadoran guerrilla factions into a unified front;
- The series of contacts between Salvadoran Communist leaders and key officials of several Communist states that resulted in commitments to supply the insurgents nearly 800 tons of the most modern weapons and equipment;
- The covert delivery to El Salvador of nearly 200 tons of those arms, mostly through Cuba and Nicaragua, in preparation for the guerrillas' failed "general offensive" of January 1981;
- The major Communist effort to "cover" their involvement by providing mostly arms of Western manufacture.

It is clear that over the past year the insurgency in El Salvador has been progressively transformed into another case of indirect armed aggression against a small Third World country by Communist powers acting through Cuba.

The United States considers it of great importance that the American people and the world community be aware of the gravity of the actions of Cuba, the Soviet Union, and other Communist states who are carrying out what is clearly shown to be a well-coordinated, covert effort to bring about the overthrow of El Salvador's established government and to impose in its place a Communist regime with no popular support.[41]

Substantial doubts about the accuracy of many of the assertions in the paper were raised by reports in major American newspapers.[42] The State Department announced on March 2 that it was sending another $20 million in emergency funds (again bypassing Congress under authority granted by Section 506A of the Foreign Assistance Act), as well as asking Congress for a $5 million "re-programming" of military assistance.[43] The funds were to be used for unspecified quantities of ammunition, arms communications equipment, and helicopter support. Documents subsequently released confirmed that the aid included 500-lb bombs, grenade launchers, helicopter gunships, fragmentation grenades and mortars.[44] The announcement coincided with the sending of additional non-combat advisers to El Salvador (see below).

In the spring of 1981, the Reagan Administration asked Congress for an additional $25 million in arms credits and $1 million in training funds for El Salvador for FY 1982 (beginning October 1, 1981). According to the Pentagon, "our security assistance program for FY 1982 is designed to enable the Government to defend itself against the insurgency, curtail the infiltration of arms and men from abroad, and pursue its policies of peaceful change and development. In this context, we are requesting FMS direct credits and guaranteed loans to enable the Salvadoran armed forces to buy transportation equipment, small arms and ammunition, and radar systems, and to upgrade its Navy and Air Force."[45] The FY 1982 request brings total U.S. military assistance to El Salvador since FY 1980 to $62 million, close to four times what the U.S. provided over the previous twenty year period.

In a lengthy letter on May 6, 1981, Amnesty International's Secretary General Thomas Hammarberg wrote Secretary of State Alexander Haig that "the recent resumption of military assistance to the Salvadoran authorities by the United States has given rise to widespread international concern regarding the impact which that aid is likely to have on the human rights situation in El Salvador, particularly in view of the December, 1980 United Nations General Assembly resolution on El Salvador which called upon governments to refrain from the supply of arms and other military assistance in the current circumstances."[46] The letter detailed human rights abuses against human rights workers, journalists, opposition leaders and supporters, the church, academics, peasants, refugees, the wounded, medical personnel and first aid workers, and the young, and concluded that

available information suggests unequivocally that all branches of the Salvadoran security forces, whether nominally military, military police, or paramilitary, have been implicated in human rights violations which have occurred on such a scale that they constitute a gross and consistent pattern of human rights abuses.[47]

Amnesty received a response on June 4, 1981 from Deputy Secretary of State William P. Clark, Jr. which played down official Salvadoran government participation in human rights violations, stating that "the tragic violence occurring in El Salvador emanates from a variety of sources, including leftist guerrilla and terrorist groups and rightist civilian death squads. As you have correctly pointed out in your letter, individuals within the Salvadoran security forces have also been identified at times with unwarranted violence. Your letter, however, focuses on only one component of a larger complex problem."[48]

1. *U.S. military personnel in El Salvador*

Mobile Training Teams (MTT's) are groups of U.S. military personnel assigned to foreign countries for training purposes. They are considered different from military advisers in that MTT's do not accompany foreign troops on military operations, and are not supposed to help plan, coordinate, or otherwise advise foreign military personnel in the performance of defensive or offensive combat operations. The United States currently has military personnel in the form of Mobile Training Teams, Technical Assistance Teams, and Technical Assistance Field Teams in scores of countries around the globe. In the vast majority of cases, these U.S. personnel are not in areas where there is generalized armed conflict, as is the case in El Salvador. U.S. military training personnel—beyond the Marine Guards and military mission stationed at the U.S. Embassy in San Salvador—were first introduced into El Salvador in November, 1979, one month after the coup that toppled the Romero government. A four-man team of U.S. Army specialists trained Salvadoran troops in non-lethal methods of riot control.[49]

In the late summer and fall of 1980, four other U.S. teams went to El Salvador, for periods of about a month each, to assist in the repair and maintenance of communications equipment and wheeled vehicles (trucks, jeeps, etc.), to survey the weapons needs of the Salvadoran Army, and to "implement a signal and motor maintenance support system."[50] The presence of these two latter teams in El Salvador was not affected by the "hold" on U.S. military assistance following the deaths of the four U.S. churchwomen in December, 1980.

In early January, 1981, in its last weeks in office, the

Carter Administration began to increase the number of military personnel in El Salvador. On January 7, an Operational and Planning Assistance Team (OPAT) arrived to provide assistance, in the words of one Pentagon official, on "how to protect the harvest against guerrillas."[51] Fourteen personnel to provide pilot training and maintenance of the six UH-1H helicopters leased to El Salvador arrived by late January. By the time the Carter Administration left office, nineteen U.S. training personnel were in El Salvador.[52]

Former U.S. Ambassador to El Salvador Robert White testified before Congress in February, 1981, that during these final days of the Carter term, U.S. Military Group Commander Col. Eldon Cummings, came to him with a message to be sent to Washington advocating the placement of seventy-five U.S. advisers in the field. White refused to send the message, maintaining that it "would totally change U.S. policy on the eve of a new Administration."[53]

On March 2, 1981, the Reagan Administration announced that it was sending additional teams to El Salvador to "train Salvadoran personnel in communications, intelligence, logistics, and in other professional skills designed to improve their capabilities to interdict infiltration and to respond to terrorist attacks."[54] As of mid-March, fifty-six U.S. military personnel were in El Salvador performing the following functions:[55]

6   Staff of U.S. Military Group at the Embassy in San Salvador (raised from a level of 4), to serve as a liaison with the Salvadoran armed forces and gather military intelligence;

14   training in the use and maintenance of helicopters;

6   naval training team to "assist the Salvadoran Navy in improving its capability to interdict seaborne infiltra-

tion of arms destined for the leftist guerrillas[56] and to survey the need for upgrading and refurbishing Salvadoran patrol boats and provide training in the maintenance of boats and other naval equipment." The team left the port of La Union in mid-April, and was subsequently replaced by a smaller team of three.

5   augment the Military Group for administrative and logistics purposes related to the presence of additional U.S. personnel;

5   Operational and Planning Assistance Team (OPAT) to assist each of El Salvador's five regional commands in the planning and improvement of intelligence, communications, and logistics, and to serve as a liaison between regional and national commands;

5   Operational Planning and Assistance Team to work with senior Army commanders at the headquarters in San Salvador to establish communications links and coordination between army units in the five military districts;

15   three small unit training teams of five men each to "provide in-garrison training for the Salvadoran's new quick-reaction force"[57] The fifteen are counterinsurgency specialists from the Special Forces. They provide training in patrolling, air mobile operations, individual soldier skills, and counter-guerrilla operations. The "quick reaction force"—named the Atlacatl Battalion after a Salvadoran Indian chief—involves an infantry unit of 2000 men supported by helicopters for rapid mobility to points of conflict.

As of July 24, 1981, one Operational Planning Assistance Team and all of the helicopter trainers had ended their tours of duty in El Salvador.[58] The Pentagon indicated in late July, however, that four medics and two specialists in helicopter security would be arriving in early August.[59]

In response to a lawsuit undertaken by the Center for Constitutional Rights in New York on behalf of 27 members of Congress, Lt. Gen. Ernest Graves declared (Defendant's Exhibit 8) that:

> at no time have United States military training personnel participated in or accompanied Salvadoran forces during offensive operations against insurgent forces. At no time have personnel from these training teams participated in the coordination and /or planning of combat operations for Salvadoran armed forces.[60]

According to accounts in the U.S. press however:

> The five-man team of communications intelligence and logistics specialists is teaching Salvadorans how to gather reports of guerrilla activity, evaluate them and coordinate military responses. Before the war room was set up, there was no central coordination for the Salvadoran army, national guard, national police, and rural police, all of which are involved in anti-guerrilla operations.[61]

2. *The use of U.S. military equipment and training*

In late June, 1981, Col. Orlando Rodriguez retired from his post as military attache at the U.S. Embassy in San Salvador. "It is very difficult to say farewell," he told his Salvadoran military colleagues, "when the blood of our brothers in arms stains red the fields of a nation that refuses to be subjugated by international communism."

"Made brothers by the cause," he continued, "we defend the same ideals of democracy and struggle against a common enemy: communism . . . we say farewell to you with a military salute of profound admiration and respect."[62]

The close relationship between the U.S. and Salvadoran

military establishments raises profound questions over the responsibility the United States may bear for human rights violations committed by the Salvadoran armed forces. At the simplest level, merely by providing unconditional assistance and advisory support to El Salvador, it would appear that the United States is associated with violence in that country. This was expressed by former U.S. Ambassador to El Salvador Robert White, in hearings before the House Appropriations Subcommittee on Foreign Operations on February 25, 1981:

As the civilian responsible for the implementation of United States foreign policy in El Salvador over the past year, I would be at a loss as to how to define the mission of military advisers in El Salvador. You know, the security forces in El Salvador have been responsible for the deaths of thousands of young people, and they have executed them on the mere suspicion that they are leftist or sympathize with leftists. Are we really going to send military advisers in there to be part of that type of machinery?"[63]

Three U.S. Congresspersons who visited Central America in January, 1981, expressed a similar view:

We believe very strongly, on the basis of our own conversations with refugees, and after consultation with others genuinely familiar with the recent history of El Salvador, that by far the greatest responsibility for violence and terrorism rests with those forces now receiving U.S. guns, helicopters, grenades and ammunition.[64]

While it is often difficult to ascertain the use of U.S. military supplies in particular incidents where human rights have been violated, it is clear that U.S. equipment is being employed by the Salvadoran armed forces in their conduct of war. Before the Salvadoran left's general offensive of January 1981, approximately half of the $5.7 million in aid approved in April 1980, had been delivered.[65]

Later, U.S. officials reported that despite emergency provisions of additional military aid, the Salvadoran military put down the offensive "without a single U.S. bullet."[66]

Subsequent U.S. shipments, however, replenished drawn-down Salvadoran stocks, and U.S. aid currently serves as the principle source of weapons for the Salvadoran armed forces. By the Pentagon's own assessment in February 1981, U.S. military aid to El Salvador was crucial because the armed forces were "not organized to fight a counterinsurgency war," and because they had "no hope" of defeating the guerrillas with existing resources.[67]

According to the pro-government Salvadoran daily *El Diario de Hoy* on March 17, 1981,

The army has begun to use the new weapons received from the United States in its struggle against local and international terrorists, according to statements made by military sources. . . . It has been stated that the most intensive operations being carried out by the army have taken place in Morazan Department. Most soldiers are reportedly engaged in that battle and, according to reports, they are using the new weapons and helicopters that the armed forces have received from the United States.[68]

Similarly, *El Diario de Hoy* reported that

At present the U.S. military advisers are training a special combat company which will go into action as soon as it is ready. The company will fight in a second phase of the military offensive that has been prepared.[69]

Reports in the U.S. and foreign press and subsequent conversations with the journalists involved have served to develop the link between U.S. equipment and training and the actions of Salvadoran government troops:

The young recruit with the new American M-16 rifle talked excitedly about the training he and other members of El Salvador's Atlacatl rapid reaction battalion are getting from U.S. Special Forces advisers here about 20 miles west of the capital. "It's much better than what we had before," he said. "Right now we are learning how to set up ambushes."

—The Washington Post, June 7, 1981

An elite Salvadoran Army unit trained by United States military advisers is engaged in a major operation in the mountains surrounding this isolated village about 42 miles northeast of the capital. For the last three days, about 1200 soldiers of the Atlacatl Battalion, El Salvador's rapid reaction force, have been taking part in sporadic and sometimes heavy combat in the densely forested mountains with leftist guerrillas. Residents in Cinquera pointed to the hills, where they said explosives had been dropped from United States-supplied helicopters. Jet fighters flew low over the hills.

—The New York Times, July 8, 1981

Combat troops trained by United States military advisers here are conducting search-and-destroy missions in the densely forested mountains against guerrilla units of the Farabundo Marti National Liberation Front. American-supplied transport trucks ferry troops across rivers where bridges have been blown up and helicopters supplied and maintained by the United States allow El Salvador's army to respond more quickly when patrols are attacked as they have been with increasing frequency in the last few weeks.

—The New York Times, July 13, 1981

According to a congressional staff aide who visited Central America in January, 1981, "there is no question that U.S.-trained soldiers are involved in search and destroy missions in the north of El Salvador."[70] No direct evidence has yet come to light, however, indicating that U.S. instructors are training Salvadoran troops in such missions, or other techniques—the razing of villages, the burning of crops—that have led to widespread human rights violations. However, Salvadoran officers themselves have described their military strategy as follows: "The subversives like to say that they are the fish and the people are the ocean. What we have done in the north is to dry up the ocean so we can catch the fish easily."[71] According to a U.S. congressional delegation, "the Salvadoran method of 'drying up the ocean' is to eliminate entire villages from the map, to isolate the guerrillas, and deny them any rural base off which they can feed."[72] Because U.S. counterinsurgency experts train Salvadoran troops alleged to be carrying out such missions, there is a high probability that U.S. personnel know of, and at some level condone, if not encourage such practices. Moreover, two U.S. Operational Planning Assistance Teams have been working with local and national Salvadoran commanders in overall skills relating to the planning and coordination of the war effort. Given this high level and in-the-field contact (see previous section), it is again unlikely that U.S. officials are unaware of tactics used by their Salvadoran counterparts, even if the United States does not directly promote such activities.

In mid-April 1981, London *Sunday Times* reporter David Blundy filed cables from Tegucigalpa, Honduras, based on conversations with Honduran Army officers, stating that U.S. military officers had met with Salvadoran and Honduran officers and

pressed for more cooperation between Honduras and El Salvador to counter the guerrillas who were using, the Americans claimed, Honduras as a safe base. "It is necessary to fight the guerrillas together," the Americans insisted. . . . According to the Honduran sources, this meeting was followed by several others in Honduras, Salvador, and Miami where the U.S. had the same message—combined operations were the only solution.[73]

The State Department has denied that such meetings ever took place. When Blundy double-checked with his Honduran sources, however, they reiterated that the above account was true.

On several occasions, Salvadoran and Honduran troops have cooperated in operations that resulted in the deaths of hundreds of Salvadoran refugees fleeing heavy fighting in El Salvador's northern provinces.

Moreover, according to one U.S. refugee worker who witnessed the crossing at the Rio Lempa, "a Salvadoran helicopter, with mounted machine gun, had passed over to the Honduran side . . . the helicopter returned . . . riveting the river up and down, both shores, with machine gun fire, and then dropped some kind of mortar into the rocky banks."[74] Said U.S. priest Father Earl Gallagher, another witness, "that was my tax money paying for American bombs to drop from American helicopters on my head."[75]

On July 17–18, 1981, several hundred Salvadoran troops using U.S. UH-1H helicopters crossed into Honduras during a "pincer operation" to root out Salvadoran guerrillas believed to be operating in the border zone. The incursion—involving helicopter pilots trained by U.S. instructors—was formally protested by the Honduran Foreign Ministry on July 27, 1981.[76] *Boston Globe* reporter Steven Kinzer, who witnessed and photographed the incident, stated later that "there is no doubt that United States helicopters were used in the operation."[77]

In March 1980, the Carter Administration, when asking Congress for $5.7 million in military aid to El Salvador, said "we would promptly reassess our policy if there were evidence that our assistance was not being used to enhance human rights in El Salvador."[78] This year, the Reagan Administration told Congress that security assistance, in addition to "enabling the Government to defend itself against the insurgency," would help El Salvador "pursue its policies of peaceful change and development."[79] The response of former Ambassador to El Salvador, Robert White, to a question by U.S. Representative

Matt McHugh, in a recent congressional hearing, brings a substantially different perspective to the situation:

McHUGH: My first question would be whether there is any evidence that, after a year, that the government has indeed become less repressive, that those proponents of reform within the government who we support have had any success whatsoever in reducing the indiscriminate killing, which most reasonable people agree has been conducted by the government we are supporting?

WHITE: Very little. . . . I have to tell you that of all the objectives we have set ourselves in El Salvador, this is the one on which we have made the least progress. . . .[80]

CHAPTER 13

LEGAL RESTRICTIONS ON U.S. INVOLVEMENT ABROAD

This chapter discusses legislation restricting the U.S. executive branch in its conduct of foreign relations that is relevant to U.S. involvement in El Salvador. Specifically, it reviews the legislation linking human rights with U.S. foreign assistance programs, its over-sight provisions, and the War Powers Resolution, which restricts the power of the executive branch to commit U.S. armed forces abroad.

A. *The constitutional role of the Executive and Legislative Branches in the conduct of foreign affairs*

The Constitution confers on both the President and Congress specific powers in the area of foreign affairs. This division of authority, and the failure of the Constitution specifically to confer general authority over foreign affairs to either branch of government, has resulted in historical controversy over the respective roles of each branch.

The specific powers given to the President are limited:

• The Power, by and with the Advice and Consent of the Senate, to make Treaties (Article 2, section 2);

- to appoint Ambassadors, other Public Ministers and Consuls (Article 2, section 2);
- to receive Ambassadors and other public Ministers (Article 2, section 3);
- to act as Commander-in-Chief of the Army and Navy of the United States (Article 2, section 2).

Despite the limited nature of the specific powers granted to the President, judicial interpretation and actual practice attribute to the President "plenary" powers in foreign affairs, limited, of course, by the prohibitions applicable to all acts of government and by implications in grants to Congress.[1]

The Constitutional grants of legislative power that give Congress authority in foreign affairs include the following:

- To regulate Commerce with foreign Nations, and among the several States, and with the Indian tribes (Article 1, section 8, clause 3);
- To define and punish Piracies and Felonies committed on the high Seas, and Offences against the Law of Nations (Article 1, section 8, clause 10);
- To declare War, . . . and make Rules concerning Captures on Land and Water (Article 1, section 8, clause 11).

Congress also has general powers that are indispensable to the conduct of foreign relations, *e.g.,* to tax and to spend for the common defense and the general welfare,[2] to do what is "necessary and proper" to carry out other powers[3] and to appropriate funds from the Treasury.[4]

One commentator has suggested that Congress' foreign commerce power, like its domestic commerce power, can be stretched "to support virtually any legislation that relates to foreign intercourse, *i.e.,* to foreign relations."[5] Thus, because of the concurrent, constitutional authority of both the executive and legislative branches in the area of foreign affairs, the actual division of authority has historically fluctuated between the two branches according to their relative strengths and the circumstances of the time.

The legislation discussed in this chapter was enacted in the Vietnam War/Watergate era, when Congress took unprecedented steps to carve itself a bigger role in the development of U.S. foreign policy. Because the President has general and specific authority to act independently in regard to most of the matters that are the subject of the legislation, the effective implementation of the legislation depends to a large extent on the legislative branch's continuing belief in it; the enforcement role of the courts is uncertain.

B. *U.S. legislation linking foreign assistance with human rights*

Beginning in the early 1970s, Congress enacted laws that condition U.S. foreign assistance and international trade and investment incentives on the human rights record of the recipient country.[6] These human rights conditions affect most forms of U.S. foreign assistance. However, given the particular concern in this report for the human rights consequences of providing military assistance to El Salvador, this section only discusses laws governing the security assistance program.

The purpose of attaching human rights conditions to foreign assistance programs is stated in Section 502B(a)(1)[7] of the Foreign Assitance Act of 1961. Recalling United States obligations under the U.N. Charter to promote human rights, Section 502(b)(a)(1) proclaims:

. . . a principal goal of the foreign policy of the United States shall be to promote the increased observance of internationally recognized human rights by all countries.

Most of the legislation linking human rights and foreign assistance follows the format of prohibiting the executive branch from providing a particular type of assistance to any country, "the government of which engages in a consistent pattern of gross violations of internationally recognized human rights." All the legislation containing this prohibition qualifies it with an exception clause allowing the executive branch to waive the prohibition under broadly specified circumstances. Finally, most of the legislation includes reporting requirements through which Congress can oversee implementation.

1. *Section 502B of the Foreign Assistance Act: substantive criteria*

Section 502B, enacted in 1974, links human rights and security assistance with the following prohibition:

No security assistance may be provided to any country the government of which engages in a consistent pattern of gross violations of internationally recognized human rights.[8]

Section 502B defines "security assistance",[9] and thus extends the human rights mandate, to include all *U.S. governmental programs* normally considered to constitute security assistance. These include:

- The Military Assistance Program (MAP),[10] under which the United States provides outright grants or loans to foreign countries of military equipment, facilities, technical assistance, repair and rehabilitations, supply operations support, and administrative support.
- The International Military Education and Training Program (IMET)[11] under which training is provided foreign military personnel on a grant basis.
- The Foreign Military Sales financing program (FMS financing)[12] under which credits and loan repayment guarantees are provided foreign governments for the purchase of defense articles, services and training.
- The Economic Support Fund (ESF),[13] under which budgetary

support (in cash form) is provided countries on a grant or loan basis.

Section 502B also defines security assistance to include the *commercial* export of all items legally classified as "defense items and services" and on the Munitions List.[14] Export of any item on the Munitions List requires a license,[15] thus giving the State Department the regulatory control necessary to implement Section 502B.

Finally, Section 502B applies to items not normally considered "security assistance" but which are known as "crime control and detection instruments and equipment." They are identified in the administrative regulations of the Export Administration Act[16] and include such items as shock batons, thumbscrews, communications equipment, and other items commonly used for internal security and surveillance purposes. Their export requires a special license. A clause in 502B includes a prohibition on the commercial export of such items to countries with poor human rights records:

(L)icenses may not be issued under the Export Administration Act of 1979 for the export of crime control and detection instruments and equipment to a country the government of which engages in a consistent pattern of gross violations of internationally recognized human rights. . . .[17]

Section 502B only applies when the government of a recipient country engages in "a consistent pattern of gross violations of internationally recognized human rights." The "Gross" human rights violations referred to in the legislation are defined to include:

torture or cruel, inhuman, or degrading treatment or punishment, prolonged detention without charges and trial, causing the disappearance of persons by the abduction and clandestine detention of those persons, and other flagrant denial of the right to life, liberty, or the security of persons.[18]

In requiring "a consistent pattern of gross" human rights violations to trigger the application of the statute, Section 502B reiterates the provisions of United Nations Economic and Social Council.

Resolution 1503[19], which authorizes a subsidiary body of the Economic and Social Council to study or investigate "particular situations which appear to reveal a consistent pattern of gross and reliably attested violations of human rights requiring consideration by the Commission."[20] By incorporating the language and standards of Resolution 1503, Section 502B reflects the intent of its drafters to conform the United States security assistance program with the norms of international law.

Finally, the statute is only relevant when the government itself engages in gross human rights violations. Consistent with the norms of the international legal system, the State Department, in private correspondence, has stated that government engagement occurs when the highest political officials of a foreign government "deliberately engage in or *tolerate abuse* (perpetrated by outside forces)."[21] (emphasis added)

The Carter Administration however, reduced assistance to various countries on human rights grounds without formally identifying them as gross and consistent violators. This approach was designed to minimize the potentially serious diplomatic repercussions of the human rights policy and to avert protracted interdepartmental conflicts over whether a particular country should be so identified. Thus, although El Salvador prior to 1979 was not formally designated as a gross and consistent human rights violator, security assistance was substantially reduced in fiscal years 1978 and 1979.[22]

The exception clause of Section 502B is very broad. It allows the executive branch to disregard the human rights prohibition in cases in which "extraordinary circumstances" warrant the provision of security assistance in spite of egregious human rights conditions in the recipient country.[23] Nothing in the language or in the legislative history of Section 502B serves to narrow the meaning of the "extraordinary circumstances" clause.[24]

2. *Section 502B of the Foreign Assistance Act: congressional oversight*

Section 502B contains several mechanisms by which Congress can oversee implementation.

a. *The country reports*

Section 502B(b) requires the Secretary of State to submit annual reports on the human rights conditions in countries proposed as recipients of security assistance.[25] Such reports are also required by Section 116,[26] which applies to the economic assistance program, but this second requirement applies to all countries that are members of the U.N. To comply, the State Department publishes one annual compilation of human rights reports, known as the Country Reports.

b. *Certification of compliance*

A certification to Congress of the extraordinary circumstances justifying assistance must be supplied:

- When "security assistance (is) provided to the police, domestic intelligence, or similar law enforcement forces of a country . . . the government of which engages in a consistent pattern of gross violations of internationally recognized human rights . . ."[27]
- When "licenses (are) issued under the Export Administration Act of 1979 for the export of crime control and detection instruments and equipment to a country, the government of which engages in a consistent pattern of gross violations of internationally recognized human rights . . ."[28]
- When International Military Education and Training assist-

ance is provided "to a country the government of which engages in a consistent pattern of gross violations of internationally recognized human rights."[29]

The executive branch has interpreted these three provisions to require the following:[30]

* The State Department must certify the existence of extraordinary circumstances *each time* a crime control equipment export license falling within the meaning of Section 502B is approved.[31]
* No individual certifications are required in the other two cases. Rather, to fulfill these requirements the State Department submits one annual certification that mentions no particular country but generally states that the Department is complying with Section 502B.[32]

c. *The resolution of request and congressional veto provisions*

Section 502B(c)[33] prescribes a procedure under which Congress can obtain a statement from the State Department regarding the human rights situation in a particular country, the justification for providing assistance to the country, and any other information deemed appropriate.

This provision requires no more from the State Department than Congress is normally entitled to under its constitutional authority for governmental spending and domestic and international commerce. The provision, however, does underscore the intent of Congress to oversee the implementation of Section 502B and may serve as a formal statement of Congressional skepticism regarding the wisdom and validity of providing assistance to the particular country. The resolution of request has in fact only been used once before the Carter administration when in 1976 the House Foreign Affairs Committee had submitted three, none of which applied to El Salvador.

The provision additionally triggers a mechanism by which Congress can reduce or terminate assistance to a country by passage of a joint resolution.[34] This veto provision of Section 502B(c) adds nothing to Congress' traditional authority to enact legislation because a joint resolution, like any law, requires Presidential signature.

d. *Summary*

While the Country Report requirement and the resolution of request procedure, if it were utilized, ensure that human rights maintain a high visibility in the State Department, the procedures established by Section 502B are limited in their usefulness for Congressional oversight and enforcement purposes. In the absence of an effective Congressional veto provision, such as a concurrent resolution clause, Section 502B fails to provide Congress a mechanism by which it can implement the legislation in the event of executive resistance. However, as the following section discusses, Congress has other, more traditional methods by which it can achieve the same purpose.

3. *Congressional oversight and enforcement procedures other than those provided for in Section 502B*

a. *The annual foreign assistance authorization and appropriation process*

Congress is most active in overseeing implementation of Section 502B during the annual process in which the foreign assistance authorization bill is prepared and enacted. At this time, Congress has before it the Country Reports on human rights and a compilation of proposed security assistance programs for the coming fiscal year. When the authorizing bill is passed, the executive branch is bound by the proposed levels of assistance presented to Congress,[35] unless Congress modifies those levels either in the authorization bill itself or in the conference reports accompanying the bill.

Thus, the annual foreign assistance authorization process sets the pattern for the assistance to be provided to a country throughout the year. Several committees attempt to incorporate human rights into the mold in the following ways:

—Where assistance is proposed for a country with a bad human rights record, committee members question administration officials regarding the purpose of the assistance and the human rights situation in the particular country. The House Subcommittee on Human Rights and International Organizations, and others, frequently hold hearings in which human rights groups testify regarding the human rights situations abroad and the impact of U.S. aid on that assistance. Congressional staff persons and State Department officials believe that the publicity and pressure generated by these hearings, and private correspondence between Congress and the State Department, serve to promote executive compliance with the human rights legislation.

—Congress frequently reduces the security assistance proposed for specific countries in the conference report accompanying the authorization bill. If a concern for human rights is the basis for the reduction, this is normally explicitly stated in the report. These reductions have the effect of law. No such reductions have ever applied to El Salvador.

—Congress may authorize the administration's security assistance proposals but condition them on the executive's certification of an improvement in the human rights situation in the country in question. This is the approach taken in regard to El Salvador in the fiscal year 1982 authorization Act (the text of the language relating to El Salvador is Appendix IV).

After enactment of the authorization act, Congress may also impose conditions on or reductions in the foreign assistance appropriation bills. For example, the appropriation act for FY 1978 prohibited foreign military credit sales to El Salvador.[36]

Beyond the annual authorization and appropriation acts, Congress normally exercises only limited control over the security assistance program. However, pursuant to its powers under the Constitution, Congress, throughout the year, could enact into law any bills related to security assistance. Additionally, Congress could reserve independent authority over the security assistance programs for particular countries by including concurrent resolution veto provisions in the authorization or appropriation acts, but this rarely occurs.

b. *Ongoing oversight mechanisms independent of the President*

Congress has enacted laws that allow it to veto by concurrent resolution the transfer of both governmental and commercial arms.[37] These laws add little to Congress' ability to enforce the human rights mandate of Section 502B, however, because they only apply to the transfer of very expensive and sophisticated weapons.

If the administration reprograms security assistance, *i.e.,* extends more assistance to a country than it proposed in the original budget proposal, it must submit a reprogramming notification to Congress 15 days prior to reprogramming the assistance.[38] Although Congress has no statutory authorization to veto the reprogramming, the appropriation committees of both the Senate and the House traditionally vote to approve or disapprove it.

In response to a reprogramming notification Congress held extensive hearings on the human rights situation in El Salvador in 1980.[39] Requesting and receiving more detailed information on the reprogramming than it regularly received, the appropriation committees voted in favor of the reprogramming. Due to the lack of statutory direction and precedent on the issue, the effect of a vote against the reprogramming is unclear.

4. *Section 660 of the Foreign Assistance Act*

Section 660[40] of the Foreign Assistance Act *absolutely* proscribes the use of security assistance funds *authorized under that act*

to provide training or advice, or provide any financial support, for police, prisons, or other law enforcement forces for any foreign government or any program of internal intelligence or surveillance on behalf of any foreign government within the United States or abroad.[41]

The security assistance programs to which Section 660 applies, *i.e.,* those authorized under the Foreign Assistance Act, include the MAP, IMET, and ESF programs. The FMS program and commercial sales are regulated by the Arms Export Control Act.[42]

Section 660 was motivated by congressional concern that assistance to foreign police under the now defunct Public Safety Program, implicated the United States in human rights violations.

United States participation in the highly sensitive area of public safety and police training unavoidably invites criticism from persons who seek to identify the United States with every act of local police brutality or oppression in any country in which this program operates. It matters little whether the charges can be substantiated, they inevitably stigmatize the total United States foreign aid effort. In undeveloped areas of the world, the costs of public safety programs are better left to be underwritten from local resources and the United States assistance effort directed toward less sensitive areas of social or economic development.

We have troubles enough with police community relations in our own society. The Committee believes that our government's efforts would be better directed to this, and our own crime problem, rather than trying to teach foreigners how to run their police departments.[43]

5. *The emergency and special authority clauses of the Foreign Assistance Act*

There are two special provisions of the Foreign Assistance Act, Section 506[44] and Section 614.[45] Under 614, the President may furnish up to $250 million in any type of security assistance to a country without regard to Sections 502B, 660 or any other provision of the Foreign Assistance or Arms Export Control Acts. Under Section 506, the President, without a prior authorization, may provide foreign countries defense articles and services and military training in an aggregate amount not to exceed $50 million in any fiscal year. This special authority is triggered upon the President's certification that:

(1) an unforeseen emergency exists which requires immediate military assistance to a foreign country or international organization; and

(2) the emergency requirement cannot be met under the authority of the Arms Export Control Act or any other law except Section 506.[46]

The President may only use the drawdown authority of Section 506 upon prior notification to Congress[47], but no special congressional authorization for any particular drawdown is required. Additionally, the President must keep Congress "fully and currently informed" of all drawdowns provided under the emergency provision.[48]

Prior to 1980, the President could provide emergency assistance under Section 506 without regard to the limitations and prohibitions normally applicable to the security assistance programs.[49] Presently, it appears that Section 506 only authorizes an expedited procedure to provide assistance. The provision of the assistance must otherwise conform with law.

On January 16, 1981, President Carter used the emergency authority of Section 506 to provide up to $5 million of assistance to El Salvador. On March 5, 1981, President Reagan used 506 to provide $20 million worth of assistance to the country.

C. *Legislation governing the involvement of U.S. forces abroad*

1. *The War Powers Resolution*

The War Powers Resolution,[50] enacted in 1973, was a direct result of the conflict between the executive and legislative branches over U.S. involvement in Vietnam. By the early 1970's many in Congress were dismayed over the war's continuation in the absence of declaration of war, which, under the Constitution, is an exclusively legislative responsibility.[51] U.S. presidents had been relying on their powers to conduct foreign relations and on their authority as Commander-in-Chief to engage troops in Southeast Asia. Over time, as U.S. military activities turned into full-fledged war, presidents relied on various congressional measures, *i.e.,* the Gulf of Tonkin Resolution and repeated Congressional appropriations, to argue, that Congress had conferred the necessary approval.[52]

Thus, without a declaration of war but with regular congressional appropriations in support of the war effort, debate over the continuation of the conflict was at a constitutional impasse. One constitutional lawyer writes that "a clear resolution (to end the war) would have bound the President and he could not have properly insisted on prosecuting the war thereafter."[53] Congress was unable to muster the votes necessary for such a resolution.

In attempting to prescribe when the engagement of U.S. troops abroad requires affirmative Congressional approval, the War Powers Resolution states that without Congressional approval within a specified time period, U.S. troop engagement must terminate. Thus, it reverses the Vietnam situation, in which affirmative Congressional action was necessary to terminate, rather than to authorize the continuation of, the involvement.

The War Powers Resolution requires the President, *in every possible instance,* to consult with Congress before introducing U.S. armed forces "into hostilities or into situations where imminent involvement in hostilities is clearly indicated by the circumstances."[54]

The statute requires the President to report to the Congress within 48 hours of introducing U.S. forces "into hostilities or into situations where imminent involvement in hostilities is clearly indicated by the circumstances."[55] In the case of protracted U.S. involvement, the President must periodically (no less than every six months) report to Congress on the status of the hostilities.[56]

Within sixty days after a report is submitted, *or is required to be submitted under the provision set forth directly above,* the President must terminate any use of U.S. armed forces with respect to which the report was submitted.[57] The three circumstances under which the President need not terminate U.S. engagement include the following:

- Congress has declared war or has enacted a specific authorization for such use of U.S. armed forces;
- Congress has extended by law the sixty-day period;
- Congress is physically unable to meet as a result of an armed attack upon the United States.[58]

Whenever U.S. armed forces are engaged in hostilities outside the territory of the United States, its possessions, or territories without a declaration of war or specific statutory authorization, such forces shall be removed by the President if the Congress so directs by concurrent resolution."[59]

There are two basic issues of fact that must be analyzed to determine whether the War Powers Resolution applies to any particular situation:

a. *Have U.S. armed forces been "introduced" into the situation?*

Before the consultation or reporting provisions of the legislation go into effect, U.S. armed forces must be "introduced" into hostilities or into a situation threatening imminent involvement in hostilities. The term "introduction of United States Armed Forces" is statutorily defined to mean the following:

The assignment of members of such armed forces to command, coordinate, participate in the movement of, or accompany the regular or irregular military forces of any foreign country or government when such military forces are engaged, or there exists an imminent threat that such forces will become engaged, in hostilities.[60]

One aspect of this factual issue turns on the specific functions the U.S. armed forces are serving in the particular situation. The United States regularly stations members of the armed forces in foreign countries to provide technical services and training in connection with the various security assistance programs. Normally, the involvement of armed forces serving in this capacity would not trigger the application of the War Powers Resolution. However, if the armed forces were assigned "to command, co-ordinate, participate in the movement of, or accompany the regular or irregular military forces of any country or government . . .," the War Powers Resolution would apply, provided the other statutory conditions existed.

The second aspect of this factual issue turns on whether the foreign military forces themselves are engaged in hostilities or there exists an immediate threat thereof.

b. *Are the U.S. armed forces introduced into the hostilities or is there an imminent threat that they will become so involved?*

This factual issue turns on the proximity, geographical and strategic, of the U.S. armed forces to the hostilities and the consequent risk that they will actually become involved in them.

A constitutional authority, Louis Henkin, predicted that the War Powers Resolution would have a limited restraining effect on the President's use of American force abroad. Recognizing the lack of a clear constitutional division of authority between the President and Congress in situations short of war, he stated:

(A)lthough the President can use force if Congress is silent, Congress can forbid or regulate even such uses of force, if only on the ground that they might lead to war. *Presidents, however, are likely to deny the control of Congress in such cases.* [61]

In reference to the difficult factual issues presented by the War Powers Resolution, Henkin anticipated a second problem that would limit its effective enforcement:

Whether such legislation would effectively restrain the President is a different question. A President who wished to act could exploit its ambiguities and uncertainties, notably the meaning of "hostilities," and when "imminent involvement" in them is "clearly indicated." [62]

To date, both of the problems raised by Henkin have limited the effect of the War Powers Resolution.

Excluding the situation in El Salvador from consideration, the President, since 1973, has authorized the use of U.S. forces abroad in eight instances in which the War Powers Resolution arguably applied: to evacuate U.S. and other personnel from Danang, Phnom Penh, and Saigon at the end of the Indochina war; to rescue the crew of the Mayaguez; to evacuate U.S. and other civilians during civil strife on Cyprus and in Lebanon; to transport European troops to Shaba province in Zaire during the tribal invasion of that area; and to rescue the American hostages in Iran.[63] Commenting on the implementation of the legislation through 1979, two observers concluded: "In no case has there been anything approximating meaningful consultation. Again the Resolution itself has several large loopholes, and these the Presidents' lawyers have exploited with alacrity. In particular, the law says that the President need only consult 'in every possible instance.' In practice, genuine prior consultation has, somehow, never proven 'possible.' "[64]

Congress received a report containing the information specified in the War Powers Resolution in only four of the eight instances enumerated above.[65] In regard to the Shaba operation, for example, former President Carter failed to report to Congress because, he argued, the operation did not pose a threat of U.S. involvement in the hostilities.[66]

Even in those instances in which reports were submitted, the President added that he was reporting "pursuant to the President's constitutional executive power and his authority as Commander-in-Chief" and as "Chief Executive in the conduct of foreign relations. . . ."[67] In other words, the President refused to concede that the War Powers Resolution altered his full and independent constitutional power to use U.S. force according to his own discretion.

Again excluding the Salvadoran situation, none of the Presidential uses of force extended beyond the War Powers Resolution's sixty-day grace period, nor has Congress ever attempted to use the concurrent resolution procedure to terminate an operation.[68] In regard to El Salvador, the present Administration denies the applicability of the War Powers Resolution to the involvement of U.S. personnel in that country; it argues that they "are not being introduced into hostilities or a situation where their involvement in hostilities is imminent."[69]

2. *Section 21(c) of the Arms Export Control Act*

As noted previously, the War Powers Resolution raises factual issues which are difficult to resolve. In the face of Executive Branch denial, it is practically impossible for Congress to ascertain whether U.S. armed forces abroad are engaged in the activities that trigger the application of the resolution, or whether they are in imminent danger of involvement in hostilities.

Section 21(c)[70] of the Arms Export Control Act, newly enacted in 1980, serves one of the purposes of the War Powers Resolution without raising all of the resolution's difficult factual issues. It prohibits U.S. personnel providing defense services from performing "any duties related to training and advising that may engage United States personnel in combat activities."[71] As does the War Powers Resolution, Section 21(c) requires the President to report to Congress "within 48 hours after the outbreak of significant hostilities involving a country in which United States personnel are performing defense services . . ."[72] The Provision does not totally eliminate the possibility of a controversy over facts because the term "significant hostilities" requires a subjective determination. However, unlike the War Powers Resolution, under this section, the activities of the U.S. personnel and the possibility of their involvement in the hostilities are irrelevant considerations.

The reporting requirement of Section 21(c) fulfills a major aim of the War Powers Resolution, and also provides much of the information necessary to determine whether that resolution applies in any particular case. The report must include:

- the identity of the country in which the significant hostilities are occurring;
- a description of the hostilities;
- the number of members of the United States Armed Forces and the number of United States civilian personnel performing

defense services related to the hostilities, their location, the precise nature of their activities, and the likelihood of their becoming engaged in or endangered by hostilities.[73]

The Reagan Administration has not submitted with regard to El Salvador the report required by Section 21(c).

D. *The use of the courts to enforce Section 502B, Section 660 and the War Powers Resolution*

No court has ever considered and decided a case arising under any of the legislation discussed above. In a case currently pending in the D.C. District Court[74], however, several Members of Congress have invoked two of these statutes, Section 502B and the War Powers Resolution, as the law supporting their request for the court to direct the defendants, President Reagan, Secretary of Defense Weinberger, and Secretary of State Haig, to "withdraw all United States Armed Forces, weapons, military equipment and aid from El Salvador and (to prohibit) any further aid of any nature."[75] In addition to Section 502B and the War Powers Resolution, plaintiffs have invoked Article 2, Section 8, Clause 11 of the U.S. Constitution, which gives to Congress the power to declare war, and several treaties and other sources of international law.

The defendants have raised two issues to support their motion to dismiss the suit. First, the defendants argue that the plaintiffs have no standing to bring the suit because the defendants' actions cause them no injury and because the law upon which they rely affords no private right of action. Second, the defendants argue that the suit should be dismissed because the issues raised are nonjusticiable under the political question doctrine.

There has been no ruling on the defendants' motion to dismiss.

APPENDICES

APPENDICES CONTENTS

APPENDIX I

SALVADORAN LEGISLATION RELATING TO HUMAN RIGHTS.

This appendix is divided in three sections: the first analyzes Salvadoran legislation concerning human rights adopted before the October 15, 1979 overthrow of President Romero. The second section deals with those laws adopted by the Revolutionary Governing Junta since the coup, which directly or indirectly affect civil, political, economic and social rights. The final section discusses the international treaties, conventions, covenants, declarations, etc. relating to human rights which El Salvador has either ratified or signed.

A. *Legislation adopted before October 15, 1979*
  1. *A brief constitutional history of El Salvador*

Throughout the republican history of El Salvador there have been reforms, derogations, and enactments of numerous constitutions. Of these, however, there have been two basic charters: the constitutions of 1886 and of 1950.

The Constitution of 1886, proclaimed by President Francisco Menendez, found its political inspiration in the Constitutions of the United States and France and its economic philosophy in the traditional laissez-faire doctrine of the epoch. This classic liberal charter, which lasted until 1939, steered El Salvador through the development and consolidation of a plantation economy, based on coffee, sugar and cotton, and its insertion into the world market.

After seven years in power, General Maximiliano Hernandez Martinez adopted in 1939 a new constitution which lasted until his overthrow in 1944. The new constitution was basically a copy of the 1886 charter, except for some functional reforms aimed at modernizing public administration and amending the prohibition barring General Martinez's reelection. In 1944 he sought to continue in power and again changed the constitutional provision relating to reelection, but he was overthrown before elections were held. The first measure taken by the new authorities was to restore the Constitution of 1886 while maintaining the reforms.

In order to return to a *de jure* constitutional order, a constituent assembly was elected in 1945. The constitution proclaimed that year was again the same as that of 1886 with a few amendments in matters of public administration. However, its application was quite limited since President Castaneda maintained a state of siege throughout his three years in office. On December 14, 1948 President Castaneda was removed from office and the Revolutionary Council that was established scheduled elections for March of 1950.

The Constituent Assembly elected that month enacted a new constitution which, at least in theory, marked a great departure from the previous economic orientation of the Salvadoran state. The charter adopted the then-prevailing concept of the socio-economic responsibility of the state towards its people. It rejected laissez-faire and postulated an active role by the state in promoting the well-being of the population. At the same time civil and political rights whose roots could be found in the 1886 Constitution were considerably enlarged.[1]

Constitutional order was broken by the coup of October 26, 1960 that set up a military-civilian Governing Junta and again on January 25, 1961 by the successful military revolt which led to the establishment of the Civil-Military Directorate. A constituent assembly was elected in that year to return the country to a regular constitutional order.

The Constitution proclaimed on January 8, 1962, which is still partially in force today, is a direct descendant of the one adopted in 1950. The only significant change that was introduced was the reduction of the presidential term of office from six to five years.

2. *The 1962 Constitution of El Salvador*[2]

Although after the coup of October 15, 1979, the Revolutionary Governing Junta originally upheld the validity of the Constitution of 1962, the Junta eventually proceeded to emasculate it by stripping away some of its fundamental precepts and, in particular, by creating a state of "constitutional uncertainty" with the adoption of Decree No. 114.

Therefore, to understand the legal order that exists in El Salvador today one must begin with a general outline of the Constitution.

a. *The State and its form of government*

The Constitution proclaims that El Salvador is a sovereign state and that sovereignty resides in the people and is limited to what is honest, just, and advantageous to society (Article 1).[3] The government is republican, democratic and representative (Article 3), composed of three branches: legislative, executive and judicial (Article 4).

The principle that a president cannot succeed himself *(alternabilidad)* is declared indispensable and violation of this rule makes insurrection an obligation (Article 5). The right of the people to insurrection is recognized, limited in its effects to the removal, as necessary, of officials of the executive branch (Article 7).

Legislative power is vested in a unicameral Legislative Assembly (Article 36), composed of members elected every two years (Article 40).

Executive power is exercised by the President of the Republic and the ministers and under-secretaries of state (Article 62). The president is elected by universal suffrage for a term of five years and may not be reelected (Articles 5, 6, 24, 28, 29, 31, 63). The President is commander-in-chief of the armed forces (Article 70).

The President appoints and removes ministers and undersecretaries of state (Article 72). The executive power must maintain the sovereignty and integrity of the Republic; preserve peace and domestic tranquility; sanction and promulgate the laws; conduct foreign affairs; make appointments; direct the armed forces and the public security corps; confer military ranks; enter into international treaties and conventions, submit them to the Legislative Assembly for ratification, and see that they are enforced; suspend and reestablish with approval of the Council of Ministers, the constitutional guarantees to which Article 175 of the Constitution refers, if the Assembly is adjourned (Article 78).

Judicial power is vested in the Supreme Court of Justice, composed of ten magistrates and the courts of second instance (appellate courts) and other tribunals established by law (Article 81, 82). The judges of the Supreme and appellate courts are elected by the Legislative Assembly and the judges of lower courts are appointed by the Supreme Court, all for a term of three years (Articles 47:8, 89:8, 91).

The Supreme Court has the duty, *inter alia,* of hearing cases of *amparo* (Article 89:1). (The writ of amparo is a remedy meant to block and redress acts or omissions of any authority or official of the State which violate the constitutional right of an individual or otherwise obstruct or limit its exercise.) The courts have the power to declare inapplicable any law or order that is contrary to the Constitution, and significantly the Supreme Court has exclusive jurisdiction to declare unconstitutional laws, decrees or regulations on the petition of any citizen (Articles 95, 96).

Public officials and employees are in the service of the state and the law shall regulate the civil service (Articles 108, 109). Strikes by public officials or employees, as well as the collective abandonment of positions, are prohibited. The civil public service may be militarized only in the event of a national emergency (Article 110).

The armed forces are established to protect the integrity of the territory and the sovereignty of the republic, enforce the law, maintain public order, and guarantee constitutional rights. They shall especially see that *alternabilidad,* the principle that the president of the republic cannot succeed himself, is not violated (Article 112). Military service is compulsory for all Salvadorans from eighteen to thirty years of age. However, in the event of war, all Salvadorans from eighteen to sixty years of age are soldiers, and if this class becomes exhausted, all Salvadorans capable of performing military service. The permanent strength of the Army shall be fixed annually by the Legislative Assembly, but in no case shall it be less than 3,000 men (Article 113). The armed forces are to be nonpolitical and essentially obedient, and may not deliberate on service matters (Article 114). Decisions of the courts martial may be appealed in last instance, before the commander-in-chief of the armed forces (i.e., the President) or before the respective chief of operations in the field. There shall be special tribunals and procedures for the trial of military offenses (Article 116), as regulated by the Code of Military Justice (described below).

b. *Individual and social rights*

Titles X and XI (Articles 150 through 209) of the Constitution define individual and social rights and establish the means to guarantee them. Individual rights include: equality before the law, freedom, asylum, the prohibition of extraditing Salvadorans and foreigners accused of political offenses, freedom of movement and residence. In addition, Salvadorans may neither be expatriated nor forbidden entry to the country (Articles 150–154). The Constitution protects human dignity and freedom, and freedom of conscience and religion, but neither the clergy nor laymen may engage in political propaganda of any kind based on religious motives or making use of the religious beliefs of the people. Likewise, the laws of the state, its government or public officials may not be criticized in religious rites or sermons in places of worship. Freedom of thought and expression, inviolability of correspondence, and the right of petition are also protected (Articles 155–162). The right to protection in the preservation and defense of life, honor, liberty, labor, property and possessions is recognized (Articles 163–164). The right to justice and due process of law is guaranteed, as well as the right of *habeas corpus.* The home is recognized as inviolable. Arbitrary detention is forbidden as is the retroactive application of laws (Articles 165–172). The Constitution also recognizes the right to dispose of property and the freedom to enter into contracts (Articles 173, 174).

c. *Economic rights*

The Constitution states that the economic system must be based essentially on principles of social justice that will ensure to all inhabitants of the country the livelihood of a dignified human being (Article 135). The State is responsible for promoting and protecting private enterprise, and private property as a social function is recognized and guaranteed (Articles 136, 137). Property may be expropriated for reasons of legally proven public utility or social interest, and after fair compensation. If the expropriation is caused by the necessities of war or public disaster or if it is for the purpose of supplying water or electric power, or for the construction of housing or roads, compensation need not be made in advance. Whenever justifiable, the amount of compensation fixed for expropriated property, in accordance with the preceding paragraph, may be paid in installments over a period not to exceed twenty years. Confiscation of property is prohibited, either as a penalty or on any other grounds (Article 138).

The state is responsible for directing monetary policy (Article 143). It may administer enterprises that render essential services to the community, for the purpose of maintaining continuity of service, if the owners or operators refuse to abide by legal provisions governing their economic and social organizations (Article 144). It is also directed to promote the development of small rural property holdings and provide small farmers with facilities for technical assistance, credit, and other means necessary for a better utilization of their lands (Article 147). Housing construction is declared to be a matter of social interest and the state is charged with the task of permitting the greatest possible number of Salvadoran families to become homeowners. It is entrusted with the duty of seeing that every farm owner provides a sanitary and comfortable home for his tenants and workers and provides facilities to enable small owners to do so (Article 148).

The chapter on social rights provides for the protection of the family, labor and social security, the right to organize and strike, education (which is free, democratic and obligatory in primary grades), academic freedom and the autonomy of the University, and public health and social assistance (Articles 179–209).

d. *Suspension of Constitutional guarantees*

The Constitution of El Salvador contains detailed provisions for the suspension of specific individual guarantees in emergency situations. In the event of war, invasion, rebellion, sedition, catastrophe, epidemic, or other general disaster, or serious disturbances of the public order, Article 175 provides that certain specified guarantees established in the Constitution may be suspended, except for meetings or assemblies for cultural or industrial purposes. The specific rights that may be suspended are: freedom of movement and residence (Article 154); freedom of thought and expression (Article 158, paragraph one); inviolability of correspondence (Article 159); and the right of assembly (Article 160). Such suspension may be put in effect in the whole or a part of the territory of the republic. The Legislative Assembly is invested with the power to decree the suspension of guarantees (Articles 47:27, and 176), but if it is in recess, the executive power, on the advice of the Council of Ministers, may decree the suspension of guarantees. Such a decree shall include by implication, the convocation of the Assembly within the next forty-eight hours to approve or disapprove the decree (Articles 78:17 and 176).

The second paragraph of Article 175 limits the period that constitutional guarantees may be suspended to no more than thirty days. However, it adds that when this period has elapsed the suspension may be prolonged for a like period by a new decree, if the circumstances that caused it continue. If such new decree is not issued, the suspended guarantees are thereby legally reestablished. When a suspension of constitutional guarantees has been declared, the military tribunals have jurisdiction in trying cases of treason, espionage, rebellion, sedition, and other offenses against the peace or independence of the state or against the law of nations (Article 177). Whenever the circumstances that gave rise to the suspension of constitutional guarantees no longer exist, the Legislative Assembly must reestablish such guarantees, but if it has adjourned, the executive power shall order their reestablishment (Article 178).

3. *The Organic Law of the Judicial Branch*[4]

The Organic Law of the Judicial Branch enacted in 1953 and later amended determines the structure and organization of the Salvadoran Judiciary. It provides that the Supreme Court shall have final jurisdiction over actions brought to determine the constitutionality of laws, decrees and regulations, and writs of *habeas corpus (recurso de exhibicion personal)* (Article 48:10). The *Amparo* Chamber of the Supreme Court is responsible for deciding writs of *amparo* and actions for unconstitutionality of laws (Article 51). The Supreme Court and the Courts of Appeal *(Camaras de Segunda Instancia)* are entrusted with the task of overseeing the country's prisons (Articles 48:27 and 52:6). One of the more important duties of the state attorneys' for the poor *(procuradores de pobres)* is to visit prisoners once a month, in order to hear their complaints and report them to the pertinent court (Article 85:2). The law also provides that the Supreme Court appoint medical examiners attached to the courts of first instance, who are required to provide all the examinations, analyses and autopsies that are required or requested by judges in criminal matters (Articles 89–92).

4. *The Law of Constitutional Procedures*[5]

The procedures for implementing the right of *habeas corpus* are spelled out in the Law of Constitutional Procedures. This law enacted in 1953 and later amended consolidates the procedures applicable to three fundamental and intimately related institutions of the Salvadoran legal system: actions for testing the constitutionality of laws (Articles 6–11), the writ of *amparo* (Articles 12–37), and the writ of *habeas corpus* (Articles 38–77).

The writ of *habeas corpus* may be invoked in any case in which there is imprisonment, confinement, custody or restriction that is not authorized by the law (Article 40). The remedy may be requested in writing before the Supreme Court of Justice or the appellate courts not sitting in the capital by the person whose freedom is restricted or by any other person. The petition should state, if possible, the type of confinement, imprisonment, or restriction of the detainee, the place of detention, and the person in whose custody he is, requesting that the writ of *habeas corpus* be issued and swearing the truth of the declaration (Article 41). If the arrested person is in the custody of an authority that is not part of the judiciary, the judge may provide that that authority place the person arrested at the disposal of the competent judge and return the writ with a report (Article 48). If the person arrested should be molested with more imprisonment or restrictions than those permitted by the law, or held in solitary confinement against the provisions of the law, the judge may decree that the illegal imprisonment or restrictions be ended and that the writ be returned to the court with a report (Article 57). In the event that the arrested person has been transferred to another place, the authority in whose custody he has been has the duty to inform the judge of the place where he is (Article 60). In any case of disobedience of a writ of *habeas corpus,* the judge must inform the Court. It may request the aid of armed force, placing it at the disposal of the judge so that the person favored may be brought before the Court and the disobedient authority may be apprehended, provided that authority is not a Justice of the Peace, a Judge of First Instance, or a Governor (Article 61). There is no authority, court, or jurisdiction which is privileged, in so far as the writ of *habeas corpus* is concerned. In all cases the writ shall be considered as the foremost guarantee of the security of the individual, regardless of nationality or place of residence (Article 74).

5. *The Code of Criminal Procedure*[6]

The procedures for implementing the constitutional standards applicable to due process and fair trial guarantees are set forth in the 1975 Code of Criminal Procedure ("C.C.P."), as amended in October of 1977.

Article 46, C.C.P., as amended by Article 27(a)–(c) of Decree 381 of October 20, 1977, stipulates that *from the moment of his* capture, the arrested person has the following rights:

- to be informed of the acts imputed to him;
- to call a lawyer or other authorized person to defend him;
- that no method of physical or moral coercion should be used against him; and
- that he not be denied or have restricted the rights and guarantees to which he is entitled as an individual.

If a person is detained in *flagrante delicto* or by a member of an auxiliary organ, i.e., the general administration of the national guard, of the national police, of the treasury agents, of the customs revenue, and of the Income Tax Service (Article 11), the arrested person must be delivered to the competent judge within *seventy-two hours of his capture.*

Article 244 states that when the prisoner is brought before a judge, that judge shall order the prisoner's detention for the initial period of the investigation—a maximum of seventy-two hours. The judge, except where clearly impossible, must take the prisoner's statement no later than *twenty-four hours* from the moment the prisoner is brought before him. Prior to taking his statement, the judge must advise the prisoner of the act(s) imputed to him and of his legal rights which, in addition to those already specified are:

- to be considered innocent until he is declared guilty by official verdict, without prejudice to the measures that the law may establish for reasons of security or public order;
- not to be compelled to testify against himself;
- to name a defender (lawyer) at any time from the start of the procedure; and
- not to have means used against him that would impede his free movement. (Article 46 (1)–(4)).

The judge, in the presence of the prisoner's defense attorney (if he has already named one), will take the prisoner's statement, but *not* under oath. The prisoner and his attorney have the right to read and approve the statement and to make any corrections or clarifications therein (Article 192).

Within *seventy-two hours* of the time the prisoner is brought before him, the judge must decree either his release or provisional arrest. He may issue such an arrest order when he determines that the existence of a crime has been sufficiently proven and that there is sufficient evidence that the accused participated in that crime (Article 247). The judge's arrest order must contain a statement of the facts upon which the order is based and the legal classification of the acts under investigation, in provisional form (Article 248).

The investigation period applicable to crimes punishable by death or imprisonment exceeding three years is 90 days, but may be extended to 120 days (Article 123). The period for investigating crimes punishable by fine or imprisonment less than three years is 45 days (Article 395). At the conclusion of the investigation period, the judge must order the case dismissed or brought to trial.

Standards concerning the admissibility and probative

value of extra-judicial confessions, which are relevant to the fair trial guarantee, are covered in the Code of Criminal Procedure.

Article 496, C.C.P., as amended by Article 40 of Decree 381 of October 20, 1977, provides that in cases of common crimes, any extra-judicial confessions made to agents of the *auxiliary organs* may be considered sufficient evidence for decreeing the suspect's provisional arrest, for bringing the case to trial, and submitting it to the jury, provided the confession meets the following requirements:

a. it was given within seventy-two hours of the time of capture; and
b. it was given before at least two witnesses, who merit the faith of the judge (and who could be members of the auxiliary).

This amended provision also states that in non-jury cases when the out-of-court confession is the only proof of the imputed crime, the judge shall apply the norms of "critical appreciation" ("Reglas de la Sana Critica"). Moreover, in cases of political offenses defined in Article 151 of the Criminal Code[7], an extra-judicial confession cannot have any probative value or be admissible as evidence (Article 496, C.C.P.).

6. *The Code of Military Justice* [8]

As stated earlier, Article 177 of the Constitution provides that when a suspension of constitutional guarantees has been declared, the military tribunals shall have jurisdiction in trying cases of treason, espionage, rebellion, sedition and other offenses against the peace or independence of the state or against the law of nations. Many of the procedures and rights accorded persons under the C.M.J. significantly differ from those applicable to ordinary criminal proceedings. These differences will be noted in the following description of the various stages of military proceedings prior, during, and subsequent to the convening of Special Courts Martial.

a. *The preliminary investigation*

Article 249 provides that only the Minister of Defense may initiate proceedings against civilians suspected of security offenses defined in the Constitution and related laws. He names the military investigation judge ("juez militar de instruccion"), a military officer of at least sublieutenant rank (Article 195), who presides over the preliminary investigation.

If the suspect is being held at a military establishment when the investigation begins, the military investigating judge must order the suspect's continued detention for the initial phase of the investigation—a maximum of *seventy-two* hours (Article 259(3)). Within this period, the judge must notify the suspect of the proceedings and of his right to defend himself or name a lawyer. (The judge will appoint a lawyer within twenty-four hours of notifying the suspect of this right, if the suspect has not acted (Articles 227–259 and 259(3)).

The judge must take the suspect's oral statement within twenty-four hours of the initiation of the preliminary investigation or from the time the suspect was brought before him (Article 260). The suspect has the right to have his lawyer present during the taking of his statement.

These particular procedures and relevant time periods essentially mirror those applicable to normal preliminary investigations under the Code of Criminal Procedure. However, although a suspect in an ordinary criminal proceeding may exercise the constitutional right against self-incrimination by not answering the judge's questions at this stage of the investigation, Article 264 clearly states that "it is the obligation of the suspect to answer the judge's questions." If the suspect refuses to answer, the judge will ask him to reflect on the fact that "his silence will not favor him."

Moreover, it does not appear that the military judge

must advise the suspect of his rights and the act(s) attributed to him prior to taking this statement, as is required by the Code of Criminal Procedure in normal criminal investigations. Article 270 simply states that *after* taking the suspect's statements, the military judge shall advise him of the reason for his detention, if the judge did not do so prior thereto. Further, the judge apparently is not required to inform the suspect of his basic rights, other than that to a lawyer, during the investigatory stage.

b. *Provisional arrest*

The standards for ordering the provisional arrest of a person under investigation by a military judge for suspected violation of crimes enumerated in Article 177 of the Constitution are materially different from those applied by criminal courts in ordering the provisional arrest of persons suspected of violent crimes, such as murder and acts of terrorism. Instead of the "sufficient elements of proof that the person participated in the offense" standard mandated by Article 247, C.C.P., the military investigating judge need only determine that there is a "simple presumption" of an Article 177 crime to order such an arrest (Article 275). Although "grave" and "simple presumption" appear to be legal terms of art, neither seems to be defined in the C.M.J., nor have a precise analogue in the C.C.P.

The judge must finish this investigatory stage within *fifteen* days, but it may be extended an additional *ten* days (Article 254). Within this period, the judge must prepare a report containing a list of crimes for which the suspect might be charged and, based on the evidence gathered, his opinion on whether the suspect should be freed or whether the proceedings should be continued. Unlike the regular criminal investigation, the military investigation phase is not *public,* but *confidential* ("reservado"), *i.e.,* only those actually participating therein (including the suspect and his attorney) supposedly know of it (Article 272).

The investigating judge's report is sent directly to the Defense Minister who, in turn, forwards it immediately to the "Auditor General," an in-house military legal advisor. The Auditor General has *five* days in which to review the report and to issue and opinion to the Defense Minister recommending, *inter alia:* the release of the prisoner; the beginning of further proceedings; and the designation of the military tribunal to judge the case (Article 280).

If the Auditor General's opinion recommends the prisoner's release or further proceedings, the Defense Minister will communicate this to the Military Trial Judge ("Juez de Primera Instancia Militar") (Article 281).

c. *The impaneling of special courts martial*

The Military Trial Judge will determine whether to convene a Special Courts Martial and will prepare the appropriate order naming the defendant and the crime imputed to him (Article 317). If at this point, the prisoner does not yet have legal counsel, the trial judge will inform the prisoner of his right thereto, and, if not exercised, the judge will appoint a defender (from the military) (Article 317). The Trial Judge also can order the prisoner freed, absolutely or provisionally, if he so determines based on the record.

If the trial judge orders the formation of a Special Courts Martial, he must so notify the prisoner, his attorney, the Military Auditor General, the Military Prosecutor ("Fiscal General Militar"), and the Defense Ministry. Within twenty-four hours of such notification, he must request from the Defense Ministry a list of military officers qualified to be members of the Special Courts Martial (Article 320). Article 207 specifically requires that a new Special Courts Martial be convened for each particular case. All Special Courts Martial are composed of seven military officers, but the Defense Minister can substitute a lawyer for one of the officers. The members of this body are chosen by lottery from the list provided by the Defense Ministry. The prisoner and his counsel have the right to be present at this lottery (Article 322) and to preemptorily strike no more than *two* persons from the list of potential members. Upon completion of the lottery, the Military Judge will formally designate the members and alternates on the Special Courts Martial and swear them in, ordinarily within two days of their selection (Articles 323–325). The Military Judge then delivers the prisoner and pertinent records to the Secretary of this special tribunal.

d. *Procedures applicable to special courts martial*

The President of the Special Courts Martial will open the proceedings by questioning the prisoner to establish his identity. The Secretary will then read (1) the report of the investigating judge, (2) the opinion of the Military Auditor General, and (3) all the evidence gathered by the investigating judge. The Military prosecutor will then state the charges, and the defendant's lawyer will enter his plea thereto (Article 308).

The Special Courts Martial is to be conducted in conformity with the rules and procedures governing the ordinary criminal trials (Articles 310–313), including a *public* proceeding. If the members of the Special Courts Martial find the accused guilty as charged, the President of this body will so advise the Military Auditor General who must give a legal opinion within *five* days on the following points:

(1) the legal classification of the crime and the applicable legal provision(s);
(2) the legal nature of the circumstances attending the crime's commission and the existence of mitigating or aggravating circumstances; and
(3) the penalty required by law for the crime.

Upon receipt of this opinion, the Special Courts Martial will pass sentence (Articles 315 & 316).

The prisoner may appeal the sentence, within twenty-four hours notice thereof, to the Commander General of the Armed Forces, who, in turn, will call a hearing within twenty-four hours of receiving the appeal notice. At this hearing, the prisoner, his lawyer and the military prosecutor may argue orally their respective positions on the sentence. The Commander General is empowered to affirm, revoke, or modify the Court's sentence (Articles 356–357). In particular, he may by amnesty or pardon commute a death sentence (Article 371). The Military Code of Justice seems to provide for provisional liberty under circumstances, for those prisoners not sentenced to death (Article 372). However, the Code makes no provision for appealing a conviction or sentence within the civilian judiciary, including the Supreme Court of Justice.

7. *Adherence to the law*

The preceeding sections describe the formal legal situation prior to the coup of October 15, 1979. However it should be noted that prior to the coup the government neither respected, nor applied these legal standards on a consistent or nondiscriminatory basis. On the contrary, the Inter-American Commission on Human Rights in a 1978 Special Report on El Salvador flatly concluded that ". . . in practice the legal remedies are not effective for protecting the persons arbitrarily deprived of their basic human rights."[9]

B. *Legislation adopted after October 15, 1979*

This section will analyze the myriad decrees, as well as the Proclamation of the Armed Forces, which the Revolutionary Governing Junta has enacted since coming to power, with the objective of presenting a concise but thorough overview of the existing Salvadoran legal order which affects civil and political rights.

1. *Statutes and decrees of a constitutional nature*
a. *Proclamation of the Armed Forces*

The day of the overthrow the successful young colonels issued a far-reaching Proclamation which has acquired fundamental importance and at the same time become the focus of much heated debate.

Originally the Proclamation of the Armed Forces appeared to be no more than a blueprint to the objectives of the new government. With the adoption of Decree No. 114, of February 8, 1980, however, it was accorded supra-constitutional standing and thereby incorporated into the emerging *de facto* legal order.

The Proclamation set forth the guidelines for an emergency program, promising to put an end to violence and corruption, to guarantee the observance of human rights, to adopt measures that bring about an equitable distribution of the national wealth while at the same time rapidly increasing the gross national product, and to channel the country's foreign relations in a positive direction.

Because of the importance of the Proclamation of the Armed Forces for the institutional and legal order of El Salvador and, in particular, for the situation of human rights, the entire text is presented as Appendix II of this Report.

b. *Decree No. 1 of October 15, 1979*

The first Decree of the Junta, at that moment composed of the Chiefs and Officers of the Armed Forces under the First Infantry Brigade, exercised the right of insurrection (which Article 7 of the Constitution recognizes as a right of the people) to remove from office the President, the Vice President, those attached to the office of the President, the Ministers and Under-Secretaries of State, the Attorney

General of the Republic and the Public Prosecutor General, the Deputies of the Legislative Assembly, the Magistrates on the Supreme Court of Justice, the Members of the Central Election Council and the President and Magistrates of the Tax Court of the Republic.

The Junta immediately assumed the legislative and executive powers and stated that these would be exercised in accordance with the powers and duties established in the Constitution in force. It recognized the validity of the current Constitution, as well as all laws, regulations, ordinances and other provisions that govern the institutional life of the Republic, then proceeded to flagrantly violate the Constitution. By closing down the Assembly and assuming the legislative function, the Junta violated Article 7 of the Constitution which states that the exercise of the right of insurrection ". . . shall be limited in its effects to the removal insofar as necessary of officials of the executive branch, who shall be replaced in the manner established in this Constitution."

Finally, the decree declared that the Junta would govern by means of decree which would have the force of laws (decree-laws).

c. *Decree No. 7 of October 29, 1979*

This was one of the first decrees adopted by the Junta after the negotiations that led to the formation of the so-called first civilian-military Junta (composed of Colonels Adolfo Arnoldo Majano and Jaime Abdul Gutierrez, and civilians Guillermo Ungo, Roman Mayorga and Mario Andino).

By this decree, the Junta ratified the provisions of Decree No. 1, which meant confirming the validity of the Constitution of 1962, while suspending the standards of organization applicable to the legislative and executive branches.

It also circumscribed the duration of the *de facto* government to that time when elections were held and all officials of the executive (President and Vice President), legislative (deputies of the Legislative Assembly) and the Municipal Council had taken office. As for a date for elections, the decree simply stated that they would be held in due course.

d. *Decree No. 114 of February 8, 1980*

On January 3, 1980, practically all the civilian members of the Junta, Cabinet, Supreme Court and other decentralized agencies resigned from the government. A few days later, on the 9th of January, two prominent members of the Christian Democratic Party (PDC), Hector Dada Hirezi and Jose Antonio Morales Erlich joined the government, beginning what is commonly called the second Junta.

With the enactment of decree No. 114, the Junta, a *de facto* government which had tried to apply and comply with a *de jure* constitutional charter, broke with the terms established by Decrees 1 and 7 by recognizing the legality of the Constitution "insofar as it is compatible with the nature of the present Regime and does not contravene the postulates and objectives of the Proclamation of the Armed Forces of October 15, 1979 and its line of government." The decree then enumerates some of those objectives as the following:

- nationalization of foreign trade;
- implementation of an agrarian reform;
- nationalization of the country's banking system;
- separation of property of the Public Treasury, assigning resources of the General Fund and establishing special systems to meet the needs posed by the structural changes and the activation and redirection of the national economy; and
- ensuring the rights of workers, especially farm workers, to form professional associations.

The decree also set forth several instances when expropriation without prior compensation could be undertaken. These measures, which were taken to facilitate the agrarian reform program, the takeover of banks and other financial institutions, etc., implied a major reform of Article 138 of the Constitution and thereby a change of the interpretation which the ruling elites had given to that provision.

However, the overriding significance of Decree No. 114 is that it places the Proclamation of the Armed Forces above the Constitution of 1962. Moreover, given the broad and vague wording of Article 1 of Decree 114, a veritable state of "juridical uncertainty" has been created since there are no certain or verifiable limits on the constitutional system.

2. *Creation of an investigative commission*
a. *Decree No. 9 of October 26, 1979*

One of the most unsettling issues during the terms of Presidents Molina (1972–1977) and Romero (1977–79) was the detention and subsequent disappearance of numerous citizens.

The members of the first Junta agreed that the clarification of the situation of these people was essential if peace and tranquility was to return to Salvadoran society. Therefore, by virtue of Decree No. 9, a Special Investigative Commission was established, composed of the Attorney General, a member appointed by the Supreme Court of Justice and an honorable citizen appointed by the Junta.

It was charged with investigating:

- the whereabouts of the individuals considered to have disappeared for political reasons;
- the existence of clandestine prisons;
- the existence of torture, wherever practiced; and
- the existence of secret cemeteries.

The Commission had 60 days to report its findings to the Junta. During this period, the Commission was granted wide powers to carry out its mission and the security forces were bound to provide full cooperation.

The Commission submitted an interim report on November 23, 1979 and a final one on January 3, 1980, the day most civilian members of the Junta resigned.

b. *Decree No. 12 of November 6, 1979*

The official paramilitary organization called ORDEN (literally "order"), which in 1978 the Inter-American Commission on Human Rights recommended be dissolved because it was responsible for "considerable loss of life", was ordered disbanded by Decree No. 12 of November 6, 1979. The law adopted by the first Junta also declared "any act done in (ORDEN's name) . . . as illegal."

Notwithstanding, according to numerous reports ORDEN still operates today with total impunity. (See Chapter II, Right to Life)

3. *State of siege and curfew*
   a. *Decree No. 2 of October 16, 1979 and Decree No. 5 of October 23, 1979*

A day after overthrowing President Romero, the Armed Forces imposed through Decree No. 2 a state of siege in the entire country. In accordance with Article 175 of the Constitution, several guarantees were suspended for a period of thirty days. However, when a few days later the civilians entered the Junta, one of their first measures was to enact Decree No. 5 lifting the state of siege.

b. *Decree No. 155 of March 6, 1980*

In the final days of the second Junta, a second state of siege was imposed at the same time that the agrarian reform program was adopted. Apparently, the imposition of the state of siege was a precautionary measure to allow a smoother implementation of the agrarian transformation.

Therefore, on the 6th of March, the state of siege was again declared throughout the entire country. The guarantees established in Articles 154, 158 paragraph 1, 159 and 160 of the Constitution were suspended for a period of thirty days.

Two essential features of the state of siege under the Constitution are its temporary nature and its restrictive interpretations due to its exceptional character. However, the state of siege has rapidly become a permanent institution since it has been extended every single month since it was implemented in March 1980.

Furthermore, Salvadoran authorities have interpreted these provisions in an abitrary manner to include the derogation of rights which under no circumstances may ever be suspended, such as the right to life.

c. *Curfew of January 10, 1981*

On the eve of the launching of the "general offensive" by the opposition FMLN guerrilla forces, the Junta signed a decree imposing a curfew from 7:00 P.M. to 5:00 A.M., which went into effect on January 10. The text of the decree or regulation imposing the curfew has not appeared in the Diario Oficial or other publication and is not publically available.[10] The information at our disposal stems from newspaper clippings and conversations with Salvadorans and reliable observers knowledgeable with the situation in El Salvador.

The curfew is also known in El Salvador as Martial Law, although there is no such law or direct authority in the Salvadoran legal system. The curfew appears to have been enacted by virtue of the authority vested in the Minister of Defense and Public Security by Article 2 of Decree 155, supported by a long established tradition.

The Minister of Defense and Public Security was authorized by Article 2 to put the state of siege decree into effect and to regulate its application. Since one of the rights suspended by the decree is the freedom of movement, its exercise has been restricted during certain hours of the day.

While few people would argue with this interpretation, under no circumstances could it be accepted that the authorities may suspend theright to life in order to enforce the curfew. Yet, when the curfew was enacted numerous people were killed for being outside during restricted hours. The Salvadoran security forces' orders after the imposition of the curfew were to shoot to kill; this is amply corroborated by events.

4. *Laws applicable to political offenses*

Since the overthrow of President Romero, there have been three distinct periods concerning the laws applicable to political offenses. The first is from October 15, 1979 to March 6, 1980.[11] During this period, the regular courts applied the established provisions of the Penal Code to persons accused of committing a political crime, as defined in its Article 151.

The second period began with the imposition of the state of siege on March 6, 1980. *Ipso jure,* the Special Courts Martial were vested with jurisdiction over civilians accused of committing treason, espionage, rebellion, sedition, and other offenses against the peace or independence of the state or against the law of nations (Article 177 of the Constitution). For all other crimes, civilians were still subject to the jurisdiction of the ordinary courts.

The third period began with the promulgation of Decree No. 507 on December 3, 1980 which introduced major changes in the administration of justice in El Salvador. This law reformed certain provisions of the Code of Military Justice applicable to persons accused of crimes set forth in Article 177 of the Constitution. With the enactment of Decree 507, the military jurisdiction has been vested with virtually unchecked discretionary powers to hold a person for 180 days on preventive detention or 120 days on corrective detention on the slightest suspicion or whim. In addition, the investigating phase of the proceedings is carried out by the military judge in *total secrecy,* in flagrant violation of the most elementary principles of the rights to due process of law and a fair trial. Finally, evidentiary rules have been stripped of all objective criteria, granting the security forces an inducement to obtain a coerced confession.

Because of the significant impact of Decree 507 on the right to personal liberty and the right to justice and due process of law, its entire text is attached as Appendix III of this Report. (See Chapter 6 for an analysis of this law.)

5. *Reforms of the penal code and the code of criminal procedures*

On May 22, 1980, the Junta promulgated Decrees Nos. 264 and 265 which added new provisions to the Penal Code and the Code of Criminal Procedure, respectively.

Article 1 of Decree No. 264 inserted two new paragraphs in Article 400 of the Penal Code which define certain acts of terrorism as crimes. These new crimes of terrorism are:

Article 400(4). Individual or collective participation in takeovers or occupations of communities or towns, either totally or partially; buildings and facilities for public use or public service; places of work or service counters, or places for any form of religious worship.

Article 400(5). Armed attacks on garrisons and other military installations.

In accordance with Article 400, anyone who commits, either individually or collectively, these acts *with* the use of explosives, arms or other violent means, shall be subject to imprisonment for five to twenty years.

Article 2 of this Decree added a subsection to Article 407 of the Penal Code which proscribes "Illicit Associations." This subsection states that in the case of takeovers or occupations of those entities enumerated in Article 400(4) that are achieved *without* using explosives, arms, and the like, any person who participates therein, either individually or collectively, shall be subject to imprisonment for three to five years.

Decree No. 265 incorporated into Article 251 of the Code of Criminal Procedure a long list of political crimes, specified in the Penal Code, for which bail could no longer be granted.

6. *Amnesty*

Another Decree of the first Junta (No. 3 of October 16, 1979) aimed at achieving "an atmosphere of harmony and peace in all sectors of the country" was the law by which a general amnesty was granted "to all those persons whose freedom was restricted for political crimes either with or without trial." The Decree added that the pardon would extend "to those individuals found to be in such circumstances as of October 15, 1979."

On the same date that the third Junta enacted the Special Law on procedures applicable to trials before military courts (Article 177 of the Constitution), it also adopted a decree (No. 508 of December 3, 1980) which declared a temporary amnesty—three months—"to all those individuals who have committed political crimes and common crimes related thereto . . . and who belong to irregular armed groups, guerrilla cells and, in general, groups whose purpose is to undermine and depose the Government." It was applicable as long as no proceedings had been initiated against the individual.

A committee was established to determine the standards to make the amnesty effective, process and make a decision on the applications received, grant protection and personal attention to applicants, and relocate them in agricultural cooperatives or any other center of work.

7. *Personal identity cards for minors*

Decree No. 76 of January 26, 1980, adopted by the second Junta, required "minors under the age of eighteen" to obtain a personal identity card. The card was to be issued by the Office of the Mayor of the place of domicile of the minor. The Mayor was ordered to "keep a Control Book, in which shall be recorded the number of the card, the name and surnames of the minor, the address of his residence and, if possible, the other data on the card." On its face this highly uncommon law made it compulsory for a seven or eight-year-old child to have a personal identity card.

Just over one year later, the third Junta issued a new law, Decree No. 589 of February 11, 1981, which established more precise regulations for the issuance of personal identity cards and at the same time repealed Decree No. 76.

This new law creates a personal identity card for minors between the ages of ten and eighteen.

Even for those under the age of ten, the authorities are empowered at their discretion to determine whether or not to issue one.[12]

The law also stipulates that "for every card issued, another card shall immediately be made that shall bear the same data and requisites, for purposes of establishing an alphabetical index; the duplicate card shall be kept in the files of the Office of the Mayor. This pulicate shall be stamped with a print of the thumb of the minor's right hand or when lacking, of any other finger."

Decree No. 589, just as in its predecessor, ordered each Mayor to keep "a control record in alphabetical order, wherein are registered the correlative number of the card and the name and surnames of the minor."

8. *Decrees dealing with public services and trade unions*
   a. *Decree No. 296 of June 24, 1980*

This decree was promulgated and published the same day that the Democratic Revolutionary Front (FDR) had called for a two-day national work stoppage.

The law declares illegal, in accordance with Article 110 of the Constitution, strikes and collective abandonment of posts by officials and employees of the state and its decentralized agencies. A strike or collective abandonment of posts is defined in the following broad and vague way:

when an official or employee abandons his work or, when at work, does not perform said work normally.

In this event, the employee must be summarily dismissed if he is one of the organizers of the interruption, if he is not, he must be suspended without pay for 6 months, and in case of a second offense, he must be dismissed immediately.

These penalties shall be imposed, whether it be because the officials or employees did not appear at the place of work, left the place of work, appeared at the place of work but did not actually work, worked unwillingly or caused disturbances of any nature that impeded or impaired the provision of services.

The decree imposes harsh penalties on any official or employee with personnel under his authority who fails to comply with the law. Penalties may be administratively imposed without adherence to procedures established in the Civil Service Law, and are not subject to any appeal or remedy.

The Salvadoran review "Estudios Centroamericanos" (ECA) stated that this law ignores "the philosophy of the Labor Code and the Civil Service Law itself, which

establishes an administrative career for state employees."
It also commented that "the legal instrument, in any
event, is quite effective for controlling labor demands or
protest from the labor sector of the public administration."[13]

b. *Decree No. 43 of August 21, 1980*

Decree No. 43 is an executive or administrative decree,
dealing with a specific issue, as opposed to a decree-law,
which deals with general provisions of public scope. By
means of the Decree, affecting the Ministries of Interior
and of Defense and Public Security, the State of El Salvador was declared to be in a national emergency, in accordance with Article 110 of the Constitution. The services
provided by the following institutions or autonomous government agencies were militarized and control delegated
to the Ministry of Defense and Public Security: the National Administration for Aqueducts and Sewage
(ANDA), the National Telecommunications Administration (ANTEL), the Hydroelectric Executive Commission
for the Lempa River (CEL), and the Autonomous Executive Commission of the Port Authority (CEPA).

All workers and employees of these institutions were
incorporated and therefore considered as having enlisted
in the Armed Forces.

c. *Decree No. 366 of August 22, 1980*

On August 22, 1980, the Junta adopted Decree No. 366
which declared that during the period of national emergency strikes, arbitrary interruption of the public services
essential to the community, acts of sabotage and other
actions agreed upon by those associations and designed to
subvert the public order and support political activities
shall be grounds for dissolution of the professional associations established in the State agencies and autonomous and semi-autonomous agencies. The decision to

dissolve any association was placed in the hands of the Executive.

This law is in apparent violation of Article 191, paragraph 2, which states:

These organizations (government autonomous and semi-autonomous associations) are entitled to juridical personality and to due protection in the exercise of their functions. Their dissolution or suspension may be ordered only in those cases and according to the formalities specified by law.

The formalities specified by law refer to the procedure for dissolution of unions set forth in Articles 619 through 626 of the Labor Code of El Salvador, which is still in force. (See Chapter 9, The rights of assembly and association.)

d. *Decree No. 44 of August 22, 1980*

Basing its authority on Article 110 of the Constitution and on Decree No. 366, which was issued that same day, executive-decree No. 44 dissolved the Union of Workers of the Hydroelectric Executive Committee of the Rio Lempa (STECEL), cancelled its legal personality and ordered its funds frozen.

9. *Decree No. 603 of February 26, 1981 which affects the University of El Salvador*

On June 26, 1980, the National Guard occupied the University of El Salvador, resulting in numerous deaths of students and civilians. Since that moment the University has been closed down.

Decree 603, adopted on February 26 of 1981, appointed a General Manager of the University as responsible for ordering payment of salaries of all employees of the academic institution. However, another provision stipulated that so long as the University remains closed, salaries, *per diem,* representation costs, etc., of the Rector, Vice Rector, Treasurer, Secretary General, External Auditor, Deans, Assistant Deans and Directors of the Regional Centers of the University, would be suspended. This has amounted to a *de facto* dismissal of the University authorities.

According to an authoritative Salvadoran source these measures are "in evident violation of Article 204 of the Constitution which compels the Government to maintain the University and to respect its autonomy in its teaching, administrative, and financial aspects."[14]

10. *Decree dealing with the electoral process*

On March 5, 1981, the Junta adopted Decree 608, appointing three members to the Central Election Council, as well as their alternates. These posts had been vacant by virtue of Decree No. 1 adopted the day President Romero was overthrown.

Decree 608 repealed Election Law No. 292, of September 12, 1961, as amended, and instructed the Council to prepare a new draft election law and submit it to the Junta in due course for its consideration.

On July 7, 1981, the Junta promulgated a provisional law on the formation and registration of political parties. This law will be in force while the Central Election Council drafts a permanent electoral law which is intended to establish the regulations for the March 1982 constituent assembly elections. The provisional law contains several sections dealing with political parties which have already been registered and with the formation of new ones.[15]

11. *Decrees dealing with economic and social issues*

Numerous laws affecting the socio-economic structure of El Salvador have been enacted by the Junta. It is beyond the scope of this report to analyze all of these complex and in some cases very controversial measures.

Among the laws in this area are the following:

- Rent control of Agrarian Lands—Decree No. 44, December 11, 1979.
- Basic Law of Agrarian Reform—Decree No. 153, March 5, 1980.
- Implementation of Agrarian Reform, Decree No. 154, March 5, 1980.
- Law of Nationalization of Banking Institutions and Savings and Loans Associations—Decree No. 158, March 7, 1980.
- Transitory Law for the Intervention of Banking Institutions and Savings and Loans Associations—Decree No. 159, March 7, 1980.
- Reform of Basic Law of Agrarian Reform—Decree No. 165, March 10, 1980.
- Reform of rent control law of Agrarian lands—Decree No. 171, March 17, 1981.
- Implementation of Agrarian Reform—Decree No. 207, April 28, 1980.
- Implementation of Agrarian Reform—Decree No. 220, May 9, 1980.
- Special Law on Rural Associations—Decree No. 221, May 9, 1980.
- Implementation of Agrarian Reform—Decree No. 256, May 29, 1980.
- Implementation of Agrarian Reform—Decree No. 33, June 17, 1980.
- Law of Economic Stabilization—Decree No. 544, December 22, 1980.

C. *International obligations of El Salvador*

Few countries on the American continent, indeed in the world, have assumed as many commitments in the field of international protection of human rights, as the Republic of El Salvador. Most of these treaties have force of law in domestic jurisdiction and some of them represent a legally binding obligation in the international sphere.

El Salvador is a founding member of both the United

Nations and the Organization of American States, and therefore, it is linked to the specific norms of its charters concerning human rights. It cast its vote in approval of both the U.N. Declaration on Human Rights and the OAS Declaration of the Rights and Duties of Man.

El Salvador ratified in 1953 the following four Geneva Conventions of August 12, 1949, concerning humanitarian law applicable in armed conflicts:

- Geneva Convention for the Amelioration of the Condition of the Wounded, Sick, and Shipwrecked Members of Armed Forces at Sea.
- Geneva Convention for the Amelioration of the Condition of the Wounded and Sick in Armed Forces in the Field.
- Geneva Convention relative to Treatment of Prisoners of Civilian Persons in Time of War.
- Geneva Convention relative to the Protection of Civilian Persons in Time of War.

During President Romero's Government, El Salvador deposited on November 23, 1978, its instrument of ratification to the two Protocols additional to the above Geneva Conventions. The Protocols entered into force for El Salvador in May of 1979.

These instruments are of particular importance in the situation of human rights in El Salvador, as well as on the role of the International Committee of the Red Cross. Of special importance is Protocol II, relating to the protection of victims of non-international armed conflicts.

El Salvador also ratified on June 23, 1978 the American Convention on Human Rights[16], an inter-American treaty under the aegis of the Organization of American States, and, on November 30, 1979 the U.N. Covenants on Civil and Political Rights and Economic, Social and Cultural Rights.[17] Although El Salvador signed the Optional Protocol of the Covenant on Civil and Political Rights, it has not yet ratified it.

In addition, El Salvador is a state party to the following treaties relating to human rights:

- Convention of the American States on Asylum (February 20, 1928);
- Convention of the American States on Political Asylum (December 26, 1933);
- Inter-American Convention on the Granting of Political Rights to Women (May 2, 1948);
- Inter-American Convention on the Granting of Civil Rights to Women (May 2, 1948);
- Convention on the Prevention and Punishment of the Crime of Genocide (December 9, 1948);
- Convention on the International Right of Correction (March 31, 1953);
- Convention of the American States on Territorial Asylum (March 28, 1954);
- Convention of the American States on Diplomatic Asylum (March 28, 1954);
- ILO Convention No. 105 on the Suppression of Forced Labor (June 25, 1957);
- International Convention on the Elimination of all Forms of Racial Discrimination (December 21, 1965);
- International Convention on the Suppression and Punishment of the Crime of Apartheid (November 30, 1973)

APPENDIX II

PROCLAMATION OF THE ARMED FORCES OF THE REPUBLIC OF EL SALVADOR OCTOBER 15, 1979

A. The Armed Forces of El Salvador, fully conscious of their sacred duties to the Salvadoran Nation and in sympathy with the outcry of all inhabitants against a Government that:

1. Has violated the human rights of the people;
2. Has fostered and countenanced corruption in the Public Administration and in the judiciary;
3. Has brought about a veritable economic and social disaster; and
4. Has disgraced the country and the Armed Forces.

B. Convinced that the problems mentioned above are the result of the antiquated economic, social and political structures that have traditionally prevailed in the country, structures that do not offer the majority of the inhabitants the minimum conditions essential for their human self-fulfillment. Further, the corruption and incompetence within the system created distrust within the private sector, which in turn caused the flight of hundreds of millions of colones, thereby exacerbating the economic crisis to the detriment of the working class.

C. Certain of the fact that the successive governments, themselves the product of scandalous election frauds, have adopted inadequate development programs wherein the timid structural changes have been halted by the economic and political power of conservative sectors, which have always defended their ancestral ruling-class privileges, even to the point of placing in jeopardy the country's socially progressive capital which has demonstrated its interest in achieving just economic development for the population.

D. Firmly convinced that the above conditions are the basic cause of the economic and social chaos and of the generalized violence at the present time, which can only be overcome by the coming to power of a government that guarantees the enforcement of a truly democratic system.

Therefore, the Armed Forces, whose members have always been identified with the people, hereby decide, based on the right of insurrection to which the people are entitled when those governing fail to comply with the law, to depose the Government of General Carlos Humberto Romero and thence to establish a Revolutionary Governing Junta, the majority of whose members shall be civilians whose absolute honesty and competence are beyond question. Said Junta shall assume the Power of the State so as to establish the conditions in our country to enable all Salvadorans to live in peace and in a manner consonant with man's dignity.

While the conditions necessary to hold free elections in which people will be able to decide their future are being established and because of the chaotic political and social situation the country is now experiencing, it is essential that an emergency program be adopted that makes provision for emergency measures designed to establish an atmosphere of tranquility and the bases for in-depth change in the country's economic, social and political structures.

The guidelines of this Emergency Program are as follows:

I. TO PUT AN END TO VIOLENCE AND CORRUPTION

A. By dissolving ORDEN and combatting extremist organizations that, through their activities, violate human rights.

B. By eradicating corrupt practices within the public administration and the judiciary.

II. TO GUARANTEE THE OBSERVANCE OF HUMAN RIGHTS

A) By creating an atmosphere appropriate to holding free elections, within a reasonable period of time.

B) By allowing the establishment of parties of all ideologies, so as to strengthen the democratic system.

C) By granting a general amnesty to all political exiles and prisoners.

D) By recognizing and respecting the right to unionize, in all labor sectors.

E) By stimulating free expression of thought, in accordance with ethical standards.

III. TO ADOPT MEASURES THAT BRING ABOUT AN EQUITABLE DISTRIBUTION OF THE NATIONAL WEALTH, WHILE AT THE SAME TIME RAPIDLY INCREASING THE GROSS NATIONAL PRODUCT

A) By laying solid foundations for undertaking the process of agrarian reform.

B) By providing more economic opportunities to the population, through reforms in the country's financial sector, taxes and foreign trade.

C) By adopting measures to protect the consumer so as to counteract the effects of inflation.

D) By implementing special development programs aimed at increasing national production and creating additional sources of employment.

E) By recognizing and guaranteeing the right to housing, food, education and health for the entire population of the country.

F) By guaranteeing private ownership as a social function.

IV. TO CHANNEL THE COUNTRY'S FOREIGN RELATIONS IN A POSITIVE DIRECTION

A) By reestablishing relations with Honduras as soon as possible.

B) By strengthening ties with the people of Nicaragua and its Government.

C) By strengthening the ties that unite us with the people and governments of the sister republics of Guatemala, Costa Rica and Panama.

D) By establishing friendly relations with all countries in the world that are willing to support the struggle of our people and to respect our sovereignty.

E) By guaranteeing fulfillment of the country's international commitments.

To achieve these goals rapidly, which the Salvadoran people have every right to demand, the Revolutionary Governing Junta shall form a cabinet composed of honest and capable men, representatives of various sectors, who shall be ever mindful of their duty to their country in the discharge of their duties.

At this time of true national emergency, the working class sectors and the country's socially progressive capital are called upon to help initiate a new era in El Salvador, under the principles of peace and effective observance of the human rights of all citizens.

Given in the city of San Salvador, the fifteenth day of the month of October of the year nineteen hundred seventy-nine.

APPENDIX III

REVOLUTIONARY GOVERNING JUNTA DECREE NO. 507

WHEREAS:

I. That all inhabitants of El Salvador have the right to be protected in preserving and defending their life, honor, freedom, work, property and ownership;

II. Certain individuals, associations and groups have dedicated themselves to the task of subverting the public order, thereby causing injury to individuals and properties and so creating a state of anxiety and malaise throughout the entire population;

III. In accordance with Article 177 of the Constitution, when a suspension of constitutional guarantees has been declared, the military tribunals shall have jurisdiction in trying cases of treason, espionage, rebellion and sedition and other offenses against the peace or independence of the state or against the law of nations;

IV. The procedure established for trying the crimes contained in Article 177 of the Constitution is the one specified in the Code of Military Justice;

V. That Code of Military Justice, having been enacted

under other circumstances, is not suited to the country's present circumstances, which is why standards must be enacted to restore effective trial and punishment of the crimes referred to in the preceding articles of the preamble, thereby laying the ground for reestablishment of the rule of law and the offender's rehabilitation;

THEREFORE,

in exercise of the constitutional powers conferred upon it by Decree No. 1 of October 15, 1979, published in the Diario Oficial No. 191, Volume 265, of that same date, and having heard the opinion of the Supreme Court of Justice,

THE REVOLUTIONARY GOVERNING JUNTA

DECREES, APPROVES AND ENACTS THE FOLLOWING:

SPECIAL LAW ON PROCEDURES APPLICABLE TO THE CRIMES REFERRED TO IN ARTICLE 177 OF THE CONSTITUTION

THE SCOPE OF THE LAW

Article 1. The purpose of the present law is to govern the procedures that apply to individuals over the age of sixteen who commit the crimes of treason, espionage, rebellion, sedition, and other crimes against the independence of the state and against the law or nations, such as those listed in Chapters I and II of Title I, part three, Articles 281 to 291 inclusive; those in section three, Chapter I, Title III, Articles 348 to 351 inclusive; those in the fourth part, Title I, Chapters I, II, III and IV, Articles 373 to 411 inclusive, and those in Title II, Single Chapter, Article 421, [of the Penal Code].

Notwithstanding the provisions contained in the above paragraph the corrective measures referred to in article 6 shall be applied to any minor under the age of sixteen who is found to be implicated in any of the above crimes.

COMPETENCE

Article 2. The judges of Military Courts of the First Instance shall try, in first instance, the crimes to which Article 1 of this law refers.

The examining phase shall be conducted solely by the military examining judges.

When a suspect is accused of crimes that fall under distinct jurisdictions, the first crimes to be tried shall be those of military jurisdiction, regardless of the penalty for the crime; when appropriate the judge of the military court of the first instance shall transmit the file to the judge of the common court, and turn the prisoner over to him, if he has said prisoner.

Article 3. The Supreme Court of Justice, at the proposal of the Ministry of Defense and Public Security, shall appoint the military examining judges necessary, who may be members of the military on active duty, discharged or retired. They shall have jurisdiction throughout the national territory and shall be permanent.

The military examining judges shall have jurisdiction to initiate the investigative proceedings for crimes set forth in this law, and the corresponding order to proceed referred to in Article 259 of the Code of Military Justice shall not be required.

PROCEDURE

Article 4. Upon arresting an individual, the auxiliary organs shall be obligated to notify any military examining judge of the arrest, within twenty-four hours. The prisoner's case must be brought before the military examining judge within a period of fifteen days of the date of arrest, though this shall not prejudice continued gathering of evidence and reporting of same to the military examining judge.

The auxiliary organs shall be obligated to continue the investigations and to pass them on when the prisoner is brought before the court, as stipulated in the preceding paragraph.

Article 5. The proceedings may begin by virtue of an accusation of an informant (denuncia), upon the presentation of an information or indictment by the military examining judge at his own initiative *(sua sponte).*

Once the proceedings have begun, the Military Examining Judge will continue the corresponding investigation and order the detention or release of the suspect within seventy-two hours, as appropriate.

The existence of any information to give one cause to believe that the suspect was a participant in the crime shall be sufficient to order provisional detention.

The extrajudicial investigation conducted by the auxiliary organs shall also serve as the basis for ordering provisional detention of the suspect, provided that those investigations establish that the suspect participated in the act.

If the auxiliary organs have arrested the suspect, the seventy-two hour period shall begin as of the date on which the prisoner's case was brought before the military examining judge.

Article 6. If by the time the seventy-two hour period has ended the judge has found no good cause to hold the suspect, but by studying the case or by any other means has established the need to subject him to security measures, he shall so decide and order his corrective detention for a period of no more than 120 days, at his discretion.

These detentions must be in special rehabilitation centers.

Once the term of corrective detention has been served, the judge may take such control measures as he deems pertinent, so that the suspect must appear periodically before the court under his jurisdiction and he may require bond (fianza de la haz) for fulfillment of this provision.

Article 7. The examining phase shall be secret and shall not exceed one hundred eighty days; within that time neither the accused nor the prosecution shall have the right to participate in the proceedings and all steps necessary to clarify the facts being investigated shall be taken and the investigation shall be referred to the Judge of the Military Court of the First Instance.

Once the Judge of the Military Court of the First Instance has received the case, he shall examine it to determine whether it contains any gaps. Should he find any flaws or gaps, he shall return the case to the Military Examining Judge to be corrected or to have any gap filled, said gaps being specified.

Having received the case or having returned it, when necessary, the Judge of the Military Court of the First Instance shall decide whether to dismiss the case or whether to take the case to plenary proceedings.

The pertinent decision having been made, the accused and the Attorney General of the Republic shall be notified, so that the latter may appoint his representative.

If the case is taken to plenary proceedings, the accused shall be advised to appoint defense counsel, or to indicate whether he shall defend himself, should he have the legal capacity to do this.

Should the accused fail to act within three days, the Judge shall appoint a public defender.

During the plenary proceedings, both the accused and the prosecution shall have the right to participate in the proceedings.

Article 8. Once plenary proceedings have begun, the parties shall present evidence for a period up to twenty days, within which time the parties may present all evidence available (that which is ordinarily admissible as well as that provided for in Article 11 of this decree).

Once the evidentiary proceedings have ended, the judge shall give the parties six days in which to argue the evidence.

Article 9. Once the arguments referred to in the preceding article have been completed, the judge shall hand down a verdict within twelve days.

Article 10. An order of dismissal or for plenary proceedings and the final verdict shall be appealable before the corresponding criminal division, which shall process the appeal in accordance with the general rules contained in the Code of Criminal Procedure.

ON THE EVIDENCE

Article 11. In addition to those established under regular law, the following shall be regarded as sufficient evidence to take the case to plenary proceedings:

1) A confession made before a judge other than the one trying the case;
2) A written extrajudicial confession; an oral extrajudicial confession verified by two witnesses, and a recording made in the manner established under regular law;
3) Objects that are related to the crime discovered either in the possession of the accused or in the place where he is found; such items include arms, munitions, explosives, incendiary devices, subversive propaganda or literature, military or terrorist plans, etc.; the record taken down by the arresting person or persons at the time of arrest, if possible, shall suffice for this purpose;
4) For the purposes of Article 376 and 407 of the Penal Code, it shall be sufficient to establish that the accused belongs to organizations that have claimed responsibility for criminal actions or events publicized or, by using any association, issues statements that threaten public order or security of the State or incites to acts that can harm the national economy. Confirmation by any national or foreign communications medium shall be sufficient to establish that an accused belongs to one of the groups mentioned;
5) Documents that are private although not yet acknowledged, that are corroborated by any other means of proof.

Article 12. The Judge shall hand down a guilty verdict when, in the trial, there is sufficient evidence to convict the accused of participation in and culpability for the criminal offense.

GENERAL PROVISIONS

Article 13. Those found guilty of these crimes shall not be eligible for early release.

Article 14. The provisions of this law shall prevail over any other law or provision that contravenes it.

Article 15. The provisions contained in the Code of Military Justice shall be applied with respect to matters not covered in this Decree.

Article 16. The present Decree shall remain in force as long as the constitutional guarantees are suspended.

Once the constitutional guarantees have been restored, the trials that are still pending will continue to be conducted in accordance with the provision of this law.

Article 17. The present Decree shall enter into effect eight days following its publication in the Diario Oficial.

GIVEN IN THE PRESIDENTIAL RESIDENCE: San Salvador, the third day of December of nineteen hundred eighty.

Col. and Ing. Jaime Abdul Gutierrez
Dr. Jose Antonio Morales Ehrlich
Dr. Jose Ramon Avalos Navarrete
Ing. Jose Napoleon Duarte
Dr. Mario Antonio Solano, Minister of Justice

APPENDIX IV

INTERNATIONAL SECURITY AND DEVELOPMENT COOPERATION ACT OF 1981 PL 97-113

TITLE VII—MISCELLANEOUS PROVISIONS

ASSISTANCE FOR EL SALVADOR

SEC. 727. (a) It is the sense of the Congress that assistance furnished to the Government of El Salvador, both economic and military, should be used to encourage—

(1) full observance of internationally recognized human rights in accordance with sections 116 and 502B of the Foreign Assistance Act of 1961;

(2) full respect for all other fundamental human rights, including the right of freedom of speech and of the press, the right to organize and operate free labor unions, and the right to freedom of religion;

(3) continued progress in implementing essential economic and political reforms, including land reform and support for the private sector;

(4) a complete and timely investigation of the deaths of all United States citizens killed in El Salvador since October 1979;

(5) an end to extremist violence and the establishment of a

unified command and control of all government security forces in this effort;

(6) free, fair, and open elections at the earliest date; and

(7) increased professional capability of the Salvadoran Armed Forces in order to establish a peaceful and secure environment in which economic development and reform and the democratic processes can be fully implemented, thereby permitting a phased withdrawal of United States military training and advisory personnel at the earliest possible date.

(b) It is the sense of the Congress that the United States economic assistance to El Salvador should put emphasis on revitalizing the private sector and supporting the free market system. The Congress recognizes that the lack of foreign exchange to buy imported raw materials and intermediate goods is a major impediment to the ability of the Salvadoran economy to provide jobs. The Congress also recognizes that the funds budgeted for economic assistance are only a fraction of the foreign exchange needed and United States economic aid should be used, wherever possible, to stimulate private sector lending. Therefore, the Congress urges the President to set aside a portion of the economic support funds to provide guarantees to private United States banks willing to give credits to the Salvadoran private sector.

RESTRICTIONS ON MILITARY ASSISTANCE AND SALES TO EL SALVADOR

SEC. 728. (a)(1) The Congress finds that peaceful and democratic development in Central America is in the interest of the United States and of the community of American States generally, that the recent civil strife in El Salvador has caused great human suffering and disruption to the economy of that country, and that substantial assistance to El Salvador is necessary to help alleviate that suffering and to promote economic recovery within a peaceful and democratic process. Moreover, the Congress recognizes that the efforts of the Government of El Salvador to achieve these goals are affected by the activities of forces beyond its control.

(2) Taking note of the substantial progress made by the Government of El Salvador in land and banking reforms, the Congress declares it should be the policy of the United States to encourage and support the Government of El Salvador in the implementation of these reforms.

(3) The United States also welcomes the continuing efforts of President Duarte and his supporters in the Government of El Salvador to establish greater control over the activities of members of the armed forces and government security forces. The Congress finds that it is in the interest of the United States to cooperate with the Duarte government in putting an end to violence in El Salvador by extremist elements among both the insurgents and the security forces, and in establishing a unified command and control of all government forces.

(4) The United States supports the holding of free, fair, and open elections in El Salvador at the earliest date. The Congress notes the progress being made by the Duarte government in this area, as evidenced by the appointment of an electoral commission.

(b) In fiscal year 1982 and 1983, funds may be obligated for assistance for El Salvador under chapter 2 or 5 of part II of the Foreign Assistance Act of 1961, letters of offer may be issued and credits and guarantees may be extended for El Salvador under the Arms Export Control Act, and members of the Armed Forces may be assigned or detailed to El Salvador to carry out functions under the Foreign Assistance Act of 1961 or the Arms Export Control Act, only if not later than 30 days after the date of enactment of this Act and every one hundred and eighty days thereafter, the President makes a certification in accordance with subsection (d).

(c) If the President does not make such a certification at any of the specified times then the President shall immediately—

(1) suspend all expenditures of funds and other deliveries of assistance for El Salvador which were obligated under chapters 2 and 5 of part II of the Foreign Assistance Act of 1961 after the date of enactment of this Act;

(2) withhold all approvals for use of credits and guarantees for El Salvador which were extended under the Arms Export Control Act after the date of enactment of this Act;

(3) suspend all deliveries of defense articles, defense services, and design and construction services to El Salvador which were sold under the Arms Export Control Act after the date of enactment of this Act; and

(4) order the prompt withdrawal from El Salvador of all members of the Armed Forces performing defense services, conducting international military education and training activities, or performing management functions under section 515 of the Foreign Assistance Act of 1961.

Any suspension of assistance pursuant to paragraphs (1) through (4) of this subsection shall remain in effect during fiscal year 1982 and during fiscal year 1983 until such time as the President makes a certification in accordance with subsection (d).

(d) The certification required by subsection (b) is a certification by the President to the Speaker of the House of Representatives and to the chairman of the Committee on Foreign Relations of the Senate of a determination that the Government of El Salvador—

(1) is making a concerted and significant effort to comply with internationally recognized human rights;

(2) is achieving substantial control over all elements of its own armed forces, so as to bring to an end the indiscriminate torture and murder of Salvadoran citizens by these forces;

(3) is making continued progress in implementing essential economic and political reforms, including the land reform program;

(4) is committed to the holding of free elections at an early date and to that end has demonstrated its good faith efforts to begin discussions with all major political factions in El Salvador which have declared their willingness to find and implement an equitable political solution to the conflict, with such solution to involve a commitment to—

(A) a renouncement of further military or paramilitary activity; and

(B) the electoral process with internationally recognized observers.

Each such certification shall discuss fully and completely the justification for making each of the determinations required by paragraphs (1) through (4).

(e) On making the first certification under subsection (b) of this section, the President shall also certify to the Speaker of the House of Representatives and the chairman of the Committee on Foreign Relations of the Senate that he has determined that the Government of El Salvador has made good faith efforts both to investigate the murders of the six United States citizens in El Salvador in December 1980 and January 1981 and to bring to justice those responsible for those murders.

REPORTING REQUIREMENT RELATING TO EL SALVADOR

SEC. 729. (a) Not later than ninety days after the date of enactment of this section, the President shall prepare and transmit to the Speaker of the House of Representatives and to the chairman of the Committee on Foreign Relations of the Senate a report setting forth—

(1) the viewpoints of all major parties to the conflict in El Salvador and of the influential actors in the Salvadoran political system regarding the potential for and interest in negotiations,

elections, and a settlement of the conflict; and

(2) the views of democratic Latin American nations, Canada, the Organization of American States, and European allies of the United States regarding a negotiated settlement to such conflict.

(b) It is the sense of the Congress that the President shall, as soon as possible, send a special envoy or use other appropriate means to consult with and gather information from appropriate representatives of the parties to the Salvadoran conflict, democratic governments of Latin America, Canada, and European allies of the United States regarding the attainment of a negotiated settlement in El Salvador.

RESTRICTIONS ON AID TO EL SALVADOR

Sec. 730. None of the funds authorized to be appropriated by this Act may be made available for the provision of assistance to El Salvador for the purpose of planning for compensation, or for the purpose of compensation, for the confiscation, nationalization, acquisition, or expropriation of any agricultural or banking enterprise, or of the properties or stock shares which may be pertaining thereto.

EL SALVADORAN REFUGEES

Sec. 731: It is the sense of the Congress that the administration should continue to review, on a case-by-case basis, petitions for extended voluntary departure made by citizens of El Salvador who claim that they are subject to persecution in their homeland, and should take full account of the civil strife in El Salvador in making decision on such petitions.

APPENDIX V

MURDERS:
JANUARY–DECEMBER 1981

Sector	Jan.	Feb.	March	April	May	June
Campesinos	176	313	1,224	1,765	187	203
Workers	36	28	40	50	31	50
Students	46	26	39	87	48	25
Employees	21	80	84	76	56	51
Teachers	10	9	9	6	5	5
Small Businessmen	12	12	17	21	16	19
Professionals	4	6	3	–	1	6
Clergy	–	–	–	–	–	3
Journalists	–	–	–	2	–	–
Health Workers	3	2	2	1	–	–
Unknown Professions	2,336	427	504	303	192	572
Total	2,644	903	1,922	2,311	536	934

Source: Socorro Juridico, January 15, 1982

July	Aug.	Sept.	Oct.	Nov.	Dec.	Total
114	110	159	174	600	98	5,123
45	34	28	15	15	15	387
27	10	19	9	8	2	346
44	30	38	32	25	17	554
6	1	3	6	–	2	62
13	17	15	22	19	20	203
2	1	1	1	–	1	26
1	1	1	–	–	–	6
–	–	–	–	–	–	2
1	–	–	–	–	–	9
293	377	208	179	152	240	5,783
546	581	472	438	820	395	12,501

RESPONSIBLE FOR MURDERS
JANUARY–DECEMBER 1981

	Jan.	Feb.	March	April	May	June
Combined Forces (Army, National Guard, National Police & Treasury Police)	1,933	508	1,405	1,795	251	341
Death Squad	–	–	–	15	–	18
Agents in Civilian Dress	–	2	19	11	17	15
National Guard	–	3	–	7	15	24
Treasury Police	–	–	–	38	–	–
Army	–	–	–	–	–	23
National Police	–	–	–	–	4	10
Committe for Civil Defense	–	–	–	–	–	–
Unidentified Paramilitary groups	711	390	498	445	249	503
Total	2,644	903	1,922	2,311	536	934

Source: Socorro Juridico, January 15, 1982

July	Aug.	Sept.	Oct.	Nov.	Dec.	Total
107	74	103	127	466	79	7,189
43	47	6	5	7	5	146
–	6	10	8	5	7	100
52	1	6	9	1	2	120
–	3	9	–	1	–	51
5	–	–	–	12	–	40
2	–	–	–	–	–	16
–	–	–	3	5	3	11
337	450	338	286	322	299	4,828
546	581	472	438	819	395	12,501

NOTES

CHAPTER 1

1. The data used here are drawn from the following sources: "El Salvador—Country Statement" Pan American Health Organization, Washington, D.C., 1981; "El Salvador Demographic Issues and Prospects," International Bank for Reconstruction and Development, Washington, D.C., October 1979; "Economic and Social Progress in Latin America," Inter-American Development Bank, Washington, D.C., 1979; "Economic Study of El Salvador" Organization of American States, Washington, D.C., 1979.

2. Melvin Burke, El Sistema de Plantacion y la Proletarizacion del Trabajo Agricola en El Salvador, *Estudios Centroamericanos (ECA),* Nos. 335–336, San Salvador, Septiembre–Octubre 1976, pp. 473–86.

3. Office of Public Safety, U.S. Agency for International Development (AID), Report on visit to Central America and Panama to Study AID Public Safety Programs, 1967, p. 23.

4. Stephen Webre, *Jose Napoleon Duarte and the Christian Democratic Party in Salvadorean Politics (1960–1972),* Louisiana State University Press, 1979, p. 178.

5. Report on the Situation of·Human Rights in El Salvador, Inter-American Commission on Human Rights (IACHR), OEA/Ser.L /V/II. 46, doc. 23 rev. 2, 17 November 1978, pp. 153–58.

6. IACHR 1979–80 Annual Report at 138.

7. "Central America 1980: Nicaragua, El Salvador, Guatemala," Findings of an investigative mission, sponsored by the Unitarian Universalist Service Committee, p. 18; Amnesty International, 1980 Annual Report, El Salvador, p. 134.

8. Country Reports on Human Rights Practices for 1979, Department of State, February 4, 1980, p. 314.

9. The Review, International Commission of Jurists, December 1979, No. 23, pp. 4–5.

CHAPTER 2

1. The sources for the data in this chapter include the following publications: "El Salvador—Country Statement," Pan American Health Organization, Washington, D.C., 1981; "El Salvador Demographic Issues and Prospects," The International Bank for Reconstruction and Development/The World Bank, Washington, D.C., October 1979; "Economic and Social Progress in Latin America," Inter-American Development Bank, Washington, D.C. 1979; "Economic Study of El Salvador," Organization of American States, Washington, D.C., 1979; (OEA/Ser. H/XIV, CEPCIES/408, 22 March 1979).

2. For 25 years after World War II, Honduras served as an escape valve for hundreds of thousands of landless Salvadoran peasants who migrated into Honduras, establishing permanent, though usually illegal residence there. A crisis provoked by El Salvador's population overspill into Honduras culminated in the invasion of Honduras by El Salvador charging persecution of Salvadorans inside Honduras. It was called the "Soccer War" since it coincided with a three-game regional championship in which both countries were engaged.

3. For a critical analysis of the reform plan itself, see L. Simon and J. Stephens, Jr., *El Salvador Land Reform 1980–1981 Impact Audit*, OXFAM America, Boston, MA., February 1981; see also, P. Wheaton, *Agrarian Reform in El Salvador: A Program of Rural Pacification*, EPICA Task Force, Washington, D.C., 1980.

4. The number of intervened farms varies from report to report. AID Monthly Status Report on Agrarian Reform in El Salvador, August 26, 1981 places the number at 315, while the July AID Status Report states the number to be 282. All previous AID reports quote numbers below 300.

5. AID Monthly Status Report on Agrarian Reform in El Salvador, August 26, 1981.

6. *Ibid.*

7. OXFAM Report at 29.

8. Interview with Leonel Gomez, former Assistant Director of ISTA, Washington, D.C., July 28, 1981, by Nina Shea.

9. AID Report on El Salvador: The Agrarian Reform, April, 1981.

10. R. Bonner, "Salvador Land Program Aids Few," *The New York Times,* August 3, 1981.

11. AIFLD Report on the Salvador Reform Situation, Washington, D.C., April 29, 1981, p. 3.

12. U.S. AID, *Agrarian Reform Organization, Annex IIA A Social Analysis,* June 1980, p. 25.

13. *Ibid.,* p. 32.

14. *Ibid.*

15. R. Bonner, "Salvador Land Program Aids Few," *The New York Times,* August 3, 1981.

16. U.S. AID, *Agrarian Reform Organization, Annex IIA A Social Analysis,* June 1980, p. 10.

17. OXFAM Report at 43.

18. R. Bonner, "Salvador Land Program Aids Few," *The New York Times,* August 3, 1981.

19. Hearings Before the Subcommittee on Inter-American Affairs of the Committee on Foreign Affairs, House of Representatives, 97th Congress, March 5 and 11, 1981, Washington, D.C., p. 233.

20. This figure is based on the estimated number of potential beneficiaries.

21. AID Monthly Status Report on Agrarian Reform in El Salvador, August 26, 1981.

22. U.S. AID, *Agrarian Reform Organization, Annex IIA A Social Analysis,* June 1980, p. 19.

23. Stated at a press conference by the Citizens' Committee on the El Salvador Crisis led by Clark Kerr, Angier Biddle Duke and Rev. Ernest Bartell, as reported in "Salvador Land Plan: Key Stage," *The New York Times,* Dec. 16, 1981.

24. AID Report on El Salvador: The Agrarian Reform, April 1981.

25. *Ibid.,* p. 8

26. AIFLD, sponsored by the AFL-CIO was created in 1962 with the financial assistance of AID, the State Department and some 90 multinational corporations. AIFLD, under an AID contract, is working in El Salvador to "strengthen free democratic trade union, and support the democratic center against both the dictatorial left and the dictatorial right."

27. U.S. AID, *Agrarian Reform Organization, Annex IIA A Social Analysis,* June 1980, p. 20.

28. *Ibid.*

CHAPTER 3

1. Legal Aid of the Archdiocese of San Salvador, *El Salvador, One Year of Repression,* Commission of the Churches on International Affairs, World Council of Churches, 1981, p. 32.

2. U.S. Department of State, *Country Reports on Human Rights Practices,* February 2, 1981, p. 429, (placing the figure at 9,000); *Socorro Juridico del Arzobispado de San Salvador,* 4 de Junio de 1981, (placing the number at 10,000).

3. Data received by telephone from Roberto Cuellar, Executive Director of *Socorro Juridico,* September 9, 1981.

4. Interview with President Jose Napoleon Duarte, San Salvador, August 28, 1981, by Morton Halperin and Aryeh Neier.

5. Interview with Colonel Jose Guillermo Garcia, San Salvador, August 28, 1981, by Morton Halperin and Aryeh Neier.

6. Anderson, Thomas P., *Matanza,* University of Nebraska Press, 1971, p. 131.

7. *Ibid.*

8. Webre, Stephen, *Jose Napoleon Duarte and the Christian Democractic Party in Salvadoran Politics (1960–1972),* Louisiana State University Press, 1979, pp. 150–51.

9. *Ibid.,* p. 189.

10. Report on the Situation of Human Rights in El Salvador, Inter-American Commission on Human Rights, OEA/Ser. L/V/11.46, doc. 23 rev. 1, 17 November 1978, p. 54.

11. *Ibid.,* p. 51.

12. McClintock, Michael, Disappearances and Security Systems: Guatemala and El Salvador, June 12, 1980.

13. Hearing before the Committee on Foreign Relations, United States Senate, 97th Congress, March 18 and April 9, 1981, testimony of Amnesty International, p. 248.

14. Fox, Donald T., Report on Mission to El Salvador: The Application of the November 1977 "Law of Defence and Guarantee of Public Order," International Commission of Jurists, September 1978, p. 4.

15. Decree No. 12 of November 6, 1979.

16. Amnesty International, Report 1980, El Salvador, p. 136.

17. *Ibid.,* p. 121.

18. *Ibid.,* p. 122.

19. *Ibid.*

20. *Ibid.*

21. *Ibid.*

22. U.S. Department of State, Report on Human Rights Practices in Countries Receiving U.S. Aid, February 8, 1979, p. 247.

23. Report of IACHR, *op. cit.*

24. Report of British Parliamentary Delegation, December 15, 1978.

25. U.S. Department of State, Country Reports on Human Rights Practices, February 4, 1980, p. 315.

26. *Ibid.*

27. The Review, International Commission of Jurists, December 1979, No. 23, p. 4.

28. Central America 1980: Guatemala, El Salvador, Nicaragua, findings of an investigative mission, Unitarian Universalist Service Committee, p. 18 (20 killed); Amnesty International, 1980 Annual Report, El Salvador, p. 134 (52 killed). Both sources are in accord that the shooting originated with the security forces.

29. Central America, *op. cit.* p. 19.
Prelates attending the funeral issued the following declaration:

> The following is what we could see from the steps of the Cathedral and its towers, and the evidence we have gathered on our rounds in the city: A) The sudden explosion of a powerful bomb was heard; several witnesses state they saw this thrown from the National Palace. B) Then bursts of fire and shots rang out; several of the priests present stated that these came from the second story of the National Palace. C) We saw or could verify the presence of the Security Forces in the streets of San Salvador and in the approaches to the city since the early hours of the morning."

30. Interview with U.S. Ambassador to El Salvador Deane Hinton, San Salvador, August 28, 1981, by Aryeh Neier.

31. The Salvadoran daily, *La Prensa Grafica* (January 12, 1981, p. 3) reported the enactment of the curfew and stated: "No citizen may circulate the streets without risking losing his life, as we were *officially informed.*" (emphasis added). Moreover, a U.S. official in San Salvador confirmed that the orders given were to shoot to kill.

32. *Ciudadanos asesinados durante el periodo que rige la ley Marcial,* Socorro Juridico, San Salvador, undated; see also, Amnesty International, Central America Special Action (CASA), El Salvador, 30 July 1981; *The Washington Post,* April 9 and 12, 1981; *London Times,* April 10, 1981; *International Herald Tribune,* April 16, 1981.

33. Data received from Roberto Cuellar, Executive Director, *Socorro Juridico,* September 9, 1981.

34. Hearings before the Committee on Foreign Relations, U.S. Senate, 97th Congress, March 18 and April 19, 1981, "Prepared Statement of Amnesty International, U.S.A.," p. 238.

35. Amnesty International, Report 1980, El Salvador.

36. *Ibid.*

37. Copies on file at the Library of the Center for National Security Studies, Washington, D.C.

38. Copies on file at the Library of the Center for National Security Studies, Washington, D.C.

39. Copies on file at the Library of the Center for National Security Studies, Washington, D.C.

40. "Scores of Bodies Found North of San Salvador," *The New York Times,* November 29, 1981.

41. "Copies on file . . .", *op. cit.*

42. "Salvadoran Army Begins Drive Against Rebels," *The New York Times,* September 15, 1981.

43. I would like to appeal in a special way to the men of the army, and in particular to the troops of the National Guard, the police, and the garrisons. Brothers, you belong to our own people. You kill your own brother peasants; and in the face of an order to kill that is given by a man, the law of God, which says "Do not kill," should prevail. No soldier is obliged to obey an order counter to the law of God. No one has to comply with an immoral law. It is time now that you recover your conscience and obey its dictates rather than the command of sin. The Church, defender of the rights of God, of the law of God, of the dignity of the human person, cannot remain silent before so much abomination.

We want the government to seriously consider that reforms mean nothing when they come bathed in so much blood. Therefore, in the name of God, and in the name of this long-suffering people, whose laments rise every day more tumultuously to heaven, I beseech you, I beg you, I command you in the name of God: cease the repression!

44. Interview with Jorge Pinto, Mexico City, August 13, 1981, by Roberto Alvarez.

45. "Copies on file . . .", *op. cit.*

46. Interview with Roberto Cuellar, Mexico City, August 14, 1981, by Roberto Alvarez.

47. "A Report on the Investigation into the Killing of four American Churchwomen in El Salvador", Lawyers Committee for International Human Rights, New York, New York, September, 1981.

48. Legal Aid, *El Salvador, One Year of Repression, op. cit.,* p. 24.

49. Amnesty International, Report 1981, El Salvador, p. 145; Legal Aid, *El Salvador, One Year of Repression, op. cit.,* p. 16.

50. Legal Aid, *El Salvador, One Year of Repression, op. cit.,* p. 16.

51. Amnesty International, Report 1981, El Salvador, p. 140.

52. See letter from Thomas Hammarberg, Secretary General of Amnesty International to General Alexander Haig, Secretary of State of the

United States, May 6, 1981. See also, *Socorro Juridico,* Persecution and Killing of Children in El Salvador, February 21, 1981.

53. *Ibid.*

54. Amnesty International, Report 1981, El Salvador, p. 139.

55. *Ibid.*

56. *Op. cit.,* p. 144.

57. *Ibid.*

58. Telex dated June 19, 1981, from the El Salvador Commission on Human Rights (Mexico City, transmitting a communique).

59. Hearings before the Committee on Foreign Relations, U.S. Senate, 97th Congress, March 18 and April 9, 1981, p. 240.

60. Legal Aid, *El Salvador, One Year of Repression, op. cit.,* p. 14.

61. Annual Report of the Inter-American Commission on Human Rights, 1979–80, OEA/Ser. L./V/II.50, doc. 13 rev. 1, October 2, 1980, p. 144.

62. Amnesty International, Report 1981, El Salvador, p. 143.

63. *Ibid.*

64. *Ibid.*

65. See *Disappearances—A Workbook,* Amnesty International U.S.A., 1981.

66. Amnesty International, Report for 1977, p. 140.

67. Amnesty International, Report for 1978, p. 121.

68. Report on El Salvador, IACHR, *op. cit.,* pp. 97–98.

69. *Ibid.,* p. 165.

70. Human Rights in El Salvador, A Report of a British Parliamentary Delegation in December 1978, pp. 50–54.

71. Personas capturadas por motivos politicos y posteriormente dadas por desaparecidas, Socorro Juridico, San Salvador. All of the 182 disappearances except one are reported to have taken place under the governments of Presidents Molina (1972–77) and Romero (1977–79).

72. Question of human rights of all persons subjected to any form of detention or imprisonment, in particular: Question of missing and disappeared persons, Report of the Working Group on enforced or involuntary disappearances, Commission on Human Rights, 37th Session, UN E/CN. 4/1435, 26 January 1981, para. 86.

73. Estudios Centroamericanos, enero-febrero 1980, pp. 136–39.

74. *Ibid.*

75. *Ibid.*

76. Ministerio Publico, Fiscalia General de la Republica, San Salvador, November 10, 1980. It is interesting to point out that the Attorney General at that time, Guillermo Antonio Guevara Lacayo, is today one of the three principal members of the Central Election Council.

77. See Desaparecidos por motivos politicos a partir del 15 de oc-

tubre de 1979, Socorro Juridico, San Salvador, undated.

   78. *Ibid.*

   79. Report of the Working Group, *op. cit.,* p. 41.

   80. *Ibid.,* p. 43.

   81. Amnesty International, Report for 1981, p. 146.

   82. *Socorro Juridico,* undated.

CHAPTER 4

   1. *Report on the Situation of Human Rights in El Salvador,* Inter-American Commission on Human Rights, (I ACHR), General Secretariat, Organization of American States, Washington, D.C. OEA/SER. L/V/ 11.46 Doc. 23, rev. 1, 1978. *Human Rights in El Salvador—* Report of a British Parliamentary Delegation in December 1978, Parliamentary Human Rights Group, House of Commons, London, 1978. *Report on Human Rights Practices in Countries Receiving U.S. Aid, 1979,* El Salvador, (Report to the Committee on Foreign Relations, U.S. Senate, and Committee on Foreign Affairs, U.S. House of Representatives by the Department of State), Washington, D.C., 1979, p. 248. *Report on Human Rights Practices in Countries Receiving U.S. Aid, 1980,* El Salvador.

   2. Report on Human Rights Practices, 1980, *op. cit.* p. 345.

   3. *Application of the November 1977 "Law of the Defense and Guarantee of Public Order",* International Commission of Jurists, September, 1978, p. 22.

   4. *Abuses of Medical Neutrality,* Report of the Public Health Commission to El Salvador, July 1980, Committee for Health Rights in El Salvador, New York, 1980, p. 4.

   5. *Ecumenical Visit to El Salvador March 22–25, 1980, Press Release,* Washington, D.C. 1980, p. 3.

   6. *Statement,* by Amnesty International on the Occasion of the Tenth Regular Session of the General Assembly of the Organization of American States, November 19–26, 1980, as quoted in *U.S. Policy toward El Salvador,* Hearings before the Subcommittee on Inter-American Affairs of the Committee on Foreign Affairs, March 5 and 11, 1981, Washington, D.C. 1981, p. 123.

   7. Amnesty International, *Annual Report 1980, op. cit.,* p. 133.

   8. *El Salvador: One Year of Repression,* documentation prepared by the Legal Aid Office of the Archdiocese of San Salvador, World Council of Churches, New York, 1981, p. 11.

   9. *Human Rights Since the Change of Government of 15 October 1979,* Amnesty International, London, England, 1980, p. 17.

   10. *Abuses of Medical Neutrality, op. cit.,* fn 4, p. 4.

11. *Testimony,* Legal Aid Office, Archdiocese of El Salvador, 1980.

12. *AI Concerns in El Salvador, Amnesty International,* Index: AMR 29/07/81, NS/CO/AD, London, 2 February 1981, p. 1.

13. *Testimony,* Human Rights Commission of El Salvador, San Salvador, El Salvador.

14. *Proceso* Mexico, 1 September 1980.

15. *Fifty-one Cases of Political Prisoners held in Santa Tecla Prison,* Legal Aid Office, Archdiocese of El Salvador, San Salvador, El Salvador, 1981, p. 1–8.

16. *Ibid.,* p. 1.

17. *Testimony,* Commission for Human Rights in El Salvador, San Salvador, El Salvador, 1981.

CHAPTER 5

1. Amnesty International, *Report 1979,* p. 63, citing a July 1978 Report by the office of Archbishop Oscar A. Romero.

2. Decree No. 9, October 26, 1979, published in Diario Oficial, November 2, 1979.

3. Decree No. 155, March 6, 1980.

4. Decree No. 296, June 24, 1980.

5. *Ibid.,* articles 2, 3, 7, 8 and 9.

6. Decree No. 43, August 21, 1980, article 1.

7. Decree Nos. 264 and 265, Diario Oficial, May 23, 1980.

8. They are: treason, espionage, rebellion, sedition, crimes against the independence of the State and against the law of Nations. And particularly: crimes against collective security, arson, explosion and offenses against means of transportation or public services; destruction of economic goods or means of production; crimes against the existence and organization of the State, against the personhood of the State (treason, espionage), against the domestic personhood of the State (rebellion, sedition) and against the public peace (acts of terrorism, etc. and the disruption of religious ceremonies).

9. Socorro Juridico del Arzobispado de San Salvador, *Instrumentos Juridicas que Legalizan la Sistemative Violacion de los Derechos* Humanes y Sociales en El Salvador, p. 12.

10. Socorro Juridico, *Cronologia de la Persecucion de la Iglesia,* in SOLIDARIDAD, Boletion Internacional, No. 22.

11. Comision Nacional de Justicia y Paz de El Salvador, Arzobispado de San Salvador, *Transcripcion de Algunas Noticias Transmitidas por YSAX La Voz Panamericana, Emisora del Arzobispado,* August 16, 1980.

12. Socorro Juridico, SOLIDARIDAD, Boletin Internacional, July 1980.

13. *Id., Violacion a los Derechos Individuales de Profesionales del Periodismo y Trabajadores de Prensa,* San Salvador, June 4, 1981.

14. Comite de Madres y Familiares de Presos y Desaparecidos Politicos de El Salvador, San Salvador, July 15, 1981.

15. FENASTRAS (National Trade Union Federation of Salvadoran Workers), *Legal-Political Report on the Situation of the Unionists Detained by the Christian-Democrat-Military Junta of El Salvador,* San Salvador, July 1981.

16. LIBERTAD, Ano II, Epoca 2. Comision de Presos Politicos de El Salvador (COPPES), Neuva San Salvador, July 15, 1981.

17. Decree No. 2996, January 14, 1960.

18. FENASTRAS, *Legal-Political Report Op. cit.* fn 15.

19. Art. 74, Constitutional Procedures Act.

CHAPTER 6

1. Decree No. 407, of November 25, 1977. For the full text of the Law see *Report on the Situation of Human Rights in El Salvador,* Inter-American Commission on Human Rights (IACHR), General Secretariat, Organization of American States, Washington, D.C., OEA/SER. L/V/II.46 Doc. 23, rev. 1, 1978, pp. 40–47.

2. Report on Human Rights Practices in Countries Receiving U.S. Aid, Department of State, February 8, 1979, p. 247.

3. IACHR Report, *op. cit.* Fn. 1, p. 109.

4. Report by Donald T. Fox on his mission to El Salvador in July 1978 to study the application of the November 1977 "Law of Defense and Guarantee of Public Order," International Commission of Jurists, September 1978, p. 11.

5. *Ibid.*

6. Socorro Juridico del Arzobispado, Instrumentos Juridicos Que Legalizan La Sistematica Violacion A Los Derechos Humanos y Sociales En El Salvador, p. 12.

7. *Ibid.,* Appendix.

8. For a full discussion of the failure of the Government of El Salvador to investigate the deaths of the American Churchwomen see Lawyers' Committee for International Human Rights. A Report on the Investigation Into the Killings of Four American Churchwomen in El Salvador, September 1981.

9. *Washington Post,* August 28, 1981, p. A-6.

10. Socorro Juridico del Arzobispado de San Salvador, Instrumentos Juridicos Que Legalizan La Sistematica Violacion los Derechos Humanos y Sociales En El Salvador, pp. 8–9.

11. *Ibid.*

12. IACHR 1978 Annual Report, p. 26.

13. U.S. Department of State *Country Reports on Human Rights Practices* El Salvador (February 2, 1981) P. 429.

14. International Commission of Jurists (ICJ) *Human Rights in the World: El Salvador,* 26 ICJ Review 3 (June 1981) p. 6.

15. Written testimony prepared for this report. Mahagua, Nicaragua, August 1981.

16. IACHR *1979–1980 Annual Report,* p. 143.

17. ICJ Center for the Independence of Judges and Lawyers (CIJL) Case Reports: El Salvador in 7 *CIJL Bulletin* 15, p. 26.

18. IACHR 1979–1980 Annual Report p. 142 In a September 10, 1981 *Washington Post* article, the Salvadoran Defense Ministry was reported to have made renewed accusations against the Legal Aid Office, "saying it favors leftist guerrillas and linking its director to the leftist Democratic Revolutionary Front." The Post's story quotes the Ministry's news release as saying, "Legal Aid has never done anything on behalf of the innumerable security agents and citizens kidnapped by subversive organizations" and "We have documents to prove that Legal Aid Director Roberto Cuellar has links with the Democratic Revolutionary Front."

CHAPTER 7

1. Testimony by Msgr. James A. Hickey before the House of Representatives, Inter-American Affairs Subcommittee, March 5, 1981.

2. *Persecution of the Church in El Salvador,* Publications of the Inter-Diocesan Social Secretariat, (San Salvador, June 1977).

3. *Ibid.,* pp. 56–57.

4. Organization of American States, Inter-American Commission on Human Rights, *Report on the Situation of Human Rights in El Salvador* (Washington, D.C., November 17, 1978).

5. *Op. cit.,* pp. 16–21.

6. *Amnesty International Report 1977,* (London, 1977) pp. 140–141.

7. Honorable Robert F. Drinan, John J. McAward, Thomas Anderson, *Human Rights in El Salvador: Report of Findings of an Investigatory Mission* (Boston, Unitarian Universalist Service Committee, 1978).

8. U.S. Department of State, *Country Reports on Human Rights Practices for 1979,* (Washington, February 1979), p. 253.

9. U.S. Department of State, *Country Reports on Human Rights Practices for 1980,* (Washington, February 1980), p. 318.

10. Testimony by person present at "El Despertar" retreat center at the time of the assassination of Fr. Octavio Ortiz.

11. Archbishop Oscar A. Romero, "Pastoral Message for the New

Situation in the Country," (San Salvador, October 16, 1979).

12. Archdiocese Legal Aid Office, weekly reports 1980–1981, (San Salvador).

13. Archdiocese Legal Aid Office, "Persecution Against the Church: October 11, 1979 to February 17, 1981," (San Salvador, March 1, 1981).

14. *Op. cit.*

15. Archbishop Oscar A. Romero, Homily of March 16, 1980, (San Salvador).

16. Communique of the Office of Social Communications, (San Salvador, October 19, 1980).

17. Idem.

18. *La Prensa Grafica,* March 30, 1981.

19. Communique of the San Salvador Archdiocese, (San Salvador, December 5, 1980).

20. Testimony by Robert Tiller, American Baptist Churches, before the House of Representatives, Inter-American Affairs Subcommittee, March 11, 1981.

CHAPTER 8

1. Report on the Situation of Human Rights in El Salvador, Inter-American Commission on Human Rights (IACHR), OEA/-SER.L/V/11/46 Doc. 23 Rev. 1 17 November 1978, General Secretariat, Organization of American States, Washington, D.C., p. 138.

2. As quoted in *Ibid.*

3. *The Review,* International Commission of Jurists, No. 20, June 1978, Human Rights in the World: El Salvador, p. 14.

4. IACHR Report, *op. cit.,* fn. 2, p. 137.

5. *Latin America: The Freedom to Write,* Report by the Freedom to Write Committee of the PEN American Center, New York, New York, 1980.

6. *Ibid.*

7. *Proclamation of the Armed Forces of El Salvador,* 15 October 1979, San Salvador, El Salvador, p. 1.

8. *Annual Report of the Inter-American Commission on Human Rights 1979–1980,* OEA/SER.L/V/11.50 2 October 1980. General Secretariat, Organization of American States, Washington, D.C. p. 144.

9. *La Prensa Grafica,* 29 March 1981, San Salvador, El Salvador, p. 1.

10. *El Comite de Prensa de la Fuerza Armada,* 2 April 1981, San Salvador, El Salvador.

11. Legal Aid Office of the Archdiocese of San Salvador as quoted in SALPRESS, 6/7/81 News Release, Washington, D.C. 1981.

12. *Index on Censorship,* Vol. 3, 1981.

13. Interview for this report with Jorge Pinto by Roberto Alvarez, August 13, 1981, Mexico City, Mexico. (Text available.)

14. *Ibid.*

15. *Ibid.*

16. *Ibid.*

17. Index, *op. cit.* fn. 12.

18. *Proceso,* September 1980; Mexico City, Mexico.

19. *Index, op. cit.* fn. 12.

20. *The Review,* No. 26, Intl. Commission of Jurists, June 1981, New York, New York.

21. "IEB raps arms to El Salvador, Urges hearings on Guatemala," *The Guild Reporter,* May 8, 1981.

22. "Journalists Seen as Targets, Press Concern is Mounting," *The News Media and the Law.*

23. "Reporters in Bulletproof Vests," *Columbia Journalism Review,* July/Aug. 1980.

24. "Get Out or Die," *Media File,* June 1981.

25. "In Salvador, Nooseprint," Jorge Pinto, May 6, 1981. *The New York Times.*

26. *72 Teachers Killed January–August 1980:* El Salvador. 24 October 1980, Submission by Amnesty International Regarding the Repression of Teachers in El Salvador, as quoted in *U.S. Policy Toward El Salvador,* Hearings March 5 and 11, 1981, before the Subcommittee on Inter-American Affairs of the Committee on Foreign Affairs, House of Representatives, Govt. Printing Office: 1981, p. 124.

27. *Ibid.,* p. 127.

28. *Ibid.,* p. 127.

29. Statement by Catholic University in El Salvador, "Jose Simeon Canas Central American University High Council Condemns Repression Against Salvadorean Educators," July 4, 1980, San Salvador, El Salvador.

30. Socorro Juridico del Arzobispado, undated mimeograph.

CHAPTER 9

1. Archbishop Oscar Romero, Third Pastoral letter, *Church in the World,* No. 5, Catholic Institute for International Relations, London, 1980, p. 8.

2. Report of the 1978 Mission to El Salvador, International Commission of Jurists, p. 5.

3. *Ibid.*

4. *Ibid.*

5. Law of the Defense and Guarantee of Public Order, (La Ley de Defensa y Garantia del Orden Publico); promulgated on November 24, 1977.

6. Report on the Situation of Human Rights in El Salvador, Inter-American Commission on Human Rights of the Organization of American States (IACHR), OEA/SER.L./V/11.46, Nov. 1978, pp. 40–71.

7. "Representation of Trade Unions in El Salvador," Amnesty International, Dec. 1978 at p. 3.

8. Amnesty International, 1980 Annual Report, pp. 132–33.

9. Proclamation of the Armed Forces of the Government of El Salvador, Guidelines II-B and II-D, October 15, 1979.

10. Amnesty International, 1980 Annual Report, p. 133.

11. *Ibid.*

12. Amnesty International, Update on El Salvador, Dec. 11, 1979 at p. 2.

13. *Id.* at p. 3

14. *Ibid.*

15. Amnesty International Submission to the Inter-American Commission on Human Rights of the OAS, March 21, 1980 at p. 5.

16. *Id.* at p. 6

17. Free Trade Union News, AFL-CIO, Vol. 36, No. 2, February 1981, p. 4.

18. Thiesenhusen, William C., "El Salvador's Land Reform: Was It Programed to Fail?", *Christianity in Crisis,* May 11, 1981, p. 135.

19. Latin America and Caribbean Labour Report, March 1981, p. 3.

20. Testimony of Hector Recinos, Latin America and Caribbean Labour Report, March 1981, p. 3.

21. Decree No. 43 of the Ministries of the Interior and of Defense and Public Security, promulgated on August 21, 1980.

22. Interview of Americo Duran of the Committee of United Trade Unions (CVS), March 1981.

23. Testimony of a leader of Andes, June 21, 1981.

24. Amnesty International, Urgent Action, June 22, 1981.

25. Report of A Delegation to El Salvador from the Social Justice Commission, Archdiocese of San Francisco, July 17–August 23, 1980.

26. Amnesty International, Testimony on El Salvador to the Subcommittee on Inter-American Affairs of the Committee on Foreign Affairs, March 5, 1981 at p. 3.

27. United States Catholic Conference Statement "U.S. Bishop Denounces Latin Troups Invasion of Catholic Church Office," July 9, 1980, p. 1.

28. Letter from Bishop Thomas C. Kelly, General Secretary of the

United States, Catholic Conference, to the Organization of American States, dated July 9, 1980.

29. Interview of Roberto Cuellar by Roberto Alvarez in Mexico City, August 14, 1981 at p. 15.

30. *Id.* at 20.

31. *Id.* at 25.

32. Human Rights Commission of El Salvador, Press Release, Not dated, p. 1.

33. Amnesty International, Submission to the OAS, March 21, 1980 at p. 6.

34. Human Rights Commission of El Salvador, Press Release, p. 2.

35. Amnesty International, Urgent Action, October 8, 1980.

36. Amnesty International, Testimony on El Salvador, *op. cit.* at p. 5.

37. Amnesty International, Urgent Action, October 8, 1980.

38. Human Rights Commission of El Salvador, Press Release, p. 2.

39. *Ibid.*

40. *Ibid.*

41. IACHR Report on the Situation of Human Rights in El Salvador, *op. cit.* at p. 130.

CHAPTER 10

1. *Report on Human Rights Practices in Countries Receiving U.S. Aid,* Feb. 8, 1979, pp. 247 & 254.

2. *Country Report on Human Rights Practices for 1979,* Feb. 4, 1980, p. 319.

3. *Report on the Situation of Human Rights in El Salvador,* Inter-American Commission on Human Rights (IACHR), OAS, 17 November 1978, Washington, D.C.

4. Proclamation of the Armed Forces of the Republic of El Salvador, Oct. 15, 1979.

5. Dickey, Christopher, *Death as a Way of Life,* in *Playboy,* October 1980, pp. 173–174

6. See his resignation, dated March 3, 1980, and his letter to the leadership of the PDC, announcing his intention, dated March 1, 1980.

7. "The Central Electoral Council Abuses Its Duties", paid advertisement in *El Diario de Hoy,* San Salvador, June 2, 1981, p. 21.

8. "Politics a-lo-Salvadoreno, But with a Touch of Foreignness", in *Informe* July 11—August 21, 1981 (A publication of Agencia Independiente de Prensa, Washington, D.C.).

9. Letter of May 11, 1981; *El Pais,* Madrid; Ignacio Ellacuria, "Elecc-

iones o Proceso de Mediacion en El Salvador?"; *El Mundo,* San Salvador, May 13, 1981.

10. Stephen Kinzer, "Salvadoran Leaders Vow to Hold March Elections", *Boston Globe,* July 19, 1981.

11. FBIS, 15 July 1981, pp. 5–6.

12. FBIS, 22 May 1981, p. 8.

13. Stephen Kinzer, *op. cit.*

14. Ungo, cited in FBIS, 29 June 1981, p. 2.

15. FBIS, 4 June 1981, p. 3.

16. Raymond Bonner, "U.S. Policy Opposed by Many in El Salvador", *The New York Times,* July 18, 1981.

CHAPTER 11

1. *UNHCR INFORMATION #1,* Central America, United Nations High Commission for Refugees, Geneva, Switzerland, June 1981, p. 1.

2. UNHCR *Background Paper for Embassies on the Refugee Situation in Northern Latin America,* UNHCR Geneva, Switzerland, June 1981, p. 1.

3. *ICRC Action in El Slavador: Situation Report and Appeal No. 2,* Comite International de la Croix Rouge, Geneva, Switzerland, June 17, 1981, p. 3.

4. Interview with Green Cross source, San Salvador, El Salvador.

5. *Press Release,* Amnesty International, 17 March 1980, p. 1.

6. *The Red Cross in El Salvador,* Comite International de la Croix Rouge, Geneva, Switzerland, March 1981, p. 2.

7. *Central America, 1981,* Report to the Committee on Foreign Affairs, U.S. House of Representatives, U.S. Government Printing Office, Washington, D.C. 1981, p. 26.

8. *Maclean's,* November 17, 1980, p. 33.

9. *Central America, 1981, op. cit.,* p. 27.

10. *On Salvadoran Refugees,* Legal Aid Office of the Archdiocese of El Salvador, San Salvador, El Salvador, March 1981, pp. 3–4.

11. "El Salvador Confines Some of Its Refugees", July 15, 1981, *The Washington Post.*

12. *On Salvadoran Refugees, op. cit.* fn. 5, pp. 5–6.

13. *Countries in Crisis:* Report of an AFSC Study Tour to Central America and the Caribbean Nov./Dec. 1980, p. 10 and "Refugees in Salvadoran Camp are forced to move by Army", July 6, 1981, *The New York Times.*

14. *Abuses of Medical Neutrality,* Report of the Public Health Commission to El Salvador, July 1980, Committee for Health Rights in El Salvador, 1980, p. 8.

15. *Ibid.* p. 2.

16. "Church World Service Asks $1.5 million for Salvadoran Refugees", National Council of Churches NEWS, 25 DOM 3/17/81, New York, New York, 1981, p. 1.

17. Resolution on Protection of Civilians, U.N., December 9, 1970, General Assembly Resolution 2675, United Nations, New York, New York.

18. *Geneva Convention* (IV) Article, 3, *op. cit.*

19. *On Salvadoran Refugees, op. cit.,* page 9, 10 (translation)

20. "Refugees in Salvadoran Camp are Forced to Move by Army", *op. cit.,* and "For War's Castaways, Prison is Home in Salvador", July 9, 1981, *The New York Times.*

21. "El Salvador Confines Some of Its Refugees" *op. cit.*

22. Interview with photojournalist, August, 1981.

23. "El Salvador Confines Some of Its Refugees" *op. cit.*

24. *Ibid.*

25. *Ibid.*

26. "For War's Castaways, Prison is Home in Salvador", *op. cit.*

27. *Background Paper for Embassies, op. cit.* p. 1.

28. Letter from O. Haselman, Chief, Americas, Iberia, and Oceania Section, UNHCR, Geneva, 29 May, 1981, to Mr. G. Cram, Chairman, Standing Conference of Canadian Organizations Concerned for Refugees.

29. *UNHCR Information #1, op. cit.* p. 2.

30. *Background Paper for Embassies, op. cit.* p. 2.

31. *Update on Salvadoran Refugees in Honduras,* Washington Office on Latin America, Washington, D.C. July, 1981

32. *Ibid.*

33. "Salvador Raids into Honduras, Refugees Charge", January 7, 1981, *The Washington Post.*

34. "Salvador Says 30,000 Refugees may be Moved Farther Into Honduras", June 27, 1981, *The New York Times.*

35. Translation by Inter-Church Committee for Human Rights in Latin America, Toronto, Canada.

36. *See e.g.* London *Sunday Times,* February 22, 1981.

37. *United Church Observer,* October 1980, p. 40.

38. "The Innocents Caught in Lempa River Massacre", April 26, 1981, London *Sunday Times.* See also *Washington Post* May 10, 1981, *New York Times,* June 8, 1981.

39. Interviews with relief personnel, July, August 1981.

40. Amnesty International *CASA Special Action,* August 1981.

41. "No Haven for Salvadoran Refugees in the U.S.", March 17,

1981, Inter-Religions Task Force on El Salvador, New York, New York, 1981, p. 1.

42. *Ibid.*

43. *Ibid.*, and "Shifting Sands of U.S. Immigration Policy Trap Salvadoran Refugees", Michael Maggio, Refugee and Human Rights Newsletter, Church World Service, Immigration and Refugee Program Volume V. No. 1, Winter 1981, New York, New York, 1981, p. 20.

44. U.S. Department of State Response to Subcommittee on Inter-American Affairs from Richard Fairbanks, Assistant Secretary of State for Congressional Relations, April 8, 1981.

CHAPTER 12

1. Center for International Policy, Aid Memo, "Total Aid Package for El Salvador May Reach $523 Million," Washington, D.C., April, 1981.

2. U.S. Department of Defense, *Foreign Military Sales and Military Assistance Facts* (hereinafter cited as FMS & MAF), Washington, D.C., 1981.

3. *The Washington Post,* March 1981.

4. Howard Blutstein, ed., *Area Handbook on El Salvador,* U.S. Government Printing Office, Washington, D.C., 1971, p. 195.

5. U.S. Department of Defense, *FMS & MAF.*

6. Michael T. Klare, *Supplying Repression,* Institute for Policy Studies, Washington, D.C., 1977, p. 38.

7. U.S. Agency for International Development, *Termination Phase-Out Study, Public Safety Project, El Salvador,* Washington, D.C., 1974, p. 1.

8. *Ibid.,* pp. 19–27.

9. *Ibid.,* p. 5.

10. U.S. Agency for International Development, Office of Public Safety, *Report on Visit to Central America and Panama,* Washington, D.C., 1967, p. 5.

11. U.S. Agency for International Development, Termination Phase-Out Study, *op. cit.,* p. 3.

12. U.S. Agency for International Development, *Report . . . , op. cit.,* p. 23.

13. U.S. Agency for International Development, *Termination . . . , op. cit.,* p. 10.

14. *Ibid.,* p. 9, 13.

15. U.S. Agency for International Development, *Report . . . , op. cit.,* p. 8.

16. *Ibid.,* p. 24.

17. *Washington Star,* May 17, 1976, and Penny Lernoux, *Cry of the People* Doubleday and Co., Garden City, New York, 1980, p. 69.

18. Documents received by the author under the Freedom of Information Act.

19. Quoted in Washington Office on Latin America, *Update,* December, 1979.

20. Quoted in *The Washington Post,* February 19, 1980.

21. Interview, U.S. Department of State, December 15, 1980.

22. *The Washington Post,* February 14, 1980.

23. Quoted in *The Washington Post,* February 19, 1981.

24. Letter from Amnesty International Secretary General Martin Ennals to U.S. Deputy Secretary of State Warren Christopher, February 29, 1980, p. 1.

25. Thomas Conrad and Cynthia Arnson, "The Aid for El Salvador is Called 'Non-lethal'," *The New York Times,* June 15, 1980.

26. Testimony of Deputy Assistant Secretary of State John Bushnell and Deputy Assistant Secretary of Defense Franklin Kramer, U.S. Congress House Subcommittee on Foreign Operations, Hearings, *Foreign Assistance and Related Programs Appropriations for 1981,* 96th Cong., 2nd sess., March 25, 1980, pp. 332, 339.

27. Testimony of Heather Foote, *Ibid.,* p. 387.

28. U.S. Department of Defense, *Congressional Presentation: Security Assistance for Fiscal Year 1981,* Washington, D.C., 1980, p. 391.

29. Conrad and Arnson, *op. cit.*

30. Letter from Amnesty International IEC Chairperson Jose Zalaquett to U.S. Secretary of State Edmund Muskie, June 24, 1980.

31. Quoted in *The Washington Post,* October 9, 1980.

32. Quoted in *The Washington Post,* October 12, 1980.

33. Documents received by the author under the Freedom of Information Act.

34. United Nations General Assembly, Report of the Economic and Social Council, "The Situation of Human Rights and Fundamental Freedom in El Salvador," December 1, 1980.

35. U.S. Department of State, *Press Statement,* December 5, 1980.

36. U.S. Department of State, *Press Statement,* December 17, 1980.

37. U.S. Department of State, *Press Statement,* January 14, 1981.

38. *Ibid.*

39. U.S. Department of State, *Press Statement,* January 17, 1981.

40. *Ibid.*

41. "Communist Interference in El Salvador," U.S. Department of State, Bureau of Public Affairs, Washington, D.C., February 23, 1981.

42. See e.g., *The Wall Street Journal,* June 8, 1981; *The Washington Post,* June 9, 1981.

43. U.S. Department of State, *Statement on Assistance to El Salvador,* March 2, 1981.

44. U.S. Defense Security Assistance Agency, August 12, 1981.

45. U.S. Department of Defense, *Congressional Presentation: Security Assistance for Fiscal Year 1982,* Washington, D.C.

46. Letter from Amnesty International Secretary General Thomas Hammarberg to U.S. Secretary of State Alexander Haig, May 6, 1981, p. 1.

47. *Ibid.,* p. 6.

48. Letter from U.S. Deputy Secretary of State William P. Clark to Amnesty International Secretary General Thomas Hammerberg, June 4, 1981.

49. See Footnote 18.

50. Documents received by the author under the Freedom of Information Act.

51. Documents received by the author under the Freedom of Information Act, and interview, U.S. Department of Defense, December 4, 1980.

52. U.S. Department of State, "U.S. Assistance to El Salvador, Fact Sheet,".

53. Testimony of Robert White, U.S. Congress, House Subcommittee on Foreign Operations, Hearings, *Foreign Assistance and Related Programs Appropriations for 1982,* 97th Cong., 1st sess., February 25, 1981, p. 24.

54. U.S. Department of State, *Statement on Assistance to El Salvador,* March 2, 1981.

55. Information for the list comes from a variety of different sources, including documents received by the author under the Freedom of Information Act; interviews, U.S. Department of State and Department of Defense; *The New York Times,* March 1, 10, 14, 29, and July 8, 13, 1981; *The Washington Post,* March 3, 10, 18, and June 7, 1981; *The Los Angeles Times,* June 7, 1981; *The Washington Star,* February 24, 1981; The Baltimore Sun, February 3, 1981. Where information has been contradictory, author has relied on Administration sources.

56. U.S. Department of State, *Press Statement,* February 28, 1981.

57. Testimony of Under Secretary of State for Political Affairs Walter J. Stoessel, Jr., before the Senate Appropriations Committee, March 13, 1981.

58. Interview, U.S. Department of Defense, August 13, 1981.

59. UPI, Washington, July 28, 1981.

60. United States District Court of the District of Columbia, Civil Action No. 81-1034, Defendant's Exhibit 8, p. 3.

61. *The Baltimore Sun,* February 3, 1981.

62. *La Prensa Gráfica,* June 22, 1981.

63. Testimony of Robert White, *op. cit.,* p. 3.

64. Testimony of Reps. Gerry Studds, Barbara Mikulski, and Robert Edgar, *ibid.,* p. 28.

65. Documents received by the author under the Freedom of Information Act.

66. Testimony of Robert White, *op. cit.,* p. 2.

67. Quoted in *The New York Times,* February 21, 1981.

68. *El Diario de Hoy,* March 17, 1981.

69. *Ibid.*

70. Interview, July 29, 1981.

71. Testimony of Reps. Gerry Studds, Barbara Mikulski, and Robert Edgar, *op. cit.,* p. 29.

72. *Ibid.,* p. 29.

73. Cables filed by David Blundy, London *Sunday Times,* April, 1981.

74. Inter-Religious Task Force on El Salvador, *Press Release,* Washington, D.C., April 13, 1981.

75. Quoted in the London *Sunday Times,* April 26, 1981.

76. U.S. Department of Commerce, *Foreign Broadcast Information Service,* July 18, 1981.

77. Interview, Washington, D.C., September 18, 1981.

78. Testimony of Deputy Assistant Secretary of State, John Bushnell, *op. cit.,* p. 433.

79. U.S. Department of Defense, *Congressional Presentation FY82, op. cit.,* p. 433.

80. Testimony of Robert White, op. cit., p. 10.

CHAPTER 13

1. Henkin writes: "(T)he broader theories and recurrent practice lend support to the view that the President's powers in foreign affairs are 'plenary'—Justice Sutherland's word—and that nothing in inherently outside his domain." L. Henkin, "Foreign Affairs and the Constitution" 50 (1972).

2. U.S. Const., Art. 1, sec. 8, cl. 1.

3. U.S. Const., Art. 1, sec. 8, cl. 18.

4. U.S. Const., Art. 1, sec. 8, cl. 7.

5. Henkin, cited *supra* note 1, at 70.

6. Section 116 of the Foreign Assistance Act prohibits the provision of U.S. bilateral economic assistance to any country the government of which "engages in a consistent pattern of gross violations of internationally recognized human rights . . . *unless* such assistance will directly

benefit the needy people in such country." 22 U.S.C. § 2151n(a) (1979) (emphasis added).

Section 701 of the International Financial Institutions Act of 1977 instructs the U.S. Executive Directors of the international financial institutions "to oppose any loan, any extension of financial assistance, or any technical assistance to any country" engaged in a consistent pattern of gross violations *"unless* such assistance is directed specifically to programs which serve the basic human needs of the citizens of such country." 22 U.S.C. § 262d(d) (1979). (emphasis added)

Section 239(1) of the Foreign Assistance Act applies the provisions of Section 116 "to any insurance, reinsurance, guaranty, or loan" issued by the Overseas Private Investment Corporation for projects in a country except where the project "will directly benefit the needy people in such country" or where "the national security interest so requires." 22 U.S.C. § 2199(1) (1979).

Section 112 of the Agricultural Trade Development and Assistance Act of 1954 states:

> No agreement may be entered into under this title to finance the sale of agricultural commodities to the government of any country which engages in a consistent pattern of gross violations of internationally recognized human rights . . . *unless* such agreement will directly benefit the needy people in such country. An agreement will not directly benefit the needy people in the country for purposes of the preceding sentence unless either the commodities themselves or the proceeds from their sale will be used for specific projects or programs which the President determines would directly benefit the needy people of that country. The agreement shall specify how the projects or programs will be used to benefit the needy people and shall require a report to the President on such use within 6 months after the commodities are delivered to the recipient country. 7 U.S.C. § 1712 (1979)

For a complete compilation of the human rights legislation, see *U.S. Legislation Relating Human Rights to U.S. Foreign Policy,* (2d ed. R. Lillich, ed., 1980).

7. 22 U.S.C. § 2304(a)(1) (1979).
8. 22 U.S.C. § 2304(a)(2) (1979).
9. 22 U.S.C. § 2304(d)(2) (1979).
10. Authorized under 22 U.S.C. § 2311 *et seq.* (1979 and Supp. 1980).
11. Authorized under 22 U.S.C. § 2347 *et seq.* (1979 and Supp. 1980).
12. Authorized under 22 U.S.C. § 2763, 64 (1979).
13. Authorized under 22 U.S.C. § 2346 *et seq.* (1979 and Supp. 1980).
14. 22 U.S.C. § 2778(a)(1) (1979).
15. *Id.,* § 2778(b)(2) (1979).

16. P.L. No. 96-72, 93 Stat. 503 (codified at 50 App. U.S.C. § 2401 *et seq.* (Supp. 1980).

17. 22 U.S.C. § 2304(a)(2) (1979).

18. 22 U.S.C. § 2304(d)(1) (1979 and Supp. 1981).

19. 48 U.N. ECOSOC, Supp. 1A, at 8, U.N. Doc. E/4832 (1970).

20. *Id.,* para. 5.

21. Letter from Brian Atwood, Assistant Secretary of State for Congressional Relations, to Representative Matthew McHugh (Oct. 1980).

22. *See* Meier, cited infra note 26, at 58–61.

23. 22 U.S.C. § 2304(a)(2) (1979). The language of Section 2304(a)(2) is less than crystal clear. It begins with the phrase "(e)xcept under circumstances specified in this section," and continues with a statement of the central mandate against providing security assistance to countries engaged in gross and consistent human rights violations. The only "circumstances specified in this section" are the "extraordinary circumstances" specified in subsections 2304(a)(2) and 2304(c)(1)(C).

24. The elasticity of the "extraordinary circumstances" clause is demonstrated in the single State Department report that has been submitted to Congress under Section 502B(c). (See Section III (B)(5)(c) of this chapter.) In this report, published in 1976, the State Department described, *inter alia,* the "extraordinary circumstances" justifying assistance to Argentina, Haiti, Indonesia, Iran, Peru, and the Philippines. Strategic and economic considerations were listed as the prime justification for assistance to many of the countries, particularly those regarded as regional leaders. In explaining the extraordinary circumstances in other countries, the State Department expressed doubt that a cut-off of assistance would have a positive effect on the human rights situation there. In regard to Haiti, the Department emphasized the humanitarian nature of the assistance. Congress expressed no objections or dissatisfaction upon receiving this report, and, thereby, apparently sanctioned the broad interpretation of the extraordinary circumstances clause contained therein.

For a description of the legislative history of Section 502B see M. Meier, HUMAN RIGHTS RESTRICTIONS ON UNITED STATES SECURITY ASSISTANCE PROGRAMS—A DESCRIPTION OF THE IMPLEMENTATION OF THE HUMAN RIGHTS RESTRICTIONS IN UNITED STATES LAW DURING THE CARTER ADMINISTRATION 14-2 (1981) (unpublished manuscript).

25. 22 U.S.C. § 2304(b) (1979).

26. 22 U.S.C. § 2151n (1979).

27. 22 U.S.C. § 2304(a)(2) (1979).

28. *Id.*

29. *Id.*

30. Interview with Stephen Cohen, former Deputy Assistant Secretary of State for Human Rights and Humanitarian Affairs (June 15, 1981).

31. Officials within the State Department claim that this interpretation of section 502B serves to deter the approval of export license applications to countries with poor human rights records. The validity of this claim is not subject to public evaluation because, at this point, there is insufficient public access to information regarding the export of police equipment. Efforts to obtain this information under the Freedom of Information Act have been consistently unsuccessful.

No individual certifications under the crime control equipment clause have been submitted since the clause was added in 1978. Whether this reflects the alleged deterrent effect of the individual certification requirement, or a failure to comply with the law, is unknown.

32. The certification applicable to the fiscal year 1979 security assistance program, which was identical to the certification applicable to the fiscal year 1980 program, state:

> In accordance with Section 502B of the Foreign Assistance Act of 1961, as amended (The Act), I have reviewed the international security assistance programs of the United States for the fiscal year 1979 in order to assure that:
>
> (1) all security assistance programs are consistent with the provisions of Section 502B of the Act concerning the promotion and advancement of human rights violations, and
>
> (2) with respect to those countries where human rights conditions give rise to the most serious concerns, the security assistance provided by the United States is warranted in each case by extraordinary circumstances involving the national security interest of the United States.

On the basis of this review, I certify that these security assistance programs are in compliance with the requirements of section 502B of the Act. Dated Feb. 24, 1979. The fiscal year 1979 and fiscal year 1980 certifications are published in 44 Fed. Reg. 18763 (1979) and 44 Fed. Reg. 69755 (1979), respectively.

33. 22 U.S.C. § 2304(c) (1979).

34. 22 U.S.C. § 2304(c)(4)(A) (1979).

35. This limit on the use of funds for the MAP, IMET and ESF programs is set forth in Section 634A of the Foreign Assistance Act (22 U.S.C. § 2394-1 (1979)), which provides that the State Department may only deviate from the figures presented in the Congressional Presentation Document for the programs authorized under the Foreign Assistance Act if it submits a specific reprogramming notification to Congress 15

days in advance of the reprogramming. The same notification requirement applies to budgeted assistance provided under the Arms Export Control Act, i.e., the FMS financing program, through provisions in each year's appropriation bill.

36. P.L. No. 95-148, § 503B, 91 Stat. 1239 (1977).

37. Section 36(b) of the Arms Export Control Act requires the President to inform Congress of any letter of offer to sell defense articles or services in the amount of *$25 million or more,* or any major defense equipment in the amount of *$7 million or more.* The President must inform Congress before the letter of offer is issued. The letter of offer shall not be issued if Congress, within 30 calendar days after receiving the notification adopts a concurrent resolution in opposition to the sale. 22 U.S.C. § 2776(b) (1979 and Supp. 1981).

Section 36(c) of the Arms Export Control Act requires the President to inform Congress of any application for a license to export any major defense equipment sold under a contract in the amount of *$7 million or more,* or any defense articles or defense services sold under a contract in the amount of *$25 million or more.* The license shall not be issued until at least 30 calendar days after Congress receives the notification. The license shall not be issued if, within the 30 day period Congress adopts a concurrent resolution in opposition to the sale. 22 U.S.C. § 2776(c) (1979 and Supp. 1981).

38. *See* note 32 *supra.*

39. Foreign Assistance and Related Programs Appropriations for 1981 (Part II): Hearings before the Subcommittee on Foreign Operations of the House Appropriations Committee, 96th Cong., 1st Sess. 323–435 (1980).

40. 22 U.S.C. § 2420 (1979).

41. *Id.* § 2420(a) (1979).

42. P.L. No. 90-629, 82 Stat. 1320.

43. S. Rpt. No. 93-1299, 93d Cong., 2d Sess. (1974).

44. 22 U.S.C. § 2318 (1979 and Supp. 1981).

45. 22 U.S.C. § 2364 (Supp. 1981).

46. 22 U.S.C. § 2318(a) (1979).

47. *Id.* § 2318(b)(1).

48. *Id.* § 2318(b)(2).

49. Before its amendment in 1980, Section 614(a) read:

The President may authorize in such fiscal year the use of funds made available for use under this section and the *furnishing of assistance under section 2318 of this title (Section 506)* in a total amount not to exceed $250,000,000 . . . without regard to the requirements of this chapter, any Law relating to receipts and credits accruing to the

United States, any Act appropriating funds for use under this chapter, or the Mutual Defense Assistance Control Act of 1951, in furtherance of any of the purposes of such Acts, when the President determines that such authorization is important to the security of the United States [emphasis added].

50. P.L. No. 93-148, 87 Stat. 555 (codified at 50 U.S.C. § 1541 *et seq.* (Supp. 1981).

51. U.S. Const., Art. 1, sec. 8, cl. 11.

52. *See* generally J. Galloway, THE GULF OF TONKIN RESOLU-TION (1970; a court held that Congress had authorized the Vietnam War in *Orlando v. Laird,* 443 F.2d 1039 (2d Cir. 1971), *cert. denied,* 404 U.S. 869 (1971).

53. Henkin, cited *supra* note 1, at 108.

54. 50 U.S.C. § 1542 (Supp. 1981).

55. *Id.* § 1543(a) (Supp. 1981); This subsection sets forth two additional situations that may trigger the application of the reporting requirement. Because these situations are not relevant to the present U.S. involvement in El Salvador, they are not discussed. *See* 50 U.S.C. § 1543(a)(2) and (3).

56. *Id.* § 1543(c) (Supp. 1981).

57. *Id.* § 1544(b) (Supp. 1981).

58. *Id.*

59. *Id.* § 1544(c) (Supp. 1981).

60. *Id.* § 1547(c) (Supp. 1981).

61. (emphasis added) Henkin, cited *supra* note 1, at 103.

62. *Id.*

63. J. Franck and E. Weisband, Foreign Policy by Congress 71 (1979).

64. *Id.* at 73.

65. *Id.* at 71.

66. Memorandum of the Legal Adviser, Department of State (June 16, 1978) (Unpublished).

67. Letters from President Ford to Carl Albert (April 4, April 12, April 30, and May 15, 1975) (published in War Powers: A Test of Compliance Relative to the Danang Sealift, The Evacuation of Phnom Penh, The Evacuation of Saigon and the Mayaguez Incident: Hearings before the Subcommittee on International Security and Scientific Affairs of the House Committee on International Relations, 94th Cong., 1st Sess. 4, 5, 7, 76 (1975).

68. Frank and Weisband, cited *supra* note 59, at 71.

69. Attachment to Memorandum from Erich Von Marbod, Director, Defense Security Assistance Agency, to Representative Zablocki, Chairman, House Committee on Foreign Affairs (August 14, 1981).

70. 22 U.S.C. § 2761(c) (Supp. 1981).

71. *Id.* § 2761(c)(1).

72. *Id.* § 2761(c)(2).

73. *Id.* § 2761(c)(2)(A) & (B).

74. *Crockett v. Reagan, et al.,* No. 81-1034 (D.D.C., filed May 1, 1981).

75. Brief for plaintiffs at 24, *Crockett v. Reagan, et al.,* No. 81-1034.

APPENDIX I

1. The social democratic constitution of 1950 was similar to other Latin American ones (*i.e.,* Cuba 1940, Guatemala 1945), but it was likewise influenced by the Universal Declaration of Human Rights, adopted by the United Nations on December 1948.

2. Constitution of the Republic of El Salvador, 1962, General Secretariat, Organization of American States, Washington, D.C., 1971.

3. The analysis in this section follows the description of the Constitution of El Salvador contained in Chapter I of the Report on the Situation of Human Rights in El Salvador, Inter-American Commission on Human Rights, (IACHR) (cited as "IACHR Report"), OEA/Ser. L/V/11.46, doc. 23 rev. 1, 17 November 1978, pp. 32–35.

4. Decree No. 1136 of September 2, 1953, as amended. Recopilacion de Leyes, Publicaciones de la Corte Suprema de Justicia, San Salvador, 1976, pp. 69–127.

5. Decree No. 2996 of January 14, 1960, as amended. *Ibid.,* pp. 139–160.

6. Recopilacion de Leyes, Publicaciones de la Asamblea Legislativa, Tomo V, San Salvador, 1977, pp. 303–466. Other statutory provisions of continuing relevance include the Labor Code, Decree No. 15 of June 23, 1962 as amended (*Id.* at 14-183) and the Civil Code, Decree of August 23, 1859, as amended.

7. Article 151, the Penal Code of El Salvador, Decree No. 270 of February 13, 1973 as amended by Article 9 of Decree No. 381 of October 20, 1977, defines the concept of political crime. The detailed acts are enumerated in Articles 373–411.

Political crimes are defined as punishable acts directed against the existence and organization of the State and against its international or domestic personality, with the exception of vilifying the nation, its symbols and the founding fathers. It specifies that political crimes include common crimes committed with political objectives, except assaults against the life or personal integrity of chiefs of state. It adds that common crimes connected with political crimes are those which relate directly or indirectly to the political crime or constitute a natural and frequently utilized method of preparing, carrying out or facilitating such crimes.

The second book of the Penal Code defines in some detail the acts that are to be sanctioned as crimes. Chapters I through IV of the Fourth Part of the second book establish the following specific political crimes:

- Acts destined to subject part of the territory or the state to a foreign power or to diminish its independence: 1–10 years (Article 373).
- Acts directed toward dissolving the unity of the state or its territorial or constitutional integrity: 7–12 years (Article 374).
- Moving frontier demarkations to lessen the territory of the state: 5–10 years (Article 375).
- Promoting, establishing, organizing or directing associations with the objective of the violent overthrow of the legal and political order of the state or attempting in any form to subvert by violent means the economic or social orders protected by the constitution: 3–5 years. Participation in subversive organizations which teach or spread propaganda favoring anarchistic or anti-democratic doctrines: 1–3 years (Article 376).
- Promoting, establishing, organizing or directing associations or branches of foreign institutes that preach anarchistic or anti-democratic doctrines: 1–3 years. Participation in such organizations: 1/2–1 year (Article 377).
- Propagating in any manner, including importation or sale of any printed or other type of material, or making propaganda for anarchistic or anti-democratic doctrines: 1–4 years (Article 378).
- Unjustified possession, either personally or in a dwelling place, office or ship in which the person works, of materials or objects referred to in the prior paragraph in such quantity as to create a presumption of an intention to spread anarchistic or anti-democratic doctrines: 1/2–1 year (Article 379).
- Knowingly cooperating in the execution of acts of propaganda or spreading anarchistic or anti-democratic doctrines; renting or allowing the use of houses or sites destined to the carrying out of acts of spreading such doctrines; or distributing propaganda, painting, drawing or fixing signs containing any element of subversive propaganda: 1/2–2 years (Article 380).
- Treason: 15–25 years (Article 381).
- Provoking war, reprisals or international enmity: 3–15 years. Disturbance of friendly relations with a foreign government or a serious upheaval of the domestic public order: 3–7 years. If the acts lead to the breaking of diplomatic relations or to hostile or abusive acts: 5–12 years (Article 383).

- Divulging political or military secrets relating to the security of the state: 2–6 years (Article 384).
- Espionage: 8–20 years (Article 386).
- Sabotage in time of war: 5–10 years. Sabotage committed for a state at war with El Salvador: 10–20 years. Sabotage in time of peace: 1–3 years (Article 387).
- Violation of treaties with foreign states: 1–3 years (Article 389).
- Rebellion not authorized by Articles 5 and 6 of the Constitution: 1–5 years (Article 392).
- Sedition: 1–4 years (Article 393).
- Fomenting riots: 1/2–1 year (Article 394).
- Vilifying the nation or its symbols: 1–6 years (Article 395).
- Riots or rebellions which are disbanded before causing damage will not cause sanctions against more participants and will cut in half sanctions against promoters and organizers (Article 396).
- Conspiracy followed by preparatory acts to commit crimes of rebellion or sedition: 1/2–2 years (Article 397).
- Public officials who do not oppose rebellion or sedition by all means within their power: 1/4–1 year (Article 399).
- Acts of terrorism: 5–20 years (Article 400).
- Attempted terrorism: 3–7 years (Article 401).
- Preparation to commit terrorism: 2–6 years (Article 402).
- Conspiracy to commit terrorism: 1–3 years (Article 403).
- Public incitement to commit a crime: 1/2–5 years (Article 404).
- Publicly praising a crime or a convict: 1/2–2 years (Article 405).
- Public incitement to disobedience of the laws, to hatred or collective violence: 1/2–1 year (Article 406).
- Membership in an organization having as an objective the commission of any crime: 1–5 years (Article 407).
- Public intimidation: 1–6 years (Article 408).
- Interference with legal meetings by violence, intimidation or hostile manifestations: 1/2–1 year (Article 409).
- Illegal possession of a firearm in public or official places: 1/2–1 year (Article 410).
- Possession of arms of war: 1–3 years (Article 411).

8. Decree No. 562 of May 5, 1964, as amended.

9. IACHR Report, *op.cit.,* footnote 3.

10. This discussion of the curfew and how it operates is based on newspaper reports and on interviews with Salvadorans and reliable foreign observers residing in El Salvador or otherwise informed about the situation in the country.

11. Since the state of siege imposed on October 16 was lifted one week

later, this brief period had no lasting effect and will not be considered as a separate stage.

12. The card must show the following data and requisites, as a minimum:

1. The correlative number of the card.
2. The name and surnames of the minor.
3. The place and date of birth.
4. The name and surnames of the parents or of the mother alone, as appropriate.
5. The address of his residence, specifying, wherever appropriate, the canton, farm or hacienda of the town indicated.
6. The name of the school or place of work, as appropriate.
7. A recent full-face photograph, stamped with the seal of the Office of the Mayor that issued the card.
8. An indication of the color of the skin, eyes, hair, and other special features.
9. The date of issuance, the actual signature of the Municipal Mayor that issued the card, or a copy thereof, the actual signature of the employee that has handed over the card, the seal of the respective office and the signature of the minor, if he knows how to write or is able to write.

13. Estudios Centroamericanos, ECA, San Salvador, July–August 1980, No. 382, p. 757.

14. Estudios Centroamericanos, ECA, San Salvador, March 1981, No. 389, p. 211.

15. Foreign Broadcast Information Service, FBIS, Daily Report, Latin America, Vol. VI No. 135, 15 July 1981.

16. See Handbook of Existing Rules Pertaining to Human Rights, OEA/Ser. L/V/11.50, doc. 6, July 1, 1980.

17. Human Rights, A Compilation of International Instruments, United Nations, ST/HR/1/Rev. 1, New York, 1978. See also, Multilateral Treaties in respect of which the Secretary General Performs Depository Functions, List of Signatures, Ratifications, Accessions, etc., as at 31 December 1977 (ST/LEG/SER.D/10; United Nations publication, Sales No. E.77.V.7) brought up to date as at January 1, 1978.